TIGHT ON THE WIND

By Peter Saxton Schroeder

Book Cover Design: Jessie Alarcon & Tara Richter

Editors: Adriana Hartman, Haley Cox, Steven Tye & Kaitlyn Johnson

Book & Picture Formatting: Kaitlyn Sanderson & Jessie Alarcon

Editorial Assistance: Julia Birdsall

Publisher: Richter Publishing LLC

ISBN-13: 978-1-954094-74-1

DISCLAIMER

This book is designed to provide information on sailing only. This information is provided and sold with the knowledge that the publisher and author do not offer any legal or medical advice. In the case of a need for any such expertise, consult with the appropriate professional. This book does not contain all information available on the subject. This book has not been created to be specific to any individual's or organization's situation or needs. Every effort has been made to make this book as accurate as possible. However, there may be typographical and/ or content errors. Therefore, this book should serve only as a general guide and not as the ultimate source of subject information. This book contains information that might be dated and is intended only to educate and entertain. The author and publisher shall have no liability or responsibility to any person or entity regarding any loss or damage incurred, or alleged to have incurred, directly or indirectly, by the information contained in this book. You hereby agree to be bound by this disclaimer or you may return this book within the guarantee time period for a full refund. In the interest of full disclosure, this book may contain affiliate links that might pay the author or publisher a commission upon any purchase from the company. While the author and publisher take no responsibility for the business practices of these companies and or the performance of any product or service, the author or publisher has used the product or service and makes a recommendation in good faith based on that experience. This book is a work of nonfiction describing real people and places. Any resemblance to persons not expressly identified, living or deceased, is purely coincidental. The opinions and stories in this book are the views of the author and not that of the publisher.

Table of Contents

Because each chapter is complete in itself, the chapters are not intended to be read in any specific order.

COVER PHOTO

Author Peter Schroeder aboard a replica of a Phoenician sailing cargo ship. Between 1500 and 300 BCE, Phoenician mariners ranged far from their Levantine ports, trading from Egypt to Spain, along the African coast and north to Britain. The vessel shown is a classic *Gaulos*, a broad-beamed merchant ship built from the Cedars of Lebanon.

ACKNOWLEDGMENTS

Thanks and appreciation go to:

Risa Wyatt, my wife, for her encouragement and for trimming many jib sheets and cleating countless docking lines.

Margaret Stewart, for thorough editing and detailed fact-checking.

Major airlines that supported trips to many of the world's outstanding sailing venues: American, British Airways, Air France, Hawaiian, Japan Air, Air Micronesia, Air New Zealand, Northwest Territorial, Scandinavian Airlines, United, Varig (defunct), and Qantas.

Independent and subsidiary airlines that brought me to remote places such as Búzios, the Great Barrier Reef, Hamilton Island, Majuro, Nouméa, Palau, Raiatea, St. Kitts, Vava'u, and Yellowknife.

Yacht companies that provided wonderful charter sailing yachts in distant parts of the world: Atlas Sailing Charters, Florida Yacht Charters, Gimli Yacht Charters, Moorings, Ocean Hunter Charters, Palmira Marina Bareboat Charters, Queensland Yacht Charters, Sail North, Sunsail, Temptress Cruises, and others...

Introduction

IT BEGAN WITH A CRASH

C-R-A-A-C-K!

Over the deafening din of stormy winds and breaking waves on Long Island's Shinnecock Bay, a sudden explosive blast shocked us. Crews on boats racing nearby turned their heads in alarm. My father at the helm and I—his seven-year-old crew—were hiked far out to windward with the leeward rail of our 17-foot sloop nearly in the water. We were beating toward the windward buoy on the second round of the triangular racecourse. We nearly tumbled overboard as the boat lurched upright and splinters from the fractured wooden mast showered down on us.

Trapped in Debris

In an instant, Dad and I were tangled up with shrouds, stays, halyards, a ripped sail, and six feet of the top section of the mast. Half lay across us; the rest trailed in the water. My heart pounded—half from fear, half from excitement. I trusted Dad would know what to do.

Instinctively, I grabbed debris floating alongside us and started to pull it aboard. To my surprise Dad brushed me out of the way and did exactly the opposite. He pushed everything away from the boat. Uncertain what was happening, I followed his lead, using a paddle to push the floating wreckage farther from the hull.

By this time, Dad had unsheathed his belted knife and slashed through sheets, downhaul, reef lines, sail remnants, and topping lift that held the floating debris dangerously close to the boat. Then, grabbing cable shears from the toolbox, he cut away at the shrouds, stays, and halyards until the remains drifted free of the boat.

Then he did something that seemed strange—something I didn't understand until later. He stopped me from using the paddle to push the tangle in the water farther away. Snatching up two handfuls of the waterborne mess, he started pulling the wreckage back on board. Taking his cue, I helped as much as I could with the heavy entanglement although, as a youngster, I wasn't much help. Finally, after we had retrieved the sodden mass of wires, lines, ripped sail, and broken mast back on board, we hailed a friendly powerboater who towed us back to the yacht club.

Once home, Dad explained what every experienced sailor already knows. After everyone on board is accounted for and safe, the greatest danger from a toppled mast in the water is the risk it will puncture the hull. To prevent this, the rigging must be immediately cut free. However, much of the associated hardware taken down by the falling spar ought to be retrieved because much of it is valuable and reusable.

The following week, Dad arranged for the fabrication of a four-foot cylindrical bronze collar to rejoin the two broken mast sections, reconfigured the standing rigging and lines, and repaired the torn sail. A week later, we were back on the starting line.

Lessons of the Sea

The excitement from the crashing mast remains vivid in my memory. In later years, while sailing my 12-foot Penguin dinghy, I would sometimes experience minor breakdowns—not as dramatic as a falling mast, but significant enough that I had to learn to make hasty repairs. Because these mishaps didn't endanger me, I relished the opportunity to see how resourceful I could be in the moment, always trying to avoid the need to call for a tow back to the docks.

I continued to learn that the sea often confronts one with unexpected threats. That's just part of sailing. On various occasions I capsized, lost equipment overboard, experienced knockdowns in severe conditions, contended with damaged equipment, been drenched by rogue waves, and, yes, fallen overboard myself.

Such incidents occur without warning and require fast thinking and a quick response. The challenges of these mishaps appeal to me and have taught me the importance of keeping a boat "ship-shape." I also gained a respect for the power of the sea.

Most problems result from inadequate preparation. Being unprepared for weather conditions that suddenly produce rough seas and severe winds can be disastrous. Major problems also can result from the failure of something as simple as a small shackle or other marine part that breaks down when challenged beyond its limit.

Lifelong Recreational Sailor

Growing up in a family of sailors, I spent spring vacations and summers sailboat racing and charter cruising. My favorite week-long charters took our family of four to the Chesapeake Bay, Long Island Sound, and Puget Sound, in addition to venues in the British Virgin Islands, Caribbean, and the Abaco Islands. These childhood experiences shaped me, giving me both a love of sailing and a deep respect for the sea. As an adult, I continued these sailing adventures with my own family whenever I could find time between the demands of a career and home life. The sea remained my place of freedom.

Health Crisis

But a sudden health crisis in my late thirties unmoored my life and ended my successful career as an international businessman. My life changed course as dramatically as the day the mast had crashed on me years earlier. I was diagnosed with a deadly form of bone marrow cancer, Multiple Myeloma. This disease can be treated but not cured, and it is ultimately fatal. My doctors suggested I get my personal affairs in order, provide for my family's future, and prepare for the inevitable. They gave me two years—at most.

I consulted with different doctors and researched medical journals, which all confirmed, as they still do today, a terminal prognosis of Multiple Myeloma. In addition to the typical Western medical interventions of surgery, chemo, and radiation, I pursued alternative medical systems. This led me and my family to a healing ashram and Ayurvedic practitioners in Pune, India, where we embraced a radically different lifestyle and types of healing. Slowly, after three years of living in a different climate with this new way of life, including embracing a vegetarian diet and learning from Indian healers, my body regained strength and I returned to the States.

My Western doctors were amazed. They didn't say I was cancer-free, but rather suggested I had a very slow-growing—indolent—Myeloma. They re-confirmed the terminal prognosis, giving me perhaps another few years.

Thanks to Social Security disability benefits—for which a terminal prognosis qualifies—and my private, long-term care insurance, I was able to purchase a home in Seattle and otherwise provide for my family. But where did that leave me? My two graduate degrees were of no use as I looked to the future. I couldn't get a job because I couldn't pass a pre-employment physical exam. Knowing that I could die any time, I didn't want to start my own company. But because I had no debilitating symptoms, and felt strong and energetic, I couldn't settle for the sedate life of a householder. I had to find something.

Banished at Forty-Two

How do people know when a phase of their lives ends, and it's time to move on? Graduations, marriages, births, and job changes are acknowledged as markers between the "then" and the "new." Other transitions are not widely acknowledged milestones but are more personally felt. In my case, I had no choice but to move on in an unknown direction.

I view the age of forty-two as significant. Five thousand years ago, Eastern mystics were first to observe that a person's seventy years on earth are broken into ten distinct 7-year periods. Each transition is accompanied by major changes and upheavals that bulldoze the old to make way for the new.

At age forty-two (42 ÷ 7 = 6), it's time to reflect upon the deeper meaning of life that gives birth to new paths. I considered my life in limbo as a form of banishment—the oldest, most severe, and perhaps most unfair punishment a human being can experience. Banishment doesn't involve a trial. Nor is there any judgment rendered finding the accused guilty or innocent. Banishment is simply a non-negotiable message: "Get Out!" At forty-two, I was exiled from my old life and had to find something new.

The precedent for banishment goes back to the Bible, with Adam and Eve's expulsion from the Garden of Eden. Adam and Eve may have covered their naked bodies with fig leaves, but I doubt they could have hidden the fear, even panic, they must have felt having nothing familiar to hold onto. This banishment left them untethered and separated—and separation is exactly what I was feeling.

Wake-Up Call

My previous life offered no reference point, no anchor that I could turn to. Yet the more I considered my situation, the more I grew to feel a tremendous sense of freedom. I had no responsibilities for anything or anyone anymore. Financially, my family would be secure without me after my looming death.

Paradoxically, my terminal diagnosis presented me with the opportunity to re-create my life, a prospect both scary and exciting. Scary—because what if I couldn't find a new direction? Exciting—because something was out there waiting to be discovered.

That's when I realized that what was waiting for me wasn't something new. My purpose was something I had loved ever since that mast crashed on me at seven years old. That broken mast was an omen. What began as a crash at age seven was a wake-up call now at forty-two. And as noted, both ages are divisible by seven.

I would live out my love for sailing and figure out how to earn an income doing it.

What is this Book About?

By becoming a sailing journalist, I did just that. For the next several decades, I embarked on worldwide sailing adventures. I wrote hundreds of articles for sailing magazines in North America and abroad about cruising waters across the globe.

This book is an anthology of published articles I have written about the sea, each updated to be relevant today. It is geared toward sailors who know the thrill of a tautly trimmed mainsail and for armchair adventurers who dream of distant horizons.

What began with a crash was, in truth, a beginning. The broken mast that once showered splinters on a frightened boy became the spark that lit a life of adventure. My hope is that these stories remind readers that every setback carries within it the seed of a new course, if only we are willing to set our sails and follow where the wind leads.

So… how was I fortunate enough to find this dream lifestyle that combined my love for the sea with a way to make a reasonable living?

Chapter 1

BECOMING A SAILING JOURNALIST

Confronted with this major turning point in my life at age forty-two, I realized that what I really long for is to return to a life of adventure—one that would once again carry me into the unknown. I miss the novelty and excitement of hopping a freight train across the country, of moving to a new city, learning new subjects, skiing again in China and Turkey, or striking out into uncharted territory. And, most of all, I want to travel.

What to do next? My passion is sailing, but it is an expensive pursuit involving costly travel, access to pricey boats, familiarity with new cruising waters, and contact with skippers and boat owners. At this moment, I have just enough money to support my family—and nothing more. How do I make money doing what I love?

Then it hits me: What if I become a sailing journalist? I could write about sailing regattas, charter cruise destinations, yacht deliveries, crewing experiences—all the things I want to be doing anyway. Better yet, I would have to live the adventures to tell them. So how can I find a way for others to pay my travel expenses while paying me for my writing? This is a world about which I know nothing, but why not look into it?

Letters to Editors

The motivation is there, but I lack the tools. Where do I start? How can I find newspaper or magazine editors who might publish my work? I devour books on how to sell articles to journals and publications, take writing and photography courses, and when I feel ready, I look for ways to get my name in front of editors. Having sailed ever since I was a child, I feel confident about my general understanding of sailing and in my ability to skipper sailboats of any size—from day sailors up to 50-foot yachts. I decide to try to get my name on the desks of the editors of the two daily newspapers here in Seattle by writing letters to both publications.

Now I need to find a controversial subject.

One day I stumble across a travel piece in the *Seattle Times* about the Indigenous peoples of the Northwest. The article refers to totem poles of U.S. and Canadian tribes. I happen to know, however, that totem poles are found only in Canada, not among native peoples in the continental U.S.

Wanting to be clever, I write a letter to the editor with the heading "Totemic Trouble" explaining the error. The newspaper runs my letter, and the editor calls to thank me for catching it. Seems like an auspicious sign.

When another article misidentifies a wolf eel in Puget Sound as an eel, when it is, in fact, a fish, I send a second letter that the editor again promptly publishes. Another opportunity comes up shortly afterwards. Being familiar with sailboat designs in the Pacific Northwest, I catch an article that incorrectly identifies a keel as a center board. I write again—published again. Each time, I telephone the editor to thank her for running my corrections. Before long, we're phone buddies.

First Assignments

When a non-sailing reporter covers a local regatta, I call my phone-buddy editor to point out the gaffes. With nine sailing Olympians and hundreds of sailing enthusiasts living in Seattle, I explain why they all must have had a good laugh when they read that article.

Shortly afterward, the suitably embarrassed editor calls back to ask if I would write a short news piece on the upcoming Whidbey Island Race Week, the premier sailing regatta in the Pacific Northwest. Suddenly, I have my first real assignment: 500 words for $125.

At the same time that I am writing letters to the editors of local newspapers, I write similar letters to *Pacific Yachting*, the Canadian boating magazine across the border in Vancouver. There's not much response for several months until I send a letter that stirs up a storm. When an article appears about a group of Vancouver sailors who cruised in the northern Vava'u archipelago of Tonga, I am interested because I had bareboat chartered there several years earlier. The charterers who wrote the article described how they distributed candy and plastic toys in the villages, thinking they were spreading happiness among the children.

Infuriated, I write a letter to the editor, pointing out that these islanders live a subsistence lifestyle with pigs and goats running freely throughout the villages, and the people have no dental or medical facilities. Introducing foods and items from the developed world disrupts their lifestyle and creates health hazards. Letters come flying back in the next issue defending the charterers who were just trying to be helpful, but this prompts another letter from me and from others who support my position.

As the wrangling continues, the editor telephones to thank me for stirring up a controversy, which every editor loves because it increases sales. "Editors love a good fight," he says. When our conversation gets around to my interests in writing, he asks if I would submit a news article on a tight deadline about the recent sinking of a sailing yacht on the west coast of Vancouver Island, an incident in which two lives were lost. Having no idea what this entails, I nevertheless immediately accept, thereby garnering my second paid assignment. Soon thereafter he assigns me to write a feature article, the first of many to come, and I feel that I'm really in the game.

More Assignments

I keep going. Throughout the summer, I continue to seek out assignments and send queries to additional local newspapers and boating magazines. As my name becomes known among editors, I pick up assignments to write about weekend sailing regattas, boating festivals, yacht launchings, and other nautical events.

In the process, I learn two important lessons: one about the type of event I never want to write about again, and the other, a direction I plan to pursue in the future.

The never-again assignment? I agreed to submit daily race reports to the *Seattle Times* from the five-day Whidbey Island Race Week Regatta held in northern Puget Sound. The Whidbey Regatta attracts 150 entries including the top sailors from the Pacific Northwest and some of the best racers from British Columbia. Two races are held each day followed by evening award celebrations with music, food, and an open bar that lasts well into the early evening.

During the days of the event, I follow the fleet out on the racecourse in a chase boat to take photos of the leaders at each buoy rounding. At the end of each day, I retreat to a quiet room in the yacht club to hammer out my story to meet the newspaper's 10:00 p.m. deadline for the morning edition. The problem is that when everyone is celebrating at the bar, I miss the fun while writing the article. I finish about the time the bar closes, and the food is gone. Never again will I write to a newspaper's tight deadline if it means missing the fun.

Interesting fact that I include in my article: Whidbey Island had recently received the distinction as the longest island in the continental United States when New York's Long Island lost that status by being legally declared a truncated peninsula.

Here is the hard-earned lesson that directs me to subjects I intend to write about in the future: When I cover stories about sailing regattas, I spend a lot of time and effort photographing the yachts on the racecourse, interviewing the skippers and crew members back on land, and learning about the features of the boats by making close-up inspections myself or speaking with the naval architects who designed them. After the story and images appear in print, I realize my notes and photos are worthless. Regattas in subsequent years feature new skippers, different boat designs, and alternate race venues. Even when I have multiple assignments for the same event and make reasonable income, I'm disappointed not to make further use of the work I have already done.

I soon wake up to the fact that my images and articles could be investments if I were more intelligent in my choice of assignments. That's when I begin writing "evergreen" articles—that is, stories and images that never go out of date. So, I shift focus. Tropical beaches don't change over time. Neither do natural landscapes, happy faces, or beautiful sunsets. Consequently, I cut back on the number of assignments about sailing regattas or time-specific events. Instead, I recycle, with minimal updates, articles and photos from assignments that I've had published at earlier dates.

Expanding Nationally and Internationally

While poking around in search of a direction for another assignment, I discover an idea that is so unusual that it has national appeal to several dozen newspapers and boating magazines throughout the U.S. and Canada. Expo '86, the 1986 World Exposition on Transportation and Communication, is scheduled to be held in Vancouver, British Columbia, from May 2 to October 13, 1986, which also coincides with Vancouver's centennial. Motels and hotel rooms are booked out weeks in advance for the duration of the Expo; however, when I contact marinas throughout the region around Vancouver, I find more than 400 moorage slips available, all considerably less expensive than land accommodations—a feasible floating alternative.

I write up my findings and send the article to every boating magazine and major newspaper in North America. To make this option available to non-boat owners, I include the dozen yacht charter companies in Washington's San Juan Islands and Canada's Gulf Islands where qualified boaters could cruise a chartered yacht up to Vancouver and book a slip.

This is my first attempt at self-syndicating. The yield proves spectacular with more than thirty acceptances, each paying an average of $300 for text and images. The lesson for me is to seek out unusual story angles that have wide appeal within the broader boating community.

Another exciting assignment falls into my lap when I receive a telephone call from the editor of New York–based *Oyster Bay Guardian*. The Six Metre North American Championship is to be held in Seattle, and several skippers from the Oyster Bay Seawanhaka Corinthian Yacht Club, one of the most prestigious yacht clubs in the country, are shipping their yachts cross-country along with their world-class ocean racing crews to compete in this event. The editor asks if I would submit daily race reports with focus on the New York boats. Because her earlier deadlines wouldn't pull me away from the after-race celebrations, I quickly accept.

Not to be outdone by the New York paper, the *Seattle Times* also asks me to submit daily race reports. Since I am writing the core of the article at an earlier time for the NY publication, I accept the assignment because it would require minimal effort by replacing the names of skippers and boats from the East Coast with those on the West Coast.

The Six Metre design, which originated more than 125 years ago, was sailed in the Olympics in the 1930s and 1940s but discontinued after 1952 at the Helsinki Olympics. Because it was always an expensive yacht to maintain, the class has been raced ever since exclusively by multi-millionaires who don't hesitate to make constant upgrades to their yachts as they ship them to racing venues around the world.

The wealth of these owners opens doors for me and secures two additional assignments. Little did I anticipate that my articles and photos would find favor with the Governing Committee of the International Six Metre Association and earn me two future assignments with all expenses paid. The first is to cover the World Championship of this iconic class the following year in New York. Two years later they pay all my expenses to write about the subsequent World Championship in the Stockholm Archipelago at the island of Sandhamn, Sweden.

Marketplace to Meditation

In retrospect, I realize I have stumbled across a two-step rhythm that will be the key to my future life as a freelance writer. The first step is to go out "somewhere" to experience a wonderful adventure. The second is returning to the quiet of "home" to reflect and recount the details on paper, as this was prior to the digital era. Adventure and solitude, excitement and contemplation. To say it another way, it's a rhythm of going into the hectic busyness of the marketplace to experience an adventure, then returning to a quiet, meditative state to reflect, recall, and record not just the events, but also the nuances and feelings of the underbelly of whatever was going on. This is how I turn my sailing passion into a writer's life: by alternating from "marketplace to meditation."

From these scant beginnings, I launched a thirty-year career that took me to the world's most acclaimed rivers, seas, and oceans to write and photograph my sailing and boating adventures. The following chapters hold updates of articles previously published in journals around the globe. Events and locales are grouped geographically, not chronologically.

~

Totem poles unique to Canadian First Nations, not found in the Continental U.S.

Wolf Eels are fish, not eels.

Chapter 2

BLUE - WATER YACHT DELIVERIES

Return to the Sea

One day, I spot an ad in a sailing magazine:

"Wanted: Experienced sailors to deliver a yacht from Hawaii back to The Mainland"

The owner had raced his 50-foot racer-cruiser in the previous year's Transpac Race from Los Angeles to Honolulu and more recently had been cruising the Hawaiian Islands for six months. Not up for the tough return passage, he was now looking for a delivery crew.

Over the phone, I describe my ocean-sailing experience. He agrees to hire me, along with two others yet to be found. He offers the usual terms: full provisions for the trip, three days of motel accommodations and meals at each end, $0.25 per mile for the skipper, and $0.05 per mile for each crew member. I will, however, need to pay for my own airfare to Hawaii.

I jump at this opportunity and book a flight to Honolulu, delighted to go back to Hawaii, where two decades earlier, I had lived for three years dividing my time between work and hanging out as a surfer dude.

Once back on the island, my first stop is the Ala Moana Yacht Basin near Waikiki Beach where I stroll the docks to admire the sleek sailing yachts glistening with mahogany decks and polished brightwork. Many of these boats are also the previous year's Transpac Race holdovers whose owners are likewise looking for delivery crews to sail them home. When I stop by one yacht to ask the captain if he is looking for a delivery crew, he replies in the affirmative. But he surprises me by explaining he is offering passage to those who want to learn about offshore sailing and is charging them each $250 plus a share of the provisioning. I politely decline his offer and inform him of the ad I answered that offered to pay me and the others in the delivery crew.

Many people fantasize about the joys of sailing from the tropical Hawaiian waters to southern California, but that's because they don't understand the Pacific High, an enormous stationary high-pressure weather system in the Northeast Pacific Ocean. Compared with the westbound route, sailing east is no easy passage. Sailors departing the North American West Coast for Hawaii benefit from quartering winds as they skirt the southern rim of the Pacific High. However, the return trip requires a course setting out northeast of Hawaii to catch favorable winds at the "top" of the weather system, which can take yachts north up toward Alaska's Aleutian Islands. Three days after departing Hawaii, sailors don long underwear and foul-weather gear, facing heavy winds and treacherous seas.

The owner who signed me on had docked his boat at Lanikai on the northeast side of Oahu. Upon my arrival, I meet the newly hired skipper, a local Hawaiian, and one other crewmember from Australia. It's not an easy beginning because rather than a comfortable motel, my pre-departure accommodation is a berth aboard the boat with showers and toilets nearby on shore. I'm surprised when the Hawaiian skipper informs the two of us that we won't provision until we arrive at Kauai, where he lives with his family, and he intends to lay over for several days before departing for California.

We need to arrive at the marina on Kauai's north shore in daylight to avoid the offshore reefs, which means we will need to depart Oahu the evening before, sailing through the night. Shortly before dusk, as we cast off, each of us eyes the others to see how much they know about sailing. As a child, I learned from my father, an accomplished sailor, that one can assess how much someone knows about boats by watching them take three steps on board. My Australian crewmate is obviously quite competent, but I am not so sure about the skipper. His excessive casualness makes me uneasy.

After we motor out of the marina, I am surprised when he calls for the jib to be raised; the usual procedure is to hoist the mainsail first. Once underway, the skipper seems unconcerned that lines are scattered across the cockpit. When I suggest they be properly coiled, he shrugs his shoulders. Experienced sailors know that wind and wave conditions in the ocean can change quickly, so everything should be kept shipshape in case the crew needs to adjust sails and lines on short notice.

When darkness falls, I remind our skipper that because we are still in the shipping lanes, we should turn on our cruising lights. Later in the evening, I notice that when he adjusts several lines, he secures them together on the same cleat. This is a definite hazard because the buried line is not immediately accessible in case it must be quickly released.

In the early dawn light, the glow of the Kilauea lighthouse leads us around the northeast coast of Kauai to the north shore where we make a landing at a small marina in Hanalei Bay. Immediately upon arrival, our leader is picked up by his family and disappears, leaving the two of us on our own without knowing his plans. After three days, I decide I've had enough. Not trusting my life to this skipper on an ocean crossing, I call to inform him I'm leaving. He seems unconcerned and simply says to get my things off the boat, which I do. The next day I'm on a plane back to Seattle because I have a different priority.

Antigua Race Week

The jewel of yacht racing in the Caribbean is Antigua Race Week, which attracts the world's elite racing and performance-cruising yachts in addition to many of the world's top-tier professional sailors. However, you don't need a high-tech boat to compete. The regatta also hosts a Club Class for regular cruising boats crewed by recreational sailors and less serious participants wanting to be in on the action.

A budget flight to Antigua lands me at English Harbor in the midst of the week-long series of races. After settling in, I stroll the docks. Bypassing the sleek racing machines with crews decked out in matching logo-emblazoned yachting clothes, I come to the modest cruising boats with ragtag crews in cutoff shorts and faded T-shirts—my kind of sailors. When I inquire at several boats if anyone is looking for an extra crew, I'm told they are fully manned. But then one skipper asks what I can do. I tell him that I can fill any position.

"How about trimming the main?" he asks.

I gulp inwardly because this is arguably the most responsible position in racing, but without missing a beat, I reply, "Sure." Quite a challenge, I reflect to myself!

The next morning I meet the crew as we go through the pre-race checkout. Once we cast off and raise the mainsail, I notice problems in the rigging and ask to have the sail lowered. I re-fit the top halyard and, once it's hoisted again, I tighten the boom vang and loosen the outhaul. Because the winds are very light, I want to create bagginess in the sail. As we execute the pre-start maneuvers, I experiment by pulling in and then letting out the mainsheet to find the optimum sail trim. The rest of the crew eyes me suspiciously and, I suspect, attributes my constant adjusting to not knowing what I'm doing.

At the crack of the starting gun we get a respectable start, although the skipper has put us in the wind shadow of the boats to windward. As we sail hard on the wind, I perceive we are pinching and losing speed. Respectfully, I ask the skipper to fall off, which he does, and as we pick up speed, we start to move through the fleet. We round the windward mark with the leaders, which apparently hadn't happened in previous races, judging by the crew's jubilance.

On the downwind leg, I try a trick my father had taught me. Although the wind is quite light and the boat is on an even keel, I ask the entire crew to sit like rail meat against the safety lines to windward with their legs dangling over the side to tip the boat as much as possible. Then I ask the smallest and lightest crew member, whose weight doesn't make much difference, to stand to leeward holding the boom as far out as possible. This raises the sail higher up above the surface of the water where it catches the slightly stronger winds aloft. Slowly we move into the lead and round first at the leeward mark.

For the next two legs, we continue to tweak the sails and, gaining more confidence in what I'm doing, I make suggestions to the jib trimmer and also ask the skipper to make certain course adjustments. We maintain our lead and are first across the finish line, which leads to a gala celebration with the crew that evening. But, sorry to say, I must decline the owner's invitation to sail the next day in the final race because I have already agreed to be part of another boat's delivery crew.

Delivery to Newport

The next morning the docks bustle with activity while competitors prepare for the last day's race. I join up with the delivery crew aboard *Matoaka*, the Powhatan name for Pocahontas, who befriended the settlers in the colonial settlement at Jamestown, Virginia. At age forty-three, I feel like the old man among the thirty-somethings group, who are to be my sail-mates on the voyage to Newport, Rhode Island. The 72-foot sloop is in immaculate condition with well-maintained teak decks, freshly varnished spars, and new sheets and halyards. Having provisioned for the trip in the days before, the crew is waiting for me to board before casting off.

We quickly settle into an easy routine, establishing a Swedish watch system in which two people stand watch for four hours at any time. To ensure a plentiful supply of hot food for those both coming on shift and those going off, three of the women who have their own rotation system serve as cooks. As the lone American among a crew of young Brits, I easily adapt to the 4:00 p.m. ritual when the entire group assembles for twenty minutes for teatime each day.

In just over a week, we cover the 3,000 miles to Bermuda, but on our approach to the channel into Hamilton, we encounter a problem that leads to much confusion. The entrance buoys seem to be in reverse position. As we attempt to enter the passage, the depth sounder indicates the water is becoming quite shallow, so we quickly shift the engine into reverse. Only after radioing to the harbormaster do we learn the source of the mix-up. Mystery solved: Bermuda's navigation system had always been the Lateral System of "red, right, returning"—the system familiar to every American sailor. But on the day of our arrival, Bermuda is changing to the European system which has exactly the opposite designation. Now that we understand, we proceed through the channel and take a slip at the main docks.

After a few days in Bermuda to refill the water tanks, take on more fuel, and add fresh provisions, we cast off. A week later we arrive safely at Newport where our group disbands.

Virgin Gorda Race Week

Not having been to the British Virgin Islands for several years, I decide to go down for the BVI Race Week. Professional skippers are brought in and paired with recreational sailors to compete in 32-foot sloops at the Bitter End Yacht Club for a five-day series of races. Upon arrival, I sign up as a volunteer crew and am paired with legendary Lowell North, Olympic gold medalist and founder of the world's largest manufacturer of sails, San Diego–based North Sails. Although in his mid-fifties, which is considered old in the yacht-racing world, Lowell is still a formidable challenger to the younger generation of upcoming racing skippers.

His skippering abilities and tactical skills on the racecourse are, indeed, flawless. What impresses me most, however, are all the little things Lowell does as he moves around the boat. He arrives at the docks only minutes before we must cast off. With a quick flick of one hand, he frees the stern line from the cleat and deftly hops aboard, while simultaneously grabbing the tiller and calling to hoist the sail as we motor away from the dock. As he must have done thousands of times in the past, he orders minute adjustments in the main and jib halyards and tightens the outhaul himself.

Lowell uses a gesture, one my father had taught me, to determine the direction of the wind. Lowell lifts his chin almost imperceptibly and moves his head left and right several times until he stops moving. By feeling the wind on his nose, he knows he's looking directly into the wind when he feels equal pressure on each nostril. He trusts this method more than the wind yarns fluttering on the stays.

The week goes pretty much as expected. Always among the lead boats of the dozen or so in our class, we end up second or third overall.

Delivering Winnie Home

At the end of the week, I spot a notice on the dock's posterboard looking for a delivery crew to sail to New England. Seeing an opportunity for blue-water cruising and as a cheap means of getting partway home, I make my way to St. Thomas in the neighboring American Virgin Islands to meet the skipper of *Winnie*, a 40-foot wooden yawl. After a few minutes of discussion and a handshake, I'm welcomed as the fourth member of the crew.

The next three days are hectic as we provision *Winnie* for the voyage from St. Thomas to New Hampshire, although my portion of the journey will end at Miami.

On departure day our spirits are high as we raise the anchor and head to the fuel dock to top off our diesel and water tanks. But uh-oh… Suddenly, an all-too-familiar sight makes our hearts sink; coming up rapidly behind us as if out of nowhere, a gigantic motor yacht is heading directly to the fuel dock. We know all too well it would take half a day for that boat to take on 2,000 to 3,000 gallons of diesel fuel and replenish hundreds of gallons in its water tanks. With the mega-monster monopolizing the entire length of the facilities, we could be forced to stand off and wait our turn or else return to our anchorage until the fuel dock is clear.

So, what to do? Some of the crew favor a waiting/drifting strategy, whereas others want to re-anchor and go ashore. But our cook Sherrie, an attractive petite brunette, suddenly lights up with an idea. Without saying a word, she glances at the name on the stern of our adversary as it overtakes us. Then she goes below and calls the vessel by name on channel 16 on the VHF. In a sultry, enticing voice that none of us has heard before, she hails the captain just as the waves in his wake begin to tumble us about. Back comes a slow, male, Texas drawl, and instinctively we know we are in luck.

None of us remembers afterward exactly what Sherrie says. We just know she does that age-old thing that every woman since Eve has been able to do to a man. The next moment the floating giant stops, and with thrusters foaming and churning the water all around, the vessel begins to back away from the dock. Quickly we position our fenders, ready the shore lines, and then slip up to the dock in the shadow of this ominous, towering hull. Five minutes and $8.75 later we pull away from the dock and are on our way.

During this interval Sherrie has disappeared below, and as we cast off, she reappears in her bikini. Once again, she hails the captain, this time by shouting up at him to thank him for his kindness. When he looks down at her, he surely feels it was all worthwhile. He smiles, she smiles, and then as *Winnie* turns to the open sea, our crew all look at each other and burst out in relieved laughter.

Beach Writing

Back home in Seattle, the summer activity settles down after Labor Day. Time to have another medical check-up. Once again, confounding the doctors, my Multiple Myeloma tests all come up negative, and I have no symptoms. The lesions and small isolated tumors are stable; however, the terminal prognosis remains unchanged, and I'm told to return to the medical center whenever the first signs of painful symptoms (typically in the long bones—thighs, femurs, backbone, and breastbone) occur.

To avoid the seasonal rains that will shortly begin, I book a flight to Hawaii and pack my camping gear. I intend to camp on a beach and employ my mechanical typewriter to write up the torrent of events that have filled my life in the four-plus years since the doctors told me to set my affairs to deal with the projected two-year prognosis. Recognizing that I must be living on borrowed time, I want to collect my thoughts and quickly record them on paper.

Makena Beach on Maui—a hippie colony of camping tents—is my destination offering white sands, clear water, and peace. The island's largest beach, more than a mile long and 100 yards wide, is home to an ever-changing mix of people who have in common the desire simply to drop out of society for a while. That's exactly my feeling as well.

I pitch my tent with a limited supply of provisions in a remote section of the beach and settle into a daily routine of swimming, walking along the beach, and writing at the edge of the ocean. With my typewriter propped up by a makeshift structure of driftwood and sand, and, with my back supported by padding placed against an ancient lava flow, I drift each day into a writer's reverie in this tropical paradise.

One morning while I'm hunched over my typewriter, a young woman who was camped nearby approaches and asks if I would be willing to type her application for law school. She hands me a hand-written draft and $15. An hour later she has her completed application, and I think nothing more about it.

But word soon gets around that I'm a "typewriter for hire." It begins as a trickle as people start stopping by requesting to borrow my typewriter—which I refuse—or asking if I will type something for them—which I agree to do. People bring résumés, job applications, official correspondence, and query letters of every sort. Within a few weeks, I am receiving a steady stream of clients.

To increase my services, on my regular weekly trips to Wailea to pick up groceries, I lay in a supply of stationery, envelopes, and stamps. When I first arrived here I had rented a post office box where I pick up my forwarded mail. Now I offer my clients the respectability of a return address rather than the indignity of General Delivery. I don't charge much for my services, but the inflow of money is sufficient to cover not only the writing supplies but also groceries and provisions. Island travel is cheap because I hitchhike everywhere. In addition, I find myself coming out of my self-imposed hermit shell as I meet new friends and join in social gatherings.

But after three months, it's time to return to home life. I fly back to Seattle just before Christmas to join my wife at the time and our twin sons, four years old, as we settle together in our recently purchased home. What a paradox that the previous five years of fun sailing adventures delivering yachts occurred after receiving the worst medical prognosis of my life! And little could I foresee the many sailing adventures that lie ahead.

~

Chapter 3

FLORIDA - UNLOCKING THE KEYS

Sailing south past the lower end of Key Biscayne, we—my current wife, two teenage sons from a previous marriage, and I—glance astern as the tips of Miami's skyscrapers melt into shimmering mirages. Released from our everyday world of schedules and agendas, we're ready to slow down and slip, like dolphins, into a world of sunlit seas and natural beauty. Awaiting us along this string of pearls trailing down from the southeastern corner of the United States is a world of wave and wind, sand and seabirds, conch and coral, and reef after reef teeming with a host of marine life. Nature reigns supreme in the Florida Keys.

Purrfection

Upon our arrival at Miami International Airport the previous day, Florida Yacht Charters' courtesy shuttle whisked us directly to the charter base at Miami Beach Marina. Here, in preparation for our morning's departure, the base manager conducted a chart briefing for our itinerary and checked out the boat's equipment and systems aboard our chartered sailing catamaran, *Purrfection.* With four spacious staterooms— one located fore and one aft in each of the hulls—joined by a by a sprawling condo-like main salon, this Fountaine Pajot Tobago 35 is a showpiece of French boatbuilding. As a courtesy, car keys left on the chart table allow us to provision and then enjoy dinner in Miami Beach.

Escaping Miami

Early the next morning, we nose *Purrfection* into the steady flow of commercial ship traffic in Government Cut. Our nerves jangle as we maneuver through the wakes of towering ocean freighters and cruise ships. When a gap opens, we dash at full throttle across the shipping lanes to the south side of Dodge Island, then turn west, passing under massive loading cranes as we head on a course that leads us practically into downtown Miami's honking traffic. A south turn at buoy 57 takes us to the Intracoastal Waterway, the start of our one-way, 150-mile cruise down through the Florida Keys to Key West.

Cruising under sail in the Florida Keys has always been risky because the average water depth—less than two fathoms—requires sailors to keep a constant eye on their depth sounders. Consequently, this region, which has long been a playground for powerboaters and day sailors, has been off-limits to keelboats. But that has all changed thanks to a charter program originally started by the Florida Yacht Charters to open the region to cruising multihulls. FYC offers a multihull charter fleet of French-designed catamarans ranging from thirty-two to fifty feet. With shallow drafts under three feet, catamarans make it possible for sailors to explore practically anywhere in the Keys while enjoying the amenities of a luxury cruising boat.

With Miami disappearing in our wake, we cruise down thirty-five-mile-long Biscayne Bay, unconcerned that the water depth is less than ten feet. The channel markers surrounding Featherbed Banks are easily visible and in agreement with the charts, giving us confidence in our ability to safely navigate the shoals and dredged channels found everywhere throughout the Keys.

Once in Card Sound, we seek out the mouth of Angel Creek, hidden in the mangrove-clustered shoreline at the northern end of Key Largo. Then we furl the sails and motorsail through the five-foot-deep passage to the eastern shore. We enter Hawk Channel on the continental shelf where the water depth is rarely more than twenty feet. Protected from Atlantic rollers by the offshore reef that extends from the Florida mainland to Key West, these waters are surprisingly calm.

Ocean Reef Club

As darkness descends, we enter the channel to the Ocean Reef Club on the northeastern side of Key Largo and secure *Purrfection* at our assigned dockage slip. Ocean Reef is a private development off-limits to cruising sailors, but permission to enter the marina is available by contacting the marina office in advance. This development consists of a 175-slip private marina surrounded by golf courses, swimming pools, a spa, game rooms, tennis courts, numerous recreation facilities, a dozen restaurants and lounges, and a 4,000-acre private residential section built up with luxury homes, condos, and villas.

We plan to dine at Gianni Ristorante, which specializes in old-world Italian fare, but are stopped short when we learn about the dress code. The three of us men have collared shirts and long pants as mandated, but we're also required to wear jackets. Thinking this would be a T-shirt-and-cutoff-shorts cruise, we have not brought jackets on our trip.

What to do? Not wanting to miss an elegant dinner, we devise a plan. Because this is a high-end resort, we search until we find a men's clothing store in the gallery of retail shops. Although we don't need more jackets, we hand over the credit card for three blue blazers. Problem solved.

Dinner at Gianni Ristorante proves to be all we had hoped for—well worth the extra outlay for additional clothing. Afterwards, feeling well-fed and grateful to have a secure slip for the night, we return to *Purrfection* where gentle waves rock us to sleep on deck under the stars.

In the morning, just for fun, we call room service and order breakfast. Twenty minutes later a waiter arrives carrying a silver tray laden with a basket of fruit, sweet rolls, coffee, and juice, plus the morning newspaper and a small vase of flowers. Accepting our invitation to come aboard, he sets a table on deck, pours the coffee, and then, seeming a bit bewildered, steps back onto land to return to his normal duties.

Into the Underwater World

For the next three days we immerse ourselves in the world of sail and snorkel. Jimmy Buffett songs play in the background while seagulls ke-ow and cow-cow-cow overhead as we sail south to John Pennekamp Coral Reef State Park, the world's first underwater park. Then it's on to Key Largo National Marine Sanctuary—now incorporated into the Florida Keys National Marine Sanctuary, which includes the only coral barrier reef within U.S. continental shores. The gentle arc of Key Largo and the southern keys prevents mainland freshwater runoff from damaging the coral growth, resulting in dozens of near-shore, world-class dive sites, each with its own special variety of corals and marine life.

Our first dive stop is Key Largo Dry Rocks, site of "Christ of the Deep," otherwise known as "Christ of the Abyss," a nine-foot bronze statue submerged in twenty-five feet of water. We snorkel above the underwater figure, peer down to the upward-gazing Christ face, then take turns diving fifteen feet to clasp the two upraised, barnacle-encrusted hands. A gift from Italy, the two-ton creation is dedicated to "all who lived for the sea and who, in the same sea, found their eternal peace."

On subsequent days we snorkel at whatever sites we chance upon—Mosquito Bank, French Reef, Molasses Reef, Hen & Chickens Reef, Big Pine Shoal, and Looe Key. Fifty feet of visibility in these crystal-clear waters opens marvelous views of reef fish within the waving forests of sea whips and fan corals. But it's the microcosm that fascinates me most: watching a clown fish dart in and out of a protective sea anemone's tendrils or seeing a pair of eyes set back beneath a rock waiting for an unsuspecting meal to swim by.

Mooring buoys are placed at all the dive spots to discourage boaters from using anchors, while other buoys encircle "core areas" where boats are not allowed. Regulations here are necessarily strict to protect the 40 types of coral and 650 species of fish in these reef systems, which attract more than one million visitors each year.

Frequently sighted in these waters are West Indian manatees, or sea cows, for which the island Vaca—"cow" in Spanish—is named. These gentle creatures migrate to the Keys as a refuge to escape the cold elsewhere. Sadly, their numbers are decreasing due to the destruction of seagrasses caused notably by dredging, and mortal woundings inflicted by collisions with boat hulls and propellers.

Every evening we return to the protective shelter of the Keys, calling ahead to inquire if our 22-foot beam can negotiate the entry channel to a particular marina. Surprisingly, about half the marinas we contact cannot accommodate this width. At Key Largo Marina, for example, the harbormaster requires us to stand by the entrance until a large tourist dive boat departs. Only then are we allowed to enter the forty-foot-wide channel to take a slip at the docks of Marina del Mar Resort and Marina.

Fortified with late afternoon margaritas, we relax on the cedar deck beside Marina del Mar's freshwater pool—claimed to be the largest in the Keys. As the sinking sun begins to paint the horizon with ever-changing golds, oranges, and crimsons, we stroll over to inspect the cordoned-off *African Queen*, the famous steamboat used in the 1951 Hepburn–Bogart film classic of the same name. Then we drop in at Coconuts Restaurant for a dinner of conch fritters served under a canopied veranda overlooking the marina.

Heart-Thumping Action

One night we moor at the Holiday Isle Beach Resort at Islamorada, the honky-tonk center of the Keys boasting four hotels, seven restaurants, ten bars, dozens of island shops, lots of rental accommodations, and Kokomo Beach made famous by the Beach Boys' hit song.

Holiday Isle is a place you either love or hate depending on whether or not you enjoy non-stop music and heart-thumping action. All day long, music blares around the swimming pools on the Isle, while tanned—or burned—bikinied bodies and brawny—or not-so-brawny—guys saunter endlessly from one beach bar to the next. Holiday Isle should be given a wide berth by those looking for beauty and peace. That's the advantage of cruising the Keys; there's enough variety around here that you can have it any way you like.

Marathon, the halfway town between Miami and Key West, serves as a reminder that most visitors to the Keys come to fish. The happy ending of the movie *Key Largo* finds Humphrey Bogart and Lauren Bacall headed for a new life with a fishing charter boat in Marathon. At nearby Faro Blanco Marine Resort, we secure a slip amidst heavily armed, million-dollar sportfishing yachts. Arriving at day's end, we watch fishermen lug their trophy-size catches—billfish from the Atlantic depths or bonefish and tarpon from the flats of the "backcountry"—onto shoreside scales before tucking in their shirts for mandatory posed photos.

Little Palm Island

On our last evening before reaching Key West, we come upon a small luxury hideaway, Little Palm Island Resort, just off Little Torch Key. This five-acre sliver of paradise, a favorite retreat of Presidents Truman and Roosevelt, sits at the entrance to Newfound Harbor Channel where fast-running tides create white-sand beaches and deep-water dockage.

After securing *Purrfection* at the dock, we wander along tropical pathways beneath tall Jamaican coconut palms leading to luxury thatch-roofed villas. At the garden bar with "Gumby Slumbers" in hand, we watch the evening wading birds and wildlife emerge from long shadows at water's edge, hoping we'll catch a glimpse of the pink rosette spoonbill or the diminutive Key deer.

Because of its resemblance to South Pacific islands, in 1962, Warner Brothers picked Little Palm Island as the location for *PT 109*, the film recounting the war exploits of John F. Kennedy. A legacy of the film is the twelve-foot-deep lagoon encircling half the island, dredged so the movie's naval vessels would have adequate draft for the near-shore scenes. Today, that trench creates handy shoreside mooring for transient sailors.

Key West and Home

Our last day's sail brings us to funky, uproarious Key West, a deep-water port at the juncture of two great bodies of water, the

Atlantic Ocean and Gulf of Mexico. At FYC's Land's End Marina, we turn *Purrfection* over to the delivery crew who will return her to Miami.

Then, like most charterers at the end of a trip, we head straight for hot showers and soft beds. We find both at the Gardens Hotel, an elegant, small boutique hotel hidden away in botanical gardens on what was once the island's largest private estate.

From our quiet refuge, we spend our final day exploring this self-proclaimed capital of America's "Conch Republic" that was once a rowdy outpost for contrabandists. We indulge in the attractions, lounge around in bars with locals—mostly dropouts and high rollers—and exhaust ourselves with the nightlife. At last, we admit we've had enough. It's time now to slip back to our other lives.

The return 150-mile trip to Miami International Airport is an easy half-day drive along Overseas Highway (U.S. 1), popularly known as the "Highway that Goes to Sea." This concrete and steel strand creates a beautiful necklace of turquoise-fringed tropical isles connected by forty-two bridges leapfrogging from key to key. During the few hours of our return drive, we relive our cruise in reverse as we pass by marinas, dive sites, and sailing grounds we had earlier enjoyed in such leisure.

As Miami's skyscrapers once again loom up before our eyes and the tumult of traffic assaults our ears, we know we will take back into our busy everyday world the restorative powers of peace and quiet we found in the natural world of America's "Caribbean" playground.

Tips & Highlights for Sailors

Best Time to Go

1. 📅 November–May – Dry season, steady trade winds, comfortable temps.
2. Avoid peak hurricane season (August–October).

Why Catamarans Rule

1. ⛵ Shallow draft (less than three feet) lets you explore reefs and anchorages off-limits to keelboats.
2. More space and stability = ideal for family cruising.

Must-See Reefs

1. Key Largo Dry Rocks – Christ of the Deep statue.
2. Molasses Reef – Classic coral towers, sea turtles, parrotfish.
3. Looe Key – Incredible biodiversity, great snorkeling visibility.

Marina Favorites

1. Ocean Reef Club (Key Largo) – Advance reservation required, upscale amenities.
1. Marina del Mar (Key Largo) – Largest freshwater pool in the Keys.
2. Faro Blanco (Marathon) – Full-service slips, close to fishing action.
3. Little Palm Island (Little Torch Key) – Five-star hideaway for a memorable last night.

Don't Miss

1. 🍹 Sunset cocktails at Islamorada or Key West.
2. 🐠 Spotting manatees and tarpon near the mangroves.
3. 🚢 Cruising the Overseas Highway by car on your return trip—forty-two bridges connecting the islands.

Breakfast service at Ocean Reef Club.

Original boat from 1951 Hepburn-Bogart Film Classic

Waterfront dining at Little Palm Island

Passing Miami enroute to the Keys

Chapter 4

OREGON/WASHINGTON - CRUISING THE COLUMBIA RIVER

The greatest misfortune of the Columbia, America's second-longest river, is that it never had a Mark Twain to record the rough-and-tumble life along its 1,000-plus-mile course—from the Canadian Rockies through the Pacific Northwest to the Pacific Ocean. The task fell to historians, naturalists, and chroniclers, whose dry—though factual—reports sadly lack color and flavor.

Consequently, we think of the Mississippi's western sister, the Columbia, not in terms of daring fur trappers and great salmon runs, but in terms of a nuclear plant upstream and wheat conveyed to market downstream. The Columbia—this deep-draft highway to world markets—exists in bland obscurity. That's a shame, because the Columbia deserves its own epic.

Living in Seattle for many years, an easy half-day drive away, I have known the river only as something I crossed when traveling to Portland. However, when I learn from local boaters that the lower Columbia—the 100 miles from Portland to Astoria, Oregon—is considered among the country's finest recreational boating areas, I resolve to see for myself.

Launching on the Lower Columbia

With a little research, I discover several yacht clubs and marinas, both public and private, on each side of this lower stretch of river. The small towns equally scattered along both shorelines are mostly out of touch with each other because only one bridge—connecting Longview, Washington to Rainier, Oregon—spans the reach from Portland to the river's mouth. Surprisingly, I don't find any yacht charter operations in the area. Boating here seems to be a private affair.

Not to be daunted, I decide to explore this section of the river on my own boat, a trailerable Monaro 21 cuddy cruiser. Equipped with a galley, head, water supply, electrical system, and two comfortable berths, one amidships and a V-berth forward, the boat draws less than two feet of depth. Powered by a 200-hp Mercury outboard, *Freelance* is perfect for cruising in the lakes, rivers, and sounds of the Pacific Northwest.

Having grown up in Louisville and learned to sail on the banks of the Ohio River, I'm keen to compare the Columbia River to the Ohio. A phone call convinces Dale, an old childhood sailing buddy and fellow Louisville river rat, to fly to Seattle and join me for a cruise down the Columbia.

With my boat in tow, I pick up Dale at the airport a week later. We make the half-day drive south from Seattle on I-5 to the Interstate Bridge between Oregon and Washington over the Columbia River, then continue to Hayden Island on the Oregon side. After provisioning at a local grocery, we launch *Freelance* at the Gleason Boat Ramp. Our goal for the next week is to explore both sides of the river as we travel along the 100 miles to its mouth at the Pacific Ocean. We plan to tie up at marinas each night along the way.

Birders' Paradise

By late afternoon, we are on our way downstream, motoring a short distance to Sauvie Island, the largest island along the Columbia. Here at the Sauvie Island Wildlife Area, we nose *Freelance* into a protected cove, drop anchor, and settle in for our first night.

Our mid-October visit coincides with the migration of ducks, geese, herons, and other waterfowl at this stopover along the Pacific Flyway. Because half the island is farmland that adequately feeds the avian population and the rest remains in natural vegetation, Sauvie Island attracts tens of thousands of birds as they pass through during migration seasons.

Most distinctive is the sandhill crane migration, the stars of the show with red crowns and six-foot wingspans backlit by the fading light, their calls trilling and echoing over the water. What an unforgettable experience to hear hundreds of cranes trumpeting overhead at once! Our evening is calm and golden.

Rising early the next morning, we enjoy a leisurely breakfast, serenaded by dozens of birds flocking in the nearby trees. As we rinse dishes over the side of the boat, we notice, to our surprise, the water is slightly brackish—we didn't expect tidal effects to reach this far upriver.

Kalama—Totem Poles and Quiet Shores

Once underway, we motor slowly and, aided by a few knots of current, arrive within an hour at Kalama on the Washington side of the river. With its totem poles piercing the sky, Kalama is impossible to miss. One 140-foot-high totem pole, the world's tallest, was carved from a 700-year-old red cedar for the 1962 Seattle World's Fair.

In the twentieth century, totem poles became a generalized symbol of "Northwest Native culture." Towns like Kalama adopted them as public art and heritage markers, even in places where they were not historically used by local tribes. Although the Cowlitz people inhabited the lower Columbia River region, monumental totem poles were a cultural tradition of coastal Northwest tribes farther north in Canada, not part of Cowlitz material culture.

With a backdrop of steep slopes overgrown with spruce and fir trees near the Gifford Pinchot National Forest, the Port of Kalama is nestled in quiet wilderness beauty. This cruising stopover is where sailors typically shed the cares of city life and rekindle their appreciation of the outdoors.

The town itself is named for a Hawaiian fur trader who married the daughter of a Nisqually chief in the mid-nineteenth century. Thus, many of the town's street names and places reflect Hawaiian themes in honor of the founder's heritage.

Inside the Port of Kalama building, we find a small exhibit with artifacts dating to the town's founding. Information brochures available for visitors provide historical facts about Kalama. Vampire film buffs may be interested to learn that Kalama High School served as a filming location for the movie *Twilight.*

Once the headquarters and terminus of the Northern Pacific Railroad, the port served as a critical transfer point for incoming ships' cargo and outbound rail-delivered shipments of forest products and canned seafood destined for ocean coastal ports. This juncture earned the town the motto "Rail Meets Sail."

Wanderings to the Sea

The Columbia is a river with a flair for the dramatic. Originating in the high country of eastern British Columbia, it initially flows north, then makes a complete turn like a fastball windup, before blasting south through the center of Washington. Temporarily weakened by a chain of mighty dams that harness its awesome power, it gathers new strength from the inflow of the Snake River, its largest tributary. Making a westerly turn, the Columbia flows peacefully along the Washington and Oregon border. Then, it smashes through the Cascades, generating strong winds that create a sailboard heaven in the Columbia River Gorge.

But once free of the interference of dams and the constrictions of mountains, the mighty river doesn't race directly westward toward the sea. Nature, in a gesture of goodwill toward recreational boaters and those seeking island getaways, called forth the forces of tectonics of the ubiquitous San Andreas Fault to double the length of the river's cruising grounds and create countless islands in the lower delta region. The river doesn't just flow here, it meanders, carving side channels and secret sloughs, creating a playground of hidden anchorages and protected bays.

Geologic pyrotechnics pushed the mighty Columbia north forty miles before allowing it to flow slowly, surrounded by enhanced beauty, into a broad delta before reaching the Pacific. Now, eight million years later, boaters and those seeking island vacation homes find idyllic cruising waters among countless small islands beginning only a few miles downstream from Portland, and much of the area has been converted to wildlife refuges and is otherwise uninhabited.

Canneries and Forests

Unlike most rivers worldwide, the Columbia has little commercial buildup along its shores in the lower delta region. Only a handful of towns are situated on each side of the river below Portland. These tend to be small, barely thriving on boating and fishing industries.

The more densely inhabited exception is our next stop, Longview, ten miles farther downriver at the junction with the Cowlitz River. Once claimed to be the site of the world's largest forest-products mill, Longview today serves as headquarters of the federally recognized Cowlitz Indian Tribe and is an ancestral burial ground for the Cowlitz people.

The city's claim to fame is the Nutty Narrows Bridge, reputed to be the only bridge in the world built strictly for squirrels. Its purpose is to avoid squirrel casualties on busy streets beneath. As part of the annual Squirrel Fest, new squirrel bridges have been periodically added over the years. Today the city boasts a total of seven squirrel bridges.

Sited across from this deep-water port upriver on the Oregon shore is the Trojan Nuclear Power Plant, the only commercial nuclear power plant to be built in Oregon. Although cloaked in controversy and decommissioned after cracks were discovered in steam-generator tubing, the hulking cooling tower of the Trojan still looms over the landscape. Scars along the inflowing Cowlitz River—scars left by the scathing mudslides and ash deposits from the 1980 Mount St. Helens' eruptions—further blot this otherwise pristine landscape.

Tucked up in a slough behind Longview, we spend another pleasant evening anchored under a ceiling of stars. The next day we negotiate the wide westerly sweep past Longview, keeping a careful lookout for outbound ships carrying timber products to the east and inbound freighters laden with Toyota and Hyundai automobiles. Pacific winds directed upriver create a rough chop against the outgoing tidal current, so we divert through the maze of sloughs and protected bays that meander among the islands forming stepping-stone hops to the sea.

Pile dikes—or wing dams—become a regular feature along the way. These long rows of pilings speed up the river's flow by deflecting water to the center of the channel. Then the downstream out-fanning of the flows creates deposits that restore and protect eroded areas.

Elochoman Slough

Elochoman Slough leads back among sandy beaches and rugged peaks to Cathlamet, a picturesque historic town nestled between forested hills on the Washington shore. Gill-netters and seiners, which typically operate at night, fill the moorage slips by day, but leave berths available at this last freshwater marina in the evening for pleasure craft seeking overnight shelter.

When we check in at the marina office, the friendly harbormaster greets us with, "We're full, but we'll find a place for you anyway. After all, there's not another marina for over twenty-five miles until Astoria, so if I say no, where else can you go?" Our conversation is constantly interrupted as he works the VHF radio guiding transient yachts into the hidden marina and warning them of tugs charging out of the sluggish waterway with large log booms or chip barges in tow.

In the morning, we spend a couple of hours at the nearby Wahkiakum Historical Society Museum, which houses artifacts that preserve the area's history. The displays include agricultural equipment that was used locally, and the centerpiece is an old Shay locomotive once used to haul timber and passengers. The displays feature tribal art and handicrafts created by people from the Chinook Indian Nation, a nation made up of the five westernmost tribes at the mouth of the Columbia River. The exhibits explore the resilience of the Chinook people and their relationship to their ancestral lands.

The picture gallery shows how, at the turn of the twentieth century, salmon, timber, and the flowing Columbia were not just mainstays of the economy but the focus of all life along the river. In those days, the dozens of canneries and sawmills dotting the shoreline never worked fast enough to process the seemingly inexhaustible supply of fish and timber.

The museum director describes these booming times when hundreds of fishing vessels, mostly small sailing skiffs, thrived off the legendary salmon. "Just imagine," he exclaims, "The runs were so dense that a person could practically walk across the mile-wide river on the backs of the silvery fish!"

From Commerce to Quiet Cruising

Although commercial activities dominated the river in the past, tourism and recreational boating are the economic mainstays today. Sternwheelers—which, contrary to popular belief, are said to have started on the Columbia, not the Mississippi—plied the waters from Portland down to the sea, conveying vacationers to their summer homes scattered throughout the hundreds of islands in the lower delta region. Because landings at Ilwaco could be made only at high tide, the connecting train that ran back along the coast departed an hour later each day than it had the previous day. Word has it that this was the only railroad in the country that ran on tide time.

Now, however, we find the Columbia River quite different from the booming times of an earlier era. Gone are the great river fishing fleets. Nothing is left of the canneries that had cantilevered out over the river except the rotting toothpicks of their pilings. The only remnants of the bustling logging era are denuded shoreline slopes increasingly eroding into the river with every passing rain. But on the bright side, the demise of these commercial ventures has opened the river to more recreational possibilities.

Nowhere are these attractions more evident than below Cathlamet. The river widens and becomes brackish at the tip of the salty wedge driven twenty-five miles upriver from the sea. As the slowing river drops accumulated silt, it creates extensive marshes spread along the shore, rich with life. You can begin to smell the ocean—and the primal decay—at low tide. Wildlife abounds, whitetail deer and elk graze at the water's edge. Overhead, ospreys, great blue herons, and bald eagles, among the 175 types of birds and migrating waterfowl that inhabit the region, patrol the skies. Alert for a quick meal, hawks and owls, aerial pest control experts, are always aloft, keeping sharp eyes on the open meadows.

These fragile tidal marshes and mudflats form the basis for a complicated food chain that is being threatened by the encroachment of humans. Most of this downstream area is protected in the Lewis and Clark and the Columbian White-Tailed Deer National Wildlife Refuges. Because the region is inaccessible by roads, it offers boaters a unique opportunity to see a rare expression of nature's beauty.

Tourism and Gourmet Foods—What the River Still Provides

Barely visible from the water are scattered quaint villages and nearly deserted cannery shanty towns—Skamokawa, Grays River, Altoona, Westport. Each has its photographic structures, which were the pride of its past. Now they're relics of an exciting bygone era when the famous migratory salmon runs and vast tracts of uncut timber meant prosperity for all who worked the river. In bygone days, subsistence was as easy as land-to-mouth compared with these days when families can barely eke out a living from the Columbia's turbid waters.

Although the salmon have all but disappeared, other native foods are gaining a national reputation in gourmet kitchens across the country. From the bayshore waters come razor clams, Dungeness crabs, mussels, crawfish, sturgeon, steelhead, trout, and limited amounts of the incomparable salmon. Shad roe provides a Northwest version of caviar known as "shaviar."

The forests offer up wild grapes to make vinegar, along with raspberries, truffles, chanterelles, nuts, morels, filberts, and salmon berries. The rich fields of the Willamette Valley grow a wide selection of fruits and vegetables, made all the tastier by the perfect growing climate. Taken all together, these gifts from the earth constitute a delectable Columbia River cuisine, especially when accented with wines from one of the area's many wineries.

Our final destination at the river's mouth is Astoria on the Oregon shore where the Columbia slows down, spreads out, and spills into the sea. Founded in 1811 by New York financier John Jacob Astor as a trading post, this first U.S. settlement west of the Rockies flourished well into the twentieth century as the salmon capital of the world. Once rivaling San Francisco in size, Astoria boasted more than fifty canneries and the country's largest fishing fleet. Today the city survives on summer tourists who flock to see the restored Victorian buildings and Columbia River Maritime Museum.

For ocean-going ships and yachts, Astoria provides a refuge from an unforgiving sea that, near the Columbia's mouth, has earned the nickname "Graveyard of the Pacific." But for us, Astoria marks our turn-around point. Taking advantage of an incoming tide, Dale and I start our long journey back upriver, grateful for a week on a river that finally has its story told—at least in part.

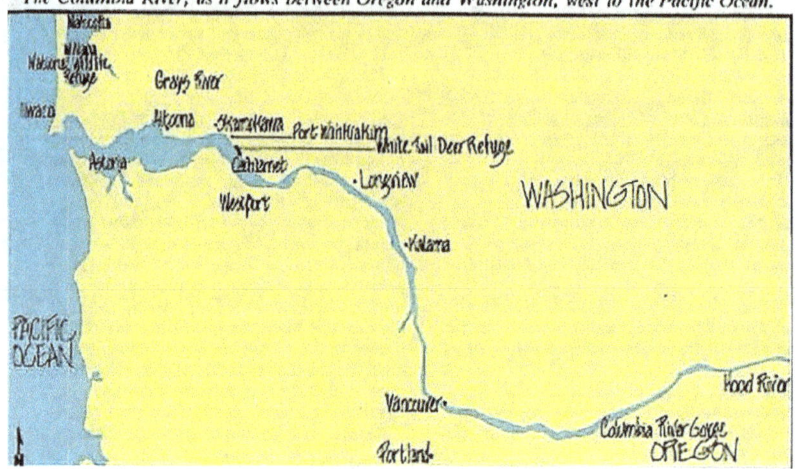

Columbia River Chart

Entering Skomokawa Marina

Redman Hall, Skomokawa

Chapter 5

WASHINGTON - WATER TO WINE IN THE SAN JUAN ISLANDS

Although my wife, Risa, enjoys boating, her ideal getaway involves visiting vineyards and wine-tasting rooms. While I'll happily quaff a glass of Pinot Noir, my heart centers on cruising aboard *Freelance*, our Monaro 21 cuddy cruiser. Fortunately, the San Juan Islands, near our Seattle home, offer both first-class ports of call and first-class pours. For two decades, we've cruised these waters, encountering breaching orcas and barking sea lions, along with secluded coves guarded by cliffs. In recent years, the islands' natural wonders have been joined by dozens of wineries and vineyards, easily reached by boat.

Just as locavores celebrate regionally grown foods, loca-pours seek wines grown near their home ZIP codes. "Let's do a wine odyssey," suggests Risa, for our annual summer cruise in the San Juans.

"We'll check out as many island wineries as we can—and see what the restaurants are pouring."

I immediately agree. Soon we're both aboard—on board with the idea and on-board *Freelance.*

Island Hopping, Wine Shopping

In a week when the weather chart displays cheerful yellow suns each day, we trailer *Freelance* north to Bellingham and cast off from Squalicum Marina. Instead of the foreboding wine-dark seas Homer wrote about, we set out on calm, cat's-paw-ruffled Bellingham Bay. Our plan for the week: explore a different vineyard each day, return to the quiet of the boat after dinner, and start fresh each morning.

Our first stop, Dynasty Cellars, just above the beach at Lummi Nation near Bellingham, is owned by Peter Osvaldik, who emigrated from the former Czechoslovakia decades ago. Although the grapes come from Les Collines Vineyard in Walla Walla, Peter oversees every aspect of the vineyard's management. He determines when to prune and when to harvest, showing up at dawn in an old truck to lend a hand.

Sourced year after year from the same blocks, the grapes include well-known Bordeaux varietals: Syrah, Zinfandel, and Tempranillo, along with other reds and whites. Peter's attention to detail shows up in the glass—especially in his Cabernet Sauvignon, rich with bold flavors of blackberry and black cherry. The tasting room is open year-round with outdoor patio seating in warmer months or indoors by a cozy fireplace in colder months.

Continuing our cruise south along Lummi Island's western shoreline, we drop the hook in Legoe Bay. After dinghying to shore, we walk a short distance to Artisan Wine Gallery, owned by Ryan

Wildstar, a retired professor at Western Washington University. "I started the shop after my wine collection outstripped the dimensions of my garage," he tells us. "The only criteria: I have to like it, and it has to be a particularly good wine."

Ryan carries vintages of top Washington labels, in addition to racks of wines from around the world. He offers classes that feature in-depth explorations of four regions in France: Alsace, Northern Rhône, Côtes du Jura, and Provence. Each class examines the connections linking the terroir—a combination of soil, climate, and environment—of a particular region's wines paired with the food, art, literature, music, and film from the same region.

As we set out the next morning to cross Rosario Strait, we encounter a familiar Northwest sea condition. The peaking tidal current—tidal exchange of fifteen feet or more is typical in Puget Sound—countered by a 20-knot wind is causing short, steep waves to churn the waters. But our Monaro, built just miles away across the border near Vancouver, is designed for weather conditions like this.

With a hull of twenty-one feet and a high freeboard, Monaros have safely circumnavigated Vancouver Island, journeyed to Alaska, cruised down the Mississippi, and performed along hundreds of miles of the wild British Columbia coast. The deep V-shaped bow, combined with the sharp forefoot, eats the chop and affords a soft dry ride—even when we occasionally fly the hull.

The seas settle as we arrive in the lee of Orcas Island, so we raise *Freelance's* trim tabs and slow-throttle through unnamed isles to Friday Harbor on San Juan Island. With 500 slips, including 150 for visiting boats, Friday Harbor Marina provides easy access to the town's premier restaurants and wine-tasting rooms.

San Juan Vineyards is more than walking distance from the marina, so we rent from Susie's Mopeds. Our Scoot Coupe—a souped-up, two-passenger go-kart—looks like a miniature Ferrari. We zip past woods, pastures, and pastoral landscapes enroute to the winery's tasting room, set in a remodeled 1895 schoolhouse.

There we chat with the winemaker, who proudly explains that although the winery makes Chardonnay, Sangiovese, and Syrah from grapes grown in Eastern Washington, the winery also produces its own island-grown Madeleine Angevine—a white grape from France's Loire Valley, in addition to Siegerrebe—a cross between Madeleine Angevine and Gewürztraminer developed in the Alsace region of Germany.

Mona, a camel that for years grazed in the pasture across the way until she died, was an island icon. She's the namesake for the winery's Mona Vino Blanc, a blend of Madeleine Angevine, Chardonnay, and Riesling.

On our way back to *Freelance*, we stop at San Juan Vineyards' second tasting room in Friday Harbor. Here, local musicians can play a baby grand piano that belonged to one of the winery's founders.

Top restaurants in the San Juans take pride in pairing island wines with local foods. "We have a bull's-eye philosophy—we want everything from this island we can get," explains Kyle Nicholson, former chef and innkeeper at The Bluff. He personally forages for island hedgehog mushrooms, bullwhip kelp, and thimbleberries to adorn his dishes.

From our dinner table on the terrace that evening, we can see *Freelance* moored among the boats below, along with the bustling passengers at the ferry docks and the full expanse of the Friday Harbor basin. Our selection of San Juan Vineyards' 2009 Afterglow—a rosé with aromas of strawberry, peach, and orange—pairs perfectly with the fried calamari accented by crystallized lemon.

Apples, Spirits, and Cider

The next morning, we set *Freelance* on course for Roche Harbor, at the western end of San Juan Island. It's a beautiful, windless day, so we strip off the canvas we put up the evening before to enclose the cockpit. Sunshine dances around the cabin as *Freelance* slices gracefully across the deep blue water. Although our usual cruising speed is 25–30 knots, today, being in no hurry, we putter at idle speed.

Once we've tied up at Roche, we rent bicycles and pedal rolling country roads to Westcott Bay Cidery and Distillery, which produces three hard ciders, along with apple eau-de-vie and Spy Hop gin. Although the region's short, cool summers challenge wine grapes, the climate is paradise for apples. In the mid-1990s, Richard Anderson planted 1,000 apple trees on his two-acre property above Westcott Bay and, with partners Susie and Hawke Pingree—longtime island residents—developed a thriving business.

The ciders use sixteen varieties of heritage apples—apples with names like Kingston Black, Yarlington Mill, Dabinett, and Sweet Coppin. "Most are 'spitters' for eating, meaning they taste bad for dessert but are perfect for cider," explains Susie. Westcott Bay ciders are made with fresh-pressed apple juice that initially runs brown with tannins, then clears to a brilliant amber-gold as it gently ferments and mellows.

Susie and Richard expanded early operations by adding gins and apple brandies made from their own fruit. Crafted in a 200-liter copper still, the gin incorporates island-grown aromatics, including blackberry, wild rose, lavender, and madrone bark.

After returning to the Roche Harbor docks, we buy a pound of live, wriggling spot prawns, our favorite summertime delicacy, and motor a few minutes to a mirror-still anchorage at Westcott Bay, one of the most protected in the San Juans. We always see wildlife here—deer grazing, blue herons and kingfishers gliding and diving, and seals lazing on the shoreline's sandbanks. This evening, a bald eagle perches atop a Douglas fir, standing sentinel over its watery realm.

We chill a bottle of Chardonnay from San Juan Vineyards by tossing it overboard in a net bag tied to a cleat. Puget Sound may be too cold for swimming, but its waters make a superb ice bucket. Risa, the designated "assassin," decapitates the prawns and sautés the tails with butter and garlic. With Puget Sound-chilled wine, we settle back to enjoy a perfect maritime meal.

Lopez Island—Slow Pedals, Serious Wines

The weatherman did not lie: a new day greets us with golden sun and calm water for our cruise to Lopez Island. Paying attention to the buoys marking the shallow entrance, we carefully motor into Fisherman Bay. Fantastical ships formed from bleached driftwood created by improvisational sculptors adorn a spit to starboard.

Resisting the temptation to fashion our own driftwood ship, we continue on to secure a slip at Lopez Island Resort and Marina. There we rent bikes—one of the best ways to get around this mostly flat, laid-back island. A one-mile pedal brings us to tiny Lopez Village, where we seek out the tasting room for Lopez Island Vineyards. "Summer Hours: 12 to 5-ish," reads the sign on the door. Luckily, we arrive on the good side of "ish."

Established in 1987, Lopez Island Vineyards is owned by Brent Charnly, the winemaker, and his wife, Maggie. Brent tells us he got bitten by the wine bug as a college student, laboring as a lark in a

Bordeaux vineyard in France. A graduate of the viticulture program at University of California, Davis, he worked a few miles up the coast at Mount Baker Vineyards before planting his own grapes on five acres on Lopez Island.

In addition to making Madeleine Angevine and Siegerrebe from organically grown estate grapes, he crafts premium wines from fruit grown at Crawford Family Vineyards in Eastern Washington. For Sangiovese, he sources fruit from Hattrup Farm's Elephant Mountain Vineyards in Wapato. He also creates fruit wines from apples, pears, blackberries, and raspberries.

The San What? Islands

The wineries in the San Juans belong to the Puget Sound AVA (American Viticultural Area), a federally designated grape-growing region. This AVA is Washington's only appellation west of the Cascade Mountains, making it the state's coolest and wettest growing region. It encompasses a wide swath of land—including numerous islands—from the Canadian border in the north through Seattle to Olympia, the state capital, to the south.

Lying at the cool extreme of viticultural survival, the islands experience a short, sweet summer, amplified by long hours of sunlight. While some local winemakers truck in grapes from Eastern Washington, others tackle the challenges of island viticulture by experimenting with different varieties of cool-weather vinifera.

Risa and I conclude our time in the San Juans at Lopez Village with dinner at Bay Café, which overlooks some of the best plonk-into-the-sea sunsets in the islands. Glasses of Lopez Island Vineyards' Madeleine Angevine enhance the flavor of the crab and shrimp cakes—all seafood, no filler—served atop a sauce accented by basil, cilantro, and plenty of lemon. This trip—a wine-and-dine cruise on the Salish Sea—has been a perfect pairing of wine and wave.

As I sip my Madeleine Angevine and review the week's adventures with Risa, I venture a suggestion: "Maybe these islands should be called the San WINE Islands!"

~

Ferries, Friday Harbor

San Juan Vineyards

Roche Harbor, San Juan Island

Dining Friday Harbor House

Chapter 6

WASHINGTON - CRUISING THROUGH THE HOOD

Things are seldom what they seem in Hood Canal. For starters, Hood Canal is not a canal. Neither is it a channel, as George Vancouver named it when he explored Puget Sound in 1792. Rather, Hood Canal is a glacial fjord, one of only two in the lower forty-eight states; the other is in Maine's Penobscot Bay.

By the way, that black shape you see lurking in the distance? It isn't a whale—although it could be. It's more likely a nuclear-tipped Trident submarine operating out of nearby Bangor Submarine Base. And you wouldn't expect to find luxury resorts or the secret family getaway homes of prominent Pacific Northwest figures—like Microsoft's Bill Gates, for example—tucked in among the hard-scrabble fishing and logging villages along Hood Canal's forested shoreline. And who could imagine that, unlike the frigid waters elsewhere in Puget Sound, Hood Canal's waters are actually swimmable?

Never mind all that. Hood Canal—this paradoxical, fishhook-shaped body of water that looks like a backward Swoosh logo, backed by glacier-capped peaks and extending deep into Washington's Olympic Peninsula—is a favorite cruising destination for our family's summer getaways: an unlikely mix of wilderness, working waterfront, and quiet luxury.

Entering the Mouth of the Hook

Stretching sixty-five miles, Hood Canal is one of the five main basins of Puget Sound. As my wife, Risa, and I enter the canal aboard our Monaro 21 cuddy cruiser, stunning views of the state's two signature mountains open up before us: 14,400-foot Mount Rainier rises to the southeast, while 10,800-foot Mount Baker towers to the northeast.

Two eighteenth century former logging towns guard the opening of the waterway, which separates the Kitsap Peninsula from the Olympic Peninsula. Port Gamble to the east, listed as a National Historic Landmark, preserves the feel of a 150-year-old New England village with pastel-painted Victorian homes. Ignoring its potential for attracting recreational boaters, however, the town has not developed its waterfront. By contrast, Port Ludlow to the west has reinvented itself as a boaters' destination with a full-service marina, a chandlery, moorage docks, and a waterfront restaurant.

After tanking up and provisioning at Ludlow's fuel dock, we enter the waterway by passing under Hood Canal Bridge This bridge is the third-longest floating bridge in the world and the only one constructed on saltwater—an engineering marvel, considering it must rise and fall twice daily with the average eleven-to-thirteen-foot tides. Even more impressive, it continues functioning with king tides up to seventeen feet. Once past the bridge, we turn sharply to port, passing at a comfortable distance from the two rocks that are well-marked on the charts. We then guide our cuddy cruiser on a southeasterly bearing to continue on our way. With an average depth of 175 feet and average width of one and a half miles, Hood Canal poses little navigational challenge.

Mind the Torpedoes

With a cruising speed of 25 knots, we traverse the entire distance in one day with time to stop at several towns along the way. We enjoy magnificent views of the snow-capped Olympic Mountains along the western shore of Hood Canal. Temperate rainforests reach down to a coastline fringed with sand beaches, gravel bars, muddy tidelands, and sheer cliffs. Five rivers—Skokomish, Hamma Hamma, Duckabush, Dosewallips, and Big Quilcene—carry snowmelt from alpine lakes in Olympic National Park and National Forest into the canal, creating perfect brackish conditions for the region's renowned shellfish.

As we cruise along, we spy the hulking shoulders of bald eagles perched on snags; ospreys, herons, swans, hawks, and cormorants also cross our path. Situated on the Pacific Flyway, the region is a major avian stopover for migratory species throughout the seasons.

Because of mishaps on earlier cruises, we're careful not only to look around us, but to watch far ahead for hard-to-see wooden stakes marking oyster farms along the shoreline shallows. On previous occasions when our attention was focused elsewhere, we found ourselves trapped in a maze of alder limbs protruding from shallow shellfish beds.

Another threat lurks in these waters as well—one we discover the hard way. As we enter Dabob Bay about twenty miles into the canal, we suddenly experience a surreal moment when a wake rolls across the water's surface. Ordinarily, a small wake is nothing unusual. But this time is different—very different: There is no sound, just an eerie silence, and there is not a boat in sight. How can this be possible? Then I recall, from earlier reading, that a series of yellow buoys marks the torpedo firing range of the Bangor Naval Submarine Base, which, in addition to stockpiling torpedoes and other conventional underwater weapons, is said to store the third-largest U.S. nuclear stockpile.

Some torpedoes are guided by noise, so the Navy issues a somber warning to boaters: Stop all propellers, motors, and other equipment generating underwater noise, or you risk becoming a target. Boaters are given plenty of advance notice about tests from naval guard boats and amber beacons, but apparently, we have somehow slipped past their security net.

In the next moment, a Navy patrol boat speeds up alongside and directs me to follow the line of flashing buoys out of danger. We quickly turn toward the eastern shore at full throttle, and within a minute are safely out of the firing range. As the locals say (in reference to the 1991 film of the same name), "Pay attention to the 'Buoys 'n the Hood!'"

When the Tide Is Out, the Table Is Set

Cruising farther along Hood Canal, we make short stops at several small towns—Quilcene, Brinnon, Seabeck, Eldon, and Lilliwaup. Although there's a fuel dock at Pleasant Harbor Marina near Brinnon, there are no marine services and not much for the tourist in any of these villages except—and this is enough in itself—arguably the freshest seafood on the planet. In these small settlements every café, sports bar, tavern, and restaurant features oysters, clams, shrimp, salmon, and Dungeness crab. Cooking styles run the gamut: baked, fried, frittered, steamed, poached, skewered, stewed, or simply served raw on the half-shell.

But we prefer to do it ourselves. We pick our own oysters and clams, reel in one of the five species of salmon that spawn in these waters, or set a shrimp trap or crab pot. Other marine creatures abound as well: cockles, moon snails, sea urchins, mussels, squid, sea cucumbers, wolf eels, and octopus. "When the tide is out, the table is set," locals claim—and we concur.

Risa and I often join other boaters on shore at one of our favorite spots, such as Eagle Creek or Mike's Beach, to grill our harvest or cook it over an open fire. Unless you purchase from a commercial source, regulations stipulate that oysters must be shucked on the beach where they are harvested, and the shells left behind, which often have new seedling oysters attached.

To complement our feast, we walk up from the public docks at Hoodsport, the southernmost village on the canal's west shoreline, to purchase chocolate truffles filled with raspberry wine at Hoodsport Winery.

"Go out on any beach any time of year, and the oysters are so thick you can't help stepping on them," Peggy Patterson tells us when we ask where to find the best shellfish. In 1978, she and her husband, Dick Patterson, founded Hoodsport Winery, one of the first wineries in the state. Today there are more than 600.

The winery earns acclaim for its award-winning grape and fruit wines, including traditional vinifera varietals such as Chardonnay, Cabernet, and a Madeleine Angevine blend, in addition to smaller productions of unique varieties like Island Belle and full-bodied cordial-style wines with names like Bella Cranberry, Stella Raspberry, and Loganberry Dream. To draw attention to the plight of orcas—often incorrectly called whales, though they're actually the world's biggest dolphins—that once fed on harbor seals in front of their winery, the Pattersons donate proceeds from their orca series of wines to support the Orca Network, a nonprofit conservation organization.

Hoodsport is renowned among scuba divers as a staging area for viewing the giant Pacific octopus. Local marine preserves such as Octopus Hole and Sund Rock offer divers the chance to see the giant octopus, in addition to wolf eels, rockfish, plumose anemones, and other marine life. Hoodsport is also popular among hikers as the gateway to the Staircase area of Olympic National Park.

Living by Tide and Timber

Life on Hood Canal still reflects its frontier roots. People who reside along the 240 miles of Hood Canal's shoreline—jagged and heavily indented with coves and small bays—are modern-day hunter-gatherers who make a living by farming the tidelands and logging the forests. It's hard to imagine that the sleepy two-lane winding road hugging the western shore—sections of which have a twenty-five miles per hour limit—is part of U.S. 101, a national highway that stretches from Canada to Mexico.

Although not accessible by boat in the marshes at the southern end of the Hood, Skokomish thrives both as a tourist town and tribal center of the Skokomish Indian Tribe. Chief Seattle, namesake for the main city on Puget Sound, was born nearby. Native peoples have been making smoked fish for centuries, prompting us to hike a few miles from Hoodsport to pick up some kipper and lox. With revenues coming from its Lucky Dog Casino, the tribe has plans to dredge an access channel and build a full-service marina and fuel dock along the town's waterfront.

Washington's Riviera

Beyond Skokomish, the sparsely settled, less-affluent west side coastal communities end, and the Hood Canal hooks sharply to the northeast at an area known as the Great Bend. The town of Union marks the start of "Washington's Riviera." Here, on the shores of Hood Canal, the family of Microsoft billionaire Bill Gates has owned a vacation home for three generations. Amenities at the compound include a helipad and, to enhance security, a secret access tunnel under the street to the beach. Locals recount how, as a kid, Bill picked oysters from the beach or walked to the Union Country Store to buy cans of SpaghettiOs, his favorite lunch. Other homes in the area are owned by members of the Nordstrom family, founders and owners of the largest upscale clothing store chain in the country, and other wealthy luminaries from Seattle.

Set amid this well-to-do neighborhood, the luxurious Alderbrook Resort and Spa blends the rustic style of the Northwestern Lodge with the amenities of a world-class resort. For us and for other transient boaters visiting the region, Alderbrook is Hood Canal's primary destination. Its T-dock offers more than 1,200 feet of side-tie moorage along with cable TV, high-speed internet, phone service, power, water, sewage, and dry-fire-system standpipes. Shoreside enticements include a world-class spa, a PGA-rated golf course, and a heated pool.

After tying up at the docks, we go ashore to book a table at the waterfront restaurant for dinner. Our table turns out to be adjacent to the small dining room reserved for the Gates family. Too bad Bill isn't around this evening!

The Alderbrook Lodge menu features outstanding Northwest cuisine and fresh seafood enhanced by locally grown ingredients from the Skokomish Valley. We choose to indulge in an oyster-focused dining experience ranging from raw and on-the-half-shell appetizers to an expertly grilled main course paired with flavorful sauces—and, of course, a bottle of a locally grown Madeleine Angevine.

The Final Stretch

To appreciate the full extent of Hood Canal, we continue northeast for the final fifteen miles to the tip of the fishhook and the town of Belfair. Here, we feel we have returned to civilization as we pass shoreside campgrounds, RV parks, and small vacation resorts. Unlike the frigid waters elsewhere in Puget Sound, the shallow depths and limited tidal exchange make this area suitable for swimming, so we don't hesitate to jump overboard.

As the canal begins to shallow, we come upon some of the most extensive salt marshes and wetlands in the state. Above the tidelands and mudflats, the shoreline disappears at Lynch's Cove into typical Northwest woodlands of cedar, alder, and fir trees.

The main deterrent to cruising the lower sections of Hood Canal for many years was the absence of marina services. Back then, the only fuel docks were at Port Ludlow and Pleasant Harbor Marina in the upper sections of the canal. But that changed when a new owner of Alderbrook Lodge, a former Microsoft executive and subsequent head of the Bill and Melinda Gates Foundation, developed Hood Canal Marina at Union. With the availability of transient moorage docks, marine fuel, a pump-out station, and boat supplies, cruising boaters can now explore the lower canal feeling secure that marina services are readily at hand.

With Hood Canal's bountiful seafood for the taking, swimmable clean water, majestic mountains soaring in nearby Olympic National Forest, and marine fuel and boat supplies readily available, all in a perfect cruising setting, boaters need not go anywhere else. Why would they ever leave?

Locals call this "Life on the half-shell."

Alderbrook Resort and Spa Docks

Mount Baker

Osprey Nest

Pleasant Harbor Marina

Chapter 7

ALASKA WEDDING - AN UNEXPECTED BONUS ADVENTURE

Sometimes my trips yield unexpected bonus adventures. Such is the case while traveling on a small cruise ship along the Inside Passage from Seattle to Whittier, near Anchorage. A young couple suddenly decides to get married, and they ask me and another journalist to serve as wedding witnesses. We quickly agree but are surprised to learn we must accompany them from our ship by helicopter to a glacier for the ceremony. Here's how the event unfolded, as recounted in my article subsequently published in the couple's hometown newspaper.

A Wedding Detour

Bald eagles wheel overhead. A murmuring salmon stream cascades into an isolated bay, lost in fog-shrouded fjords. Here on a rocky beach beside a 10,000-year-old glacier in the Alaskan wilderness, Nancy and Scott—both from a small town in Ohio—stand, hand in hand, and exchange vows.

"We wanted to get away from the hoopla of a big wedding with rice in my face and tears in the eyes of family," explains the bride, who is an executive secretary at a small manufacturing company at home. "It was perfect because we don't know anyone here and want only the blessing of a minister. This is as close to God's country as we could possibly get."

The couple chartered a helicopter from the small village of Petersburg in Alaska's southeastern panhandle. Once we're all aboard, they direct the pilot to find the most isolated wedding site possible.

A Glacier for a Chapel

Flying among the 4,000-foot-high sheer granite cliffs, the pilot gives them a view of the Stikine Icefield stretching for hundreds of miles among the peaks of the Coast Mountains across the Alaskan border into Canada. These massive packs of ice and snow feed into the LeConte Glacier about twenty-five miles south of Wrangell, which proves to be the perfect spot for the occasion. The pilot lands at an open clearing by the water's edge not far from the glacier, and the small wedding party quickly unloads flowers and champagne on the rocky beach.

Standing at the shoreline with a hastily recruited Presbyterian minister beside them, the couple gazes in silence across the bay at the awesome glacier. Thunderous sounds fill the air as huge chunks of ice calve off the 300-foot jagged face of this southernmost tidewater glacier in North America and crash into the bay below. Waves break the stillness of the water as they roll up onto the surrounding gravelly shores.

When the bay is once again calm, the bride and groom, dressed in jeans and sneakers, turn to each other as the minister conducts a brief yet heartfelt service.

A Shared Secret Dream

"We wanted to do this in our own special way," explains Scott, a Kent State graduate who is a sales engineer for a computer company in Ohio. When the couple met two years earlier, they discovered they each harbored a secret dream of seeing Alaska. With Seattle-based Alaska Sightseeing Tours, they booked a week-long cruise through the Inside Passage of Alaska's southeast panhandle from Juneau to Ketchikan on the 90-foot motor vessel *Sheltered Seas*.

According to Scott, it was a last-minute decision to get married while on the trip, prompted by the allure of the wild beauty of Alaska's remote wilderness. "It's been amazing to see as much wildlife as we have—mountain goats, whales, sea lions, porpoises—far more than what we expected," explains Scott. "These sights plus the wild beauty of the land kept us entertained the whole way."

The bride said the biggest problem in arranging the ceremony was finding time during the trip. The only opportunity was the free half-day while the tour boat was in Petersburg, a Norwegian fishing community founded in the late nineteenth century, which is known for its warm hospitality.

The Town Steps In

Although the bride and groom wanted to keep the wedding secret, it wasn't long before word leaked out. When the people of Petersburg learn of the pending marriage, many step in to help. The town magistrate waives the waiting period and blood test so that the paperwork won't be delayed. The charter air service cancels its normal flights that day due to fog but manages to take the wedding party into the fjords during a short break when the weather clears.

Upon our return to Petersburg, wine, champagne, and food come out of nowhere, courtesy of the staff at a local motel. That evening at a Norwegian folk dance and heritage festival, a traditional Scandinavian multi-tiered wedding cake mysteriously appears. After sharing their good fortune with everyone, the couple still has enough cake to feed more than 100 well-wishers.

Hoopla After All

Indeed, there was no rice and no tears in the eyes of family members. But there was hoopla. Overwhelmed by the festivities—after what had started as a very private ceremony—the bride simply comments, "It was perfect."

~

Marriage of Nancy & Scott

Minister bestows blessing on newlyweds

Chapter 8

BRITISH COLUMBIA/WASHINGTON - CRUISING THE SALISH SEA

Ah... It's that time again. Early autumn, when cruising under sail in the San Juan and Canadian Gulf Islands is at its best. As summer crowds depart, Nature swirls bright hues of gold and crimson from her palette across the landscape and unleashes from her bag the steady sailing winds that have been confined all summer. Once released, the winds frolic among the island waters where, until a few weeks ago, bare-masted sailboats under power were an all-too-common sight.

Paradoxically, during this glorious period, prices throughout the region fall. Moorage fees, charter rates, restaurant prices, and costs for supplies all tumble by fifteen to fifty percent.

Bareboat Charter

My family heeds the advice of local long-time sailors: never consider cruising under sail in the islands in summer, lest we simply drift around, impatient for winds that never materialize. Therefore, this year we decide to charter a bareboat sloop in early fall.

Bareboating is the simple, no-fuss, hassle-free way to find the right boat. The beauty is that once we've chosen the boat and finished provisioning, we can slip the mooring lines and get underway.

We will be a crew of five—my then-wife, Paula, and I, plus our preteen twin sons, Belden and Seton, and thirteen-year-old Rasila. But cruising with children creates different sets of priorities. Paula and I enjoy scenic views. Kids don't go for scenery. We can be sailing through the most dazzling surroundings, and their only thought is, "How soon before we get there?" and "When can we go swimming?" I learn this lesson once again this fall on our week's cruise through the San Juan and Gulf Islands.

A yacht charter company in Bellingham, a convenient jumping-off location for the islands, has just the boat we need—a new, comfortable, well-equipped Pearson 34. This East Coast boat is perfect for our family—small enough to maneuver through tight gunkholes, yet beamy enough for three children to spread out with books and toys. To preserve our sanity, there are forward berths for the youngsters well separated from a double berth for Paula and me in the stern. After a quick checkout by the charter yacht manager, we load provisions and cast off.

Once clear of the Bellingham breakwater, we practice man-overboard drills with everyone learning to start the engine and taking a turn at the helm as we maneuver to pick up a floating fender that simulates the hapless victim. Next is a review of knot tying, a lesson motivated by the threat that those who don't learn to tie a bowline correctly would be sent aloft in the bosun's chair secured with their own knot.

Rasila takes the wheel while Belden and Seton lend my wife and me a hand in hoisting sails. *Gezellig* practically flies down Bellingham Channel in the 12-knot southerly on this warm, sunny morning. As we learn during the cruise, the boat is a high performer that outpoints and outsails any boat our size that comes near us. After negotiating Hale Passage, we head west around the northern tip of Lummi Island into the Strait of Georgia, riding the incoming tide around the northern bend of Orcas Island.

On the rocks at Puffin Island, seals sun themselves undisturbed as we pass close by. The tall ferns on Matia give way to a massive section of arid land, an unlikely phenomenon that only geologists and meteorologists can explain. Behind us, the snows of Mount Baker, suspended in light, cast a sparkle on the water. As Mount Constitution slides past to port, the pronounced color changes of foliage at higher elevations add a fiery gloss to the water's shimmer—a sailor's dream.

Sucia Island

Sucia Island soon looms before us, its craggy rock fingers reaching out to beckon us deep into its protected anchorages. Regardless of the number of other boats, Northwest yachtsmen know they can always find here a private spot to drop the hook. My favorite anchorage is on the east side of Echo Bay, which offers unobstructed views of the morning sun as it rises slightly south of east over the Cascade Mountains. Within this narrow confine, a slender segment presents a vista of snow-capped Mount Baker towering almost 11,000 feet to the northeast.

Once snug at anchor, the five of us set out in the dinghy to explore Sucia's renowned sandstone formations, a meeting place for cruising kids throughout the region. Centuries of wind and water have worn these surfaces into every contorted shape that ever filled a child's imagination. We scamper across iguana heads, walk into dinosaur mouths, and clamor over the backs of monsters—all weathered into the thirty-foot wall along the water's edge. Not only is this a great opportunity for bone-stretching, but Paula and I enjoy some great scenery without complaints from the younger generation.

Into Canada's Gulf Islands

The next day we reach due west across Boundary Passage into Canadian waters, arriving at, Bedwell Harbor on South Pender Island by late afternoon. After clearing customs, I walk, embarrassed, to the general store to restock fruit and potatoes. Our inventory was depleted a few minutes earlier because I had forgotten that these foods are not allowed across the border. Our U.S. fruit and potato supply is now with Canadian customs officials.

In addition to a small shopping arcade, a pub, and a restaurant, the resort at Bedwell offers what every kid desperately wants—a swimming pool. While they go wild in the water—for them, this is the whole point of cruising—Paula and I explore the nearby gardens and park. Half an hour later, we coax the water rats back to the boat and are soon underway sailing past Prevost and Mayne Islands up Trincomali Channel into the Canadian Gulf Islands. This is Northwest cruising at its finest. We sail under sunny skies as a gentle southwest breeze pushes us past elongated strips of autumn color beside us and across the rich blues of the deeply gouged channels below.

As lengthening shadows climb up to attach themselves onto the island peaks, the wind dies as we ghost into Ganges Harbor, Saltspring's outpost known for its arts and crafts. After anchoring, we row ashore and, upon seeing a poster on the community bulletin board, head over to the advertised outdoor jazz concert. Afterwards, we find a quaint restaurant near the waterfront park that specializes in fresh fish—although the kids opt instead for the usual burgers and fries. Back aboard, we settle into our berths where we're lulled to sleep by the gentle rocking of the boat accompanied by the soft slap of waves against the hull.

Our kids are up early the next morning to complete the mandatory three pages of arithmetic, a condition they have agreed to fulfill each morning in exchange for missing their first week of school. Afterward, they scramble into the dink and aim it toward hundreds of grapefruit-sized jellyfish that are thick enough to almost walk on. Armed with pots and strainers, they scoop up the harmless blobs, vying for the largest catch. I don't think the marine creatures mind, since they all make it safely back into the water. The kids forget about scenery and just have fun. As Belden pronounces, this is like morning Jellyvision.

More sun and moderate winds make for adventurous sailing among the islands bordering the Strait of Georgia. We tack into the buffeting currents of Active Pass between Galiano and Mayne Islands, keeping a careful eye for the 300-foot ferries that connect the mainland with Vancouver Island. The ferries monopolize practically the entire width of this narrow passage as they plow through at 14 knots. When two of the leviathans pass each other, our best hope is to open the throttle and zoom out of their way.

Butchart Gardens

For the next few days, we continue to explore the Gulf Islands, alternating between anchorages in isolated coves and moorages in small island villages. Soon we begin to head south toward the destination I have been looking forward to the entire cruise. Under blue skies we sail around the north ends of Moresby and Portland Islands and then nose *Gezellig* around Moses Point on Vancouver Island's Saanich Peninsula into Saanich Inlet.

We haven't been to Butchart Gardens—the fifty-acre floral showpiece of the Pacific Northwest—for several years and are excited about arriving for the first time by water. On previous visits, feeling oppressed by the crowds that spilled from the steady flow of Victoria tour buses, I had always found my way past the Japanese Gardens to the tiny cove on Tod Inlet, where boaters arrived. I noted that there was no ticket booth by this rear entry. Therefore, in addition to beating the crowds, arrival by boat would offer an economic advantage.

Concerned that I might miss this tiny indentation of water, I hug the shoreline as I enter Brentwood Bay. Suddenly, out of nowhere, tiny Tod Inlet opens up, marked by a small sign with a bright rose pointing to Butchart Gardens. We throw out the anchor, send the kids ashore in the dinghy with a stern line to secure to a tree root, and then row together to the dinghy dock.

I try to hide my disappointment when I see a newly built wooden structure. "Oh yes, we installed this ticket booth because boaters were sneaking in back here without paying," explains the attendant in response to my question. My look of disbelief probably isn't very convincing as I hand over my money.

A short walk through the woods brings us to the famous gardens that were built by Mrs. Robert Butchart to mask the landscape blight resulting from her husband's limestone quarrying operations. Entering the meticulously cared-for grounds, I'm struck by another benefit of fall cruising. Not only do we have the anchorage practically to ourselves, but the busloads of tourists from Victoria are nowhere to be seen. We are, for the moment, the Butchart family strolling through our own gardens while a few others—presumably our houseguests—are far enough away in another part of the gardens so as not to disturb us.

For the next several hours, it's as if we are wandering through the pages of a coffee-table horticultural book where high-gloss floral blooms are framed in an explosion of fall colors. We conclude the afternoon with leisurely dining beside the formal Italian Gardens. The open-air musical revue on the concert lawn lends a perfect finishing touch to another full day.

Dinghy Dinged

The next morning we awaken to reflected sunlight bouncing around the cabin. Light winds force us to motor to the mouth of the Saanich Inlet where the southerly winds fill in again. We hoist sail and reach eastward past Piers Island, Knapp Island, and the Swartz Bay ferry terminal where 300-foot behemoths ping-pong back and forth to Vancouver every hour.

Entering Haro Strait with the hills of Seward Island serving as a benchmark, I notice a strange current pattern around the buoy at Arachne Reef. The tide table indicates an ebb period, but what I see by the marker shows an opposite flow. There are times when I'm glad there are no witnesses nearby because what happens next would have made me a laughingstock to any onlookers.

Approaching the buoy from downwind and what appears to be the down-current side, I should have noticed the swirling flotsam entrapped in the so-called tidal current. By the time I recognize the turbulent water for what it is—a convergence zone, or "junk line," of surface rips that just happen to end beside the buoy, giving the appearance of a tidal current—it is too late. Indeed, I had read the tide table correctly. Suddenly, *Gezellig* is swept through this watery chaos toward the buoy. There is no time to start the engine. Falling off wind, I gain a marginal amount of added distance—and just miss. By mere inches, *Gezellig's* stern avoids crashing into the buoy.

As I breathe a sigh of relief, I suddenly hear a grinding sound—maybe something like a dinghy climbing over a channel buoy? In horror, I look back just in time to see the dinghy, being towed fifteen feet off our stern, first try to pass on the other side of the swaying marker, then go airborne, climbing up and over the six-foot iron obstacle. Of course, all this happens in front of the unbelieving eyes of my wife and children who, when they see all is safe, break into hilarious laughter.

Roche Harbor—After the Yachts Depart

It isn't until that evening, after we clear U.S. Customs at Roche Harbor and are comfortably seated at the resort's waterfront deck lounge with a couple of drinks under our belts, that Paula carefully brings up the subject. The children are off at the pool, *Gezellig* is anchored at a scenic corner of the harbor, and I have inspected the dink and am satisfied there has been no damage other than my wounded ego. Paula reminds me that, at the start of the charter, the yacht manager had told us how proud he was of the rugged design of the 9-foot fiberglass dinghies that go out with each charter and how they were practically indestructible. He had said, "They are easy to row, to tow, and to stow. All you have to do is make it flow." We had certainly given his rugged dinghy the ultimate test.

Roche Harbor has in recent years acquired a fast-paced image as California-registered mega-yachts have become standard fixtures along the docks throughout the summer. A telling sign of the times is the availability of the *Wall Street Journal* and a Federal Express drop-off box at the end of the main pier. Vacationing executives can relax at Roche yet still monitor the business world and remain in overnight contact with corporate headquarters.

But again, we're talking fall cruising. Delivery of the *WSJ* has been suspended for the fall season, the FedEx mailbox is disbanded, and the boats at the docks all have Washington registries. The yellow fire bricks on the road in front of the waterfront Hotel de Haro are matched by the fading leaves along the pathways.

Hotel de Haro and the other facilities of Roche Harbor grew out of the fortunes of Robert McMillan, who developed the largest lime works west of the Mississippi. Old photographs in the hotel show smoke-belching furnaces and dozens of tall sailing ships at anchor—testimonials to the area's past glory as a major Northwest industrial center. Today the smokestacks are gone and the quarries abandoned, leaving a peaceful setting of elegant gardens, charming turn-of-the-century buildings, and a network of paths that lead to isolated beaches, undiscovered blackberry thickets, and a thought-provoking family mausoleum.

"Band Practice"

Although the next day brings more sun, blue skies, and good winds, Rasila's words create instant gloom. "Daddy, I can't get the toilet to flush." Unclogging a plugged head isn't my idea of how to spend a cruise. But cruising without a head? That would risk mutiny from my family, so I change course to Friday Harbor. While the others stroll off to explore this crossroads of the San Juans, I set out hoping, but not really expecting, to find someone who would say, "Oh yes, a Pearson 34. I can fix the head in five minutes. No problem. And it won't cost you a cent."

Wind 'n' Sails is sympathetic but doesn't have a mechanic available. The service manager at San Juan Marina says he can get parts in three days. In the meantime he lends me a plunger, the well-known "Plumber's Helper." Whereas I have been fairly anonymous up to this point, as I walk back to the boat I become an instant celebrity. Heads turn in my direction and nod sympathetically. "Sure hope it works," calls out one sailor. Another asks, "You going to band practice?" A third contributes, "I know how it is. I got kids on my boat as well." But of course, the plunger does no good, as everyone can tell as I retrace my steps along the dock to return the plunger.

I am about to telephone for a mechanic when I hear someone say, "You really can't tell what the problem is or how much it will cost until you tear the whole thing apart…" That was the omen I needed. "Okay, everyone uses the shore toilet and gets back on board," I order when I track down my family leisurely eating lunch at a dockside restaurant. Ten minutes later, bladders empty and sails full, we depart for Jones Island, a state marine park where we tie up to one of the mooring buoys in the south cove.

Our first stop ashore is the outdoor toilet vaults. Then we meet up with nearby wildlife. The deer that roam the island have never known danger from man, so they are almost pesky as they beg for food. Coming right up to eat from our hands without hesitation, they show no fear. When Rasila holds a piece of apple high overhead, they get up on their hind legs, almost climbing on her head to get the apple.

We inspect the island's interior, shaded year-round by the ancient stands of red cedar and Douglas fir that soar well over 100 feet. At water's edge we discover tidal pools and encroach upon the world of crabs, snails, sea stars, and barnacles. Such an abundance of these marine creatures brings out the collector in all of us, but in the end, we decide they all will be happier staying in the watery world they inhabit rather than joining us in an urban environment.

A late afternoon sail brings us back to our moorage for the night at Friday Harbor. We hike up the hill to the whale museum, a visit that demands more than the half-hour we have until it closes. But sometimes a short, intense visit can be as meaningful as a comprehensive tour, and that proves true for us on this visit. We leave with orca-emblazoned T-shirts and a supply of brochures, pamphlets, and books about whales—resource material for school science projects.

Rosario Resort—Pools, Pavilions, and Peace

The next day we continue our tour of swimming pools by threading between Shaw and Lopez Islands into Orcas Island's East Sound to our next destination, the toilets at Rosario Resort. Constructed by shipwrights, the historic mansion, built by industrialist Robert Moran to escape from corporate pressures and the hassles of life, offers complete spa facilities, indoor and outdoor pools, and several restaurants.

Throughout the sprawling grounds, Moran created a feeling of casual relaxation that visitors still enjoy today. Payment of a nominal moorage fee gives us access to all resort facilities. The kids go their way to frolic in the pools and devour hamburgers from the poolside café, while we of the older generation savor our last evening of quiet in the formal dining room, watching through picture windows as twilight creeps over East Sound.

A few years after our visit, we learn that the property had been sold and was closed for major renovation. Call ahead before you go.

Foggy Ending

The morning of our last day brings an unwelcome surprise—a heavy blanket of fog has settled during the night. Nevertheless, we need to return *Gezellig* to Bellingham by noon, necessitating a dawn departure despite zero visibility. We feel our way south to Obstruction Pass by sailing close to the shoreline, barely able to make out the contour of the land. However, once we start across Rosario Strait, which is known for its heavy commercial barge and ship traffic, we must rely strictly on dead reckoning.

As everyone becomes noticeably nervous because the fog has not lifted by mid-morning, as I had predicted, I decide to turn the navigation problem into a game. With pencils and paper, we work out the calculations for our landfall at Cypress Island across the strait. While it is unnerving not to have reference bearings, the fog injects an element of excitement into our last day. There is something almost cleansing about being enveloped in white, as if an enormous cotton ball were swabbing the San Juans.

When the fog finally lifts late in the morning, the peak of Lummi Island is exactly where it should be, with Mount Baker standing guard in the background. The sun breaks through for our final run up Bellingham Bay as we end the trip on an exhilarating note. At this time of year in the San Juans, there's a special nurturing environment that every Northwest boater knows—one that keeps drawing us back to these glorious cruising grounds year after year. And as I later reflect, this was the only day there were no complaints from the junior crew about too much scenery!

~

Bedwell Habor Marina, South Pender Island

Tide Pool

Chapter 9

BRITISH COLUMBIA - WINING & DINING IN THE GULF ISLANDS

"I Brake for Wine" reads a popular bumper sticker in wine country. My current wife, Risa, and I can relate. We have our own nautical version when boating on *Freelance*: "We Anchor for Wine."

I'm a lifelong boater at heart. Risa, a food-and-wine writer, is drawn to sampling local produce and vintages, and—as owners of a small winery in California—we both enjoy wine.

With more than a dozen easily reached vineyards, in addition to 200 islands offering charming anchorages, breaching orcas, barking sea lions, and playful river otters, Canada's Gulf Islands are ideally suited for indulging our combined interests.

Meandering Up to Canada with a Corkscrew

After launching *Freelance* from Squalicum Marina in Bellingham, Risa and I pass through the San Juan Islands, cross Boundary Pass into

Canadian waters, and make landfall at Bedwell Harbour on South Pender Island. Here we clear customs and, after securing a moorage slip, make our way up the hill to Poets Cove Resort and Spa where we enter another world.

The front door of this elegant waterfront resort welcomes well-dressed tourists who arrive in limousines, town cars, and taxis; the marina-facing back door welcomes those of us in T-shirts and shorts who sleep aboard our boats. No matter how we all enter, everyone meets halfway in the resort restaurants to enjoy local fare paired with island wines.

Gulf Islands' vineyard owners, winemakers, and even the grapes themselves must adapt to demanding growing conditions that include short summers and a rainy marine environment. Some grape varieties that manage to thrive here originated in cooler climates such as France's Loire Valley, Austria's Wachau Region, or Germany's Moselle Valley. But if you think vinyl cushions mildew fast, imagine the effect dampness can have on a thin-skinned grape!

North Pender Island—Sea Stars and Sea Star

After a peaceful night on the hook at Poets Cove with moonlit waves gently rocking us to sleep, morning finds Risa and me cruising to Port Browning on North Pender Island, a twenty-minute hop in protected waters. Wanting to "meet" the grapes in their natural habitat, we catch an island taxi to Sea Star Vineyards on the island's southeastern corner. Sea Star began as Morning Bay Vineyards, which was purchased in 2013 by David Goudge, who produced wines to much acclaim, earning gold and silver medals at the Northwest Wine Competition. Needing more grapes, David bought the derelict Saturna Island Vineyards and resuscitated the property with new equipment, a climate-controlled barrel cellar, and an updated wine shop.

"I named our winery Sea Star because you always see sea stars in these waters," explains David. "They typify summer here in the Salish Sea." Sea Star produces several reds: an Alsatian Pinot Noir grown on the premises and a Meritage made from grapes sourced elsewhere in British Columbia. Farm-grown crabapples, blackberries, and raspberries go into Sea Star's dessert wines. Located in an old-growth forest, the winery's sleek tasting room opens onto a garden patio and features live music on summer weekends—a favorite with local boaters.

For personal reasons, David put both Sea Star and Saturna Island Vineyards on the market in 2019. In 2022, Traci Warkentin purchased both vineyards and renamed the Saturna Island property as Sage Hayward Vineyards.

Traci continues to produce great wines but brings animal ethics and environmental values to the forefront. Don't expect to find Sea Star wines on the lists of restaurants that serve what she calls "cruelty" foods like foie gras or veal. To reduce the winery's carbon footprint, she changed from bottles made in China to lighter bottles made in California, ordered label stock made with recycled paper, and offers some larger volume wines in recyclable kegs instead of bottles. In addition, the winery allocates revenue from some of its wine sales to the Raincoast Conservation Foundation.

Once back aboard *Freelance* following our visit to Sea Star, we motor around to the eastern coast of North Pender Island, where we find a slip at the docks in Hope Bay. The sole restaurant—Café at Hope Bay but subsequently renamed The HUB—certainly lives up to its rave reviews when we dine there that night, and Sea Star's wines pass with highest honors.

The chef at The HUB uses local ingredients from his vegetable patch located behind the restaurant, so the produce is always fresh.

Risa enjoys a glass of Maréchal Foch paired with lamb and blackberries surrounded by a medley of perfectly cooked vegetables. I opt for Pinot Noir with the pork dinner—the chef's special that night. Offering reasonably priced selections on an eclectic menu that globetrots from Hawaii to India to Morocco, this restaurant, which juts out over the water, provides fantastic views across Plumper Sound. It certainly deserves multiple visits.

Feeling well fed, we return to *Freelance* and motor a short distance from the slip to a mooring buoy in Plumper Sound in a protected lee at the mouth of Hope Bay. Here, under a cloudless sky on a windless night, we fall asleep, feeling secure because scattered islands protect us from every quarter—except the southeast, which isn't a concern. Around 3:00 a.m., the boat's gentle rocking escalates to wild pitching as winds fill in from—where else?—the southeast. Wide-eyed for the rest of the night, we are reminded never to take benign weather for granted.

Salt Spring Island—Orcas, Then Oenophiles

Intending to gunkhole around a few of the smaller islets scattered throughout the Gulf Islands, we set course for a relaxing cruise to Salt Spring Island. Before we can do so, we notice several large vessels making rapid beelines to the north. Twenty years of cruising have taught us that you don't watch for whales—you watch for whale-watching boats. We follow. Ten minutes later, we spot a pod of adult orcas cavorting north to the mouth of the Fraser River to feed on salmon. One newborn stays close to its mother while making commendable efforts to keep up with the elders. The youngsters are called "flying pickles" because of their short but mighty leaps.

After following these magnificent creatures at a safe distance for twenty minutes, we thread our way west among the islets of Trincomali Channel and arrive at Ganges, the main harbor at Salt Spring.

Salt Spring Island's four wineries are located in the interior. To check them out, we engage Western Splendour Tours and Charters for the day to shuttle us from the marina. Although we boaters tend to know about reefs and rocks along a coastline, we can sometimes overlook the soul of an island. So, it's fortunate that Ryan, our guide, fills us in on the island's culture and history. Among other tidbits, we learn that in the 1930s, 1,200 African American settlers from California moved here, drawn by British Columbia's offer of land and rights to Black immigrants willing to farm the land. Many descendants from the original families are still here today.

Later, Western Splendour was acquired by Jason Griffin, who changed the name to Tour Salt Spring. Jason expanded the offerings to include a variety of sightseeing tours, wine and libation tours, and private charter tours.

Nowadays the island's population is composed of artists, retirees, farmers, and escapees from the urban lifestyle. The mantra for Salt Spring Island is perhaps summed up by a bumper sticker that read: "Relax—This ain't the Mainland." Indeed!

The region's only certified organic winery, Mistaken Identity Vineyards, grows ten grape varieties on seven acres. The winery supplements the estate wines with grapes sourced from Vancouver Island and interior British Columbia. The property also produces heritage apple and blackberry dessert wines, and a sparkling blush wine.

"Organic farming is difficult under the best of circumstances," the winemaker tells us. "But here in a marine environment, more challenges abound, including erratic weather and the need to truck in water for irrigation." But on this warm summer day, such hurdles are far from our minds as we bask on the patio sampling wine and tasty cheeses while enjoying live music—a Saturday staple throughout the summer.

Later, new owners took over the vineyard and renamed it Kutatás (Koo-Tah-Tash), a Hungarian term for research, exploration, or quest. Winemakers Mira Tusz and Daniel Dragert found this term inspiring because it relates their venture to a shared Hungarian heritage that describes their experimentation with new wine-making techniques. The property is dry farmed to ensure small berry size and achieve maximal fruit concentration.

The newest of Salt Spring's wine-grape growers is Vivezza Vineyard, which is unfortunately closed the day of our visit. With the establishment of their own estate vineyard on Salt Spring Island in 2019, Paul and Corinna Troop opened Vivezza in 2022. Their fungus-resistant grape varieties, known as PIWI blends, are hybrid grapes that produce very different wines with their aroma profiles and new taste experiences.

The last stop on our tour is seven-acre Salt Spring Winery, the island's oldest winery. We introduce ourselves to the husband-and-wife owners, both retired physicians. Dev McIntyre, who oversees the vineyard, is a surgeon; his wife Joanne is a general practitioner. As we chat with them about the winery, we learn that Dev successfully experimented with innovative cold-climate varieties that ripen sooner and are disease resistant—such stars as Evolution White, Evolution Red, and Petite Milo.

Surrounded by pretty gardens, a picturesque pond, quaint gazebo, and cozy seating areas connected by meandering pathways, we understand why boaters often congregate here for a Wine-Down party on Friday afternoons and for music in the vineyard on Sundays. The owners also operate a bed-and-breakfast that offers rooms for guests who want to sleep amidst vineyards, an enticement we can't resist. Without giving it a second thought, we decide to stay overnight.

But before turning in, we need dinner. Unfortunately, the only food services are in Ganges, which requires taking the local bus back to town. But with a gesture of trust and hospitality, Joanne lends us her two-seat Miata for the evening.

Large in ambition, huge in charm, and culinary savvy—that describes Feast, formerly House Piccolo, which is our choice for dinner that evening in Ganges. The menu presents a challenge. You have a choice of "small feasts" (appetizers) or "large feasts" (entrées). The small feasts are too large to be appetizers, and the large feasts are meant to be shared among two to four people. That means choosing a large feast that two people are happy to share, or you are limited to the short "small feasts" menu with very basic plates. The "feasts" concept could be appealing, but it's questionable whether it works. Best to go for a celebration dinner with a small group of friends.

Unfortunately, the McIntyres sold the vineyard several years ago. The new owners were unsuccessful and were forced to sell it shortly after they purchased it. It is hoped that the current owners will engage a winemaker to restore the prestige these wines once enjoyed.

The next morning, the local bus delivers us back to *Freelance*, where we navigate north around Salt Spring, then down the west side to Burgoyne Bay Provincial Park. After tying up at the dock, we hike twenty minutes along a heavily canopied lane to Fulford-Ganges Road. Half a mile beyond lies Garry Oaks Winery, named for the white oaks native to the area that once covered this valley.

The vineyard, planted in 1999 in Pinot Gris, Pinot Noir, Gewürztraminer, and Zweigelt, spreads over a ten-acre terraced, south-facing slope that was once a sheep farm. Proprietor Nalini

Samuel has a passion for blending varieties and has introduced a sparkling and dessert wine program.

Seated outside the tasting room under the distinctive peak of Mount Maxwell, we overlook the vines and enjoy a view into the lush Burgoyne Valley. After sampling a selection of vintages, we fall in love with their Zweigelt, full of black cherry and raspberry flavors, and purchase several bottles on the spot.

Galiano, Mayne, and Saturna—Three Islands, Many Courses

Located at the eastern edge of the Strait of Georgia, Galiano Island is home to one of the most notable restaurants in the Gulf Islands. A short walk on the path from our dockage slip at popular Montague Harbour Marine Provincial Park leads us beneath Douglas firs and western red cedars until we come to a log cabin hidden in the forest. Pilgrimme Restaurant looks like the Northwest version of a hobbit house, and we hasten our footsteps as enticing smells wafting through the air further stimulate our appetites.

Thanks to the culinary creativity of Jesse McCleery—both the owner and chef—the restaurant has created quite a buzz among boaters since its opening in 2014. McCleery has worked at Noma in Copenhagen, which is often seriously cited as one of the world's best restaurants. To garnish dishes at Pilgrimme, the chef and his team forage ingredients from forest and shore, bringing home sea lettuce, spruce tips, wild mushrooms, and miner's lettuce.

Multi-course meals are a signature feature of Pilgrimme. We are barely seated when, without yet seeing the menu, we are presented with three *amuse-bouches*. And that isn't all. We order a typical meal consisting of appetizer, salad, entrée, and dessert. But between each course, the chef sends out additional delectable tidbits. Staying true to the British Columbia theme, the wines and beers are all locally sourced.

To cap off this wonderful gourmet meal, following our dessert of the house's traditional roasted parsnip and pear cake with caramel cream cheese icing, we are offered a complementary digestif. When we add up all these "mini-servings" together with our main meal, we figure it counts as a ten-course meal, yet all is reasonably priced.

Set at the south end of Galiano Island at Sturdies Bay by the ferry landing, Galiano Inn welcomes boaters to tie up at the floating dock. At the inn's Atrevida Restaurant and Lounge, we look out through ceiling-to-floor windows to magnificent views of the narrow passage where ferries shuttle between Vancouver and the Gulf Islands. The menu here highlights fresh fish such as Arctic char accompanied by cilantro, chimichurri, black rice, and a fine selection of island wines.

The next day takes us to the southeast side of Mayne Island, where we need to pay strict attention to the charts that show a maze of islets, shoals, and reefs. After tying up at Mayne Island Resort's dock that evening, we feast at Bennett Bay Bistro while sitting on a sweeping deck overlooking the namesake waters.

To round out our explorations, we head south along Plumper Channel to Saturna Island, easternmost of the Gulf Islands. At Crocker Point on the southwest coast, we tie up at a rickety dock in a sheltered cove to check out Saturna Island Winery. Re-opened in 2022 as Sage Hayward Vineyards, it is a sweeping sixty-acre site encompassing four vineyards. Although the growing season is short, the south-facing slopes are sheltered by 1,600-foot cliffs that block cold northern winds and reflect the sun's heat onto the vines below. The tasting room and beautiful café terrace face south across Boundary Pass.

Moving on, we dock at Saturna Lighthouse Pub with a sunny seafront deck at Lyall Harbour's ferry dock. Although we don't usually indulge at lunch, we order two glasses of Saturna Island Pinot Gris to go with our fish and chips.

A Hold Full of Bottles

Feeling fortunate for all we have seen on our journey, we also feel melancholy. It is time to turn *Freelance* toward home. Risa and I drink a toast to the hearty wine pioneers of these islands, men and women who are confronted with arguably the most demanding growing conditions imaginable—a short growing season, limited sunshine, a hostile marine environment, the threat of frost, and the legendary Northwest rain. But despite these inherent challenges, Gulf Island winegrowers produce award-winning wines, an ample selection of which we stow safely aboard *Freelance* to enjoy in the months ahead.

Tips for Skippers

1. **Boaters' Guides:** Peter Vassilopoulos' *Gulf Islands Cruising Guide*, colorfully illustrated, gives detailed information on routes, anchorages, marinas, facilities, and historical notes. *The Dreamspeaker Cruising Guide: Gulf Islands and Vancouver Island* offers charts, tips, and shoreline plans of selected marinas and small-boat anchorages.

2. **Canadian Customs:** Boaters arriving from U.S. waters can clear customs and get information at government docks (painted red) on Vancouver Island at Sidney and Victoria or on South Pender Island at Poets Cove. It's illegal to stop or anchor in Canadian waters before checking in. Contact Canadian customs for current restrictions on food and other items.

3. **Ferries:** They're big and seem to be everywhere, suddenly appearing out of nowhere just as they round an island's tip. The BC Ferries fleet includes the world's largest double-ended ferries, which can carry 370 vehicles and 1,650

passengers. They cruise at 16–18 knots even when navigating the narrowest of channels.

4. **Tides:** Be alert for the "king tides" (the highest). These can range from fifteen to nineteen feet and cause churning rapids and swift currents. Prudent boaters wait for slack before navigating narrow passages.

5. **Orcas:** This cruising area is home to seventy-five orcas in three resident pods as along with several transient pods. If you encounter orcas, Canadian regulations require you to slow to less than 7 knots within 400 yards and keep at least 100 yards away.

6. **Swimming:** The water is generally too cold for swimming. But there are local secret warm-water areas, notably on the west side of Thetis Island and the islands farther north where there's limited tidal exchange.

7. **Weather**: Expect rain from November to May; summer months are remarkably rain-free. Prevailing winds average 5 to 10 knots and range from Northwest to Southwest. Average daytime summer temperatures in Fahrenheit range from the high 60°s to the mid-80°s. Beware of sudden winds, fog, and storm conditions that can quickly channel through the islands.

Crocker Point Dock Access to Saturna Island Vineyard

Ganges Fish Restaurant, Salt Spring Island

Gary Oaks Winery

Pilgrimme Restaurant, Montague Harbour

Pilgrimme Restaurant, Montague Harbour

Galiano Inn's Atrevida Restauraunt

Chapter 10

WINNIPEG - SAILING THE PRAIRIE SEA

Who would have guessed there'd be a sailing charter base in the middle of Canada's Prairie Provinces? When I get wind of it, two sailing friends from Seattle and I decide to check it out. After a flurry of phone calls, we track down a charter operation at the Gimli Yacht Club in Gimli, Manitoba, and arrange for a weeklong cruise on Lake Winnipeg aboard one of their yachts—a Canadian-built Tanzer 26.

"Because Manitoba is thousands of miles from the ocean, most people think we're nothing but a prairie of grain," explains the commodore of the Gimli Yacht Club on our arrival. "Only local sailors know about our great sailing on Lake Winnipeg, the tenth-largest freshwater lake in the world. If you count Hudson Bay, our province actually has more saltwater coastline than several Maritime Provinces. And the river systems that brought in trappers, settlers, and canoe brigades provide plenty of freshwater, too."

My crew and I are advised to load up with provisions for the entire trip before we set out, because once underway, we'll find few lakeside villages where we can restock. Lake Winnipeg has no tides, but wind-driven movement of water from one end of the lake to the other creates standing waves that cause changes in water levels among the islands—a phenomenon known as a seiche. In addition, because the lake is shallow and capricious, high winds can cause steep waves that develop quickly, leaving little time to seek shelter. Further, the cruising grounds are essentially wilderness, with few navigation aids, so we're advised to be extra cautious.

The Heart of New Iceland

Deciding to delay our departure by one day, we take time to learn about Gimli, a unique town midway along Lake Winnipeg's western shore. Our visit coincides with Gimli's annual Icelandic Festival held the first weekend in August. Settled originally by Icelanders, Gimli—an Icelandic name drawn from Norse mythology—is the world's largest Icelandic settlement outside Reykjavík and the Icelandic cultural heartland of Canada.

The festival features local Icelandic-themed artwork and handicrafts, traditional Nordic dishes, and an interactive Norse village where reenactors perform tasks such as blacksmithing, crafting, and boatbuilding. The festival highlight is a daily reenactment of a Norse shield-wall battle, a military formation common in medieval warfare, in which soldiers stand shoulder to shoulder with overlapping shields.

To learn more about Gimli's Icelandic origins, we visit the New Iceland Heritage Museum, which is dedicated to preserving the history and artifacts of the large population of Icelanders who migrated to New Iceland, the Interlake Region of Manitoba.

In addition, we go to the Gimli Glider Museum. Gimli made world news in 1983 when an Air Canada Boeing 767 ran out of fuel over southern Manitoba and successfully glided nine miles to a landing at Gimli Motorsport Park. This near-disaster occurred because the fuel had been erroneously measured in pounds instead of kilograms at a time when Canada was converting to the metric system. The aircraft incident became known as the Gimli Glider, and the story is told in depth with video and personal recollections at the museum.

Victoria Beach—A Peninsula of Cottages

The next day, after a thorough checkout of our boat's features with the charter base manager, we set sail in a mild northerly breeze on a fifteen-mile reach to Victoria Beach on the eastern shore. The sunny morning skies seem to validate Manitoba's claim to have more sunshine than any province in Canada.

But all too soon, the bright puffy clouds turn a threatening gray. Before we know it, we're deluged by a sudden rain squall and strengthening winds, soon topping 25 knots. According to the cruising guide, this is typical weather here, and although Lake Winnipeg may look tame, when the wind kicks up, the shallow depths make for dangerous, choppy seas.

We scramble to put a double-reef in the mainsail as our little boat struggles through steep waves. Decision time: Should we turn back to Gimli? Figuring we are already about halfway to Victoria Beach, we opt to maintain our course.

Once docked at Victoria Beach's wharf, we tidy the jumble of provisions, charts, and gear strewn about the cabin. We're still amazed at how the peaceful lake had suddenly taken on such a fury. With the wind still gusting, we disembark to explore this cottage community.

Victoria Beach developed in the 1930s, when a now-abandoned railroad line brought the well-to-do from Winnipeg out to their weekend retreats. The village lies on a narrow peninsula that extends into Lake Winnipeg and is almost completely surrounded by the lake. More than 1,000 cottages were built throughout the heavily wooded area, and a ban, still in effect, was imposed on motorized vehicles. The main attraction of this waterfront community is the soft, white silica-sand beach. Walking barefoot at water's edge is like strolling through a giant sugar bowl.

Gull Harbour Marina—Gateway to the Narrows

A southerly wind shift overnight makes for a perfect, sunny off-wind sail the next day for our forty-mile run to the north end of the lower basin. Lake Winnipeg—technically a subarctic lake—is shaped like a tilted hourglass. A watershed for the eastern Canadian Rockies, Prairie Provinces, and for four U.S. states, Lake Winnipeg is the seventh-largest body of water in North America.

Some of the best cruising is among the fragmented islands and bays in the narrow, forty-mile passage that separates the lower and upper basins. To protect these cruising grounds against development, the government has incorporated the region into Hecla-Grindstone Provincial Park.

The smaller lower basin, seventy-five miles long and twenty-five across, begins less than an hour's drive from Winnipeg, capital of Manitoba. A network of roadways and small villages lines the western shoreline, separating the lake from seemingly endless miles of prairie that reach across the continent to the Canadian Rockies.

The eastern shore is roadless and uninhabited except for occasional villages of Indigenous bands. It remains in its original state of forest and muskeg bog. The huge upper basin, 150 nautical miles long and 50 wide, is surrounded by a subarctic boreal forest. Accessible only by boat or floatplane, the region remains a wilderness.

On our way to the narrows, we sail past sparsely populated fishing villages. The people here seem to lead a simple life—fishing, farming, and building small boats. At the end of a long day of sailing, we edge into a slip at Gull Harbour Marina on the north end of Hecla Island, the gateway to Lake Winnipeg's prime cruising area. On shore we stretch our legs by exploring nature trails and white beaches in Hecla-Grindstone Provincial Park.

As evening falls, we chance upon a Gull Harbour Sailing Association party. Lacking a clubhouse, the GHSA members are celebrating around a picnic table, their bar and entertainment center, which sits out on the main dock in a way that obstructs all traffic. With only inches to spare on each side between the table and water's edge, those walking to their boats must struggle to pass this festive blockade by edging around those at the table. The result is that everyone joins the party!

Eastern Shore—Where Roads End

The next day we cruise into wilderness. While sailing twenty miles to the eastern side of the lake takes only three hours, it also represents a several-billion-year step back in geological time. The western coastal limestone formations give way to the eastern side's four-billion-year-old Precambrian Shield undulations. The eastern shoreline is strewn with low-lying islands clearly marked on the chart, but hundreds of unmarked rocky islets make for tricky navigation. We pass along the north shoreline of Black Island, dazzled by white silica beaches, and pick our way carefully through the maze of rocky obstacles.

Upon reaching the eastern shore, we follow a makeshift buoy system—plastic bottles tied to shrubs—that guides us to the mouth of the Rice River. Several hundred yards upstream, we drop a stern anchor, then nose the bow close to shore to tie off to a tree.

This is what we have come for—a wilderness anchorage. Around us rise steep cliffs and ancient black rocks studded with a mixed forest backdrop of ash, jack pine, spruce, birch, tamarack, and aspen. The geologic struggle is in full swing as the tough shield tries to resist fragile mosses and lichens that push roots into the rock, breaking it down into soil while sucking out nutrients.

Feeding off the vegetation is an abundance of wildlife. Some 260 species of birds and 25 mammals inhabit the region. The marshes, located on North America's central flyway, attract tens of thousands of migrant waterfowl.

Exploring upriver by dinghy, we inspect beaver lodges and edge close to shore to examine deer, moose, and wolf tracks in the muskeg bog. Bald eagles soar above while kingfishers, ducks, herons, and white pelicans wheel and turn over the glade-laced marshlands and grassy meadows. Wild rice grows in abundance at the water's edge. Our small outboard sounds like an intruder in the stillness of the setting, but we can imagine Indigenous people paddling quietly along the shoreline, bending the rice stalks into their canoes and tapping them gently to knock off the grains.

As beautiful as this scene is by day, nighttime is even more awesome. Around midnight the heavens suddenly begin to shimmer with tinted streams of color. Flickers of green, blue, pink, and purple light waver momentarily in narrow bands like wisps of cloud, only to disappear, then reappear seconds later with different hues. The Northern Lights, interpreted by Inuit as dancing departed spirits, shoot out long, billowy streaks from the northern sky before fading like muted lightning into a distant horizon. To catch these nightly displays, pick our anchorages with clear overhead views.

By day we gunkhole among small granite coves, explore abandoned fish camps, stroll along white beaches, and cautiously examine old Indian settlements. Jumbled rock formations and jagged cliffs are signature landmarks of the area. New forms are created every spring when wind-driven massive ice floes shove up upon the beaches, colliding with the rocky cliffs and causing them to shatter explosively.

Wild Sailing, Wilderness Anchorages

With more time, we could have continued into Lake Winnipeg's immense upper basin. In contrast to the waters in the lower basin that are brownish, colored by the shallow fine sand-silt bottom, the deeper upper basin runs clear blue. However, we are running out of time and need to return to the charter base in Gimli.

We leave Lake Winnipeg having found what we were looking for—true wilderness, reserved for those who can survive on their own resources. Our weeklong cruise confirms that Lake Winnipeg ranks among the top sailing-charter destinations anywhere—even among Manitoba's endless fields of grain.

~

Dock Party, Gull Harbour Sailing Association

Fisherman descendant of original Icelandic settlers

Gimli Yacht Club

Grindstone Point

Gull Harbour

Gunkholing Rice River

Wilderness anchorage

Chapter 11

YELLOWKNIFE - ARCTIC SAILING UNDER THE MIDNIGHT SUN

The idea for my next sailing adventure hatches while I'm chatting one day with a Canadian sailor. When exchanging stories with Mike Stilwell, a businessman from Yellowknife, Northwest Territories, about the world's great places to sail, I tell him I particularly enjoy cruising in isolated waters well away from civilization, citing as examples my adventures in Tonga and Baja California. Mike challenges me, "If you want to sail in the remotest of all waters, come to Great Slave Lake in Canada's Arctic region. Check out my sailing charter company Sail North and my fleet of Canadian-built, compact-cruiser Tanzer yachts." Mike claims his company is the world's northernmost sailing-yacht charter company. I don't know if that's true, but it certainly seems remote.

Northwest Territories and Great Slave Lake

After pondering his invitation for several months, I decide to follow up with Mike. In short order, we arrange for a ten-day charter on one of his larger Tanzer yachts. He explains that we can't confirm a date until the ten-foot-thick ice sheet melts. Ten feet thick? This gives me pause—and a lot of time to research what I might be getting into.

Knowing very little about the Northwest Territories and never having heard of Great Slave Lake, I do some reading about this part of Canada. All I learn is that it's big and way up north somewhere. I also know I want to go. Mike explains that sailing season is early June to late September for the prudent, and into October for others, so we agree on a charter date in mid-June.

As I delve further, I'm overwhelmed by the impressive statistics of this federal territory in northern Canada. It spans five time zones, is larger than India, and represents almost fifty percent of Canada's landmass. It lies in the realm of the magnetic and geographic North Poles but has a population of only 41,000 scattered among thirty-five communities. Great Slave Lake, the deepest lake and fifth largest in North America, is frozen eight months of the year, but summer temperatures reach upward of 80° Fahrenheit with constant sunny skies.

Nature's Still in Charge

The first tip-off of the remoteness of our destination is seeing snowshoes in the emergency gear of our NWT Air jet as we take off from Edmonton, Alberta, for Yellowknife—the capital and the only city in the entire Northwest Territories. At this desolate outpost of 21,000 inhabitants, Sail North runs its charter operations between the breakup and freeze-up of Great Slave Lake's (GSL) ice sheet. This is the land of muskox and caribou, wolf packs and bears. There's an uneasy truce between people and beast, but Nature's still in charge.

Living not far south of the Arctic Circle, Yellowknifers survive nine months in a subarctic winter of near-total darkness with temperatures in the minus 40°s. But after the long wait, they emerge from hibernation to welcome a glorious, albeit short, spring-into-summer that is green and warm enough to lure migrating birds and, more recently, cruising sailors.

Sailing is a Little Different Here

Upon arrival in Yellowknife, Sail North's founder greets the three of us with much enthusiasm and a non-stop monologue extolling the attractions of cruising GSL. We are a congenial trio, having cruised together on Lake Winnipeg, all adventurous gunkholers at heart. Mike assures us that if we thought sailing Lake Winnipeg was adventurous, GSL will exceed our expectations. I sure hope he's right!

At our checkout the next day, Mike explains, "Sailing here is a little different from the usual cruising, but it's quite safe as long as you use good judgment. We encourage people to be adventuresome. There are no restrictions about night sailing, and charterers aren't required to be in port before dark. That's because there is no night, and there are no ports in the cruising region of this 11,000-square-mile lake."

Our charter begins not at the start of a new day but at 10:30 p.m., prompting us to adjust our body rhythms to constant daylight. Mike agrees to accompany us the first several days to help navigate through the look-alike, low-lying islands. We nose *Misty Too*, a Tanzer 26, into Yellowknife Channel and set sail in a brisk polar easterly.

Twenty-Four Hours of Daylight

After passing the village of Dettah, home to a band of Slavey Dene people (after whom Great Slave Lake is named), we enter the main body of the lake. The northern end is shallow and teems with reefs, so Mike keeps a sharp eye on the depth sounder. After a three-hour sunset, the sun nibbles the northwest horizon, then slides northeast. The cool blue hues of day turn into night's warm yellows. Land features take on a surreal look with islands appearing silky black and trees twisting into contorted shapes against the pale night. Just for commemorative purposes, I photograph the face of my watch at midnight—in natural light, or, perhaps, in night-light—and get a clear image.

We fight not to let our bodies lag as the light keeps our minds active. The extended sunset gives way to a protracted sunrise and the new day's golden light. By 4:30 a.m., we have sailed thirty miles. We anchor near an abandoned Jesuit mission at Drybones Bay, named for the practice of leaving the bones of the dead on the rocks to dry. As we slip into bedrolls, we're grateful for the blackout curtains.

East Arm

The sun hasn't moved much higher by the time we awaken. Mike reaches over the side of *Misty Too* and fills the coffee pot from the lake. "This is the purest water you'll ever find," he explains as he sets it on the burner. "The water on the boat is only for washing dishes." We laugh as we recall this is the exact opposite to the usual procedures when sailing anywhere else.

Three hours under sail brings us to the cutoff of East Arm, our cruising destination. We turn east into Devil's Channel, a scenic, twisting waterway where mergansers, eiders, and loons work the shallows in the marsh at water's edge while bald eagles stand as sentinels from perches high above on craggy limbs. More than 200 species of birds are found in the region, as are elk, bears, and moose. The 80° air temperature and a sheltered bay tempt us to brave a swim. One quick dip is enough just to say we did it; there are no encores.

Once through the windless narrows of Devil's Channel, we hoist sail and enter the labyrinth of islands crowding the entrance of the East Arm. The twisting coastline hides sheltered bays, many containing sizeable island groups of their own. Much of the region remains unexplored except by trader voyageurs of the previous centuries.

Bones of the Earth

A white speck on the horizon promises to materialize into an iceberg. As the hours pass, we draw nearer, and it looms before us, refracting the ever-present light into bands of color. Because ice floes are common in early summer within the East Arm, cruisers need never worry about running out of ice!

We head for a rendezvous at a fishing camp in Lady Jane Bay where the guests delight in having new ears to listen to their angling stories. In the world of freshwater sportfishing, GSL is world-class. It has trophy fish—grayling, trout, whitefish, and northern pike—and the records to prove it.

Although it's past midnight when we return to *Misty Too*, our body clocks tell us it's still early evening, so we weigh anchor and set sail. By 3:00 a.m. the rolling terrain along the shore changes to jagged cliffs. Against a 250-foot vertical face at Hole-in-the-Wall, we drop anchor, put up the blackout curtains, and turn in.

The next day we scale the cliff, getting our first up-close look at the land. Delicate lichen and moss, which see the first light of a new year only after it's almost half over, cover the subtle pink rock outcropping of the all-pervading Precambrian Shield. Called the Bones of the Earth by the Dene, these rock formations date back almost four billion years, making them some of the oldest in the world. We don't see any wildlife, but wild orchids and tiny white-petaled mountain avens, the territorial flower, grow in clumps along the cliff seams and narrow crevasses. Avens flowers are a hardy little member of the rose family with white, buttercup-like petals, yellow centers, and silky, feathery seed heads that look like tiny spinning pinwheels.

You're on Your Own

Mike points out several oil drums similar to those we'd seen throughout our journey. These are caches of fuel and supplies placed for anyone who might get in trouble. A small problem could escalate into a disaster, and there's no technological safety net out here. He explains that this is a wilderness, and sailors must prepare for every contingency; outside help cannot be expected.

The Cruising Guide to Great Slave Lake warns that drawings and observations are personal and subjective. Sketches are to no particular scale, and depths are observed, not measured. Many of the findings represent the experience of one cruiser on one occasion. Notations scribbled in the margins contradict or confirm the original charts.

There are no marinas, no radio communications, and no Coast Guard. Only two official charts of this region are available, and depth soundings are sometimes miles apart. In other words, once you're here, you're completely on your own. And we love it.

Mirages

By the third day I feel completely disoriented as if my body rhythms are suspended in a space-and-time warp. Sleeping and eating no longer correspond with any pattern. Mike reassures us that this is common among first-time sailors on GSL. Even compasses often start hunting because of the proximity of the magnetic north pole, which slowly roams the Arctic.

The light makes an astounding impression, and mirages contribute to the confusion. Instead of the usual six or seven-mile visibility, the crystal sharpness of the air brings landmarks fifty miles away within easy sight. The temperature inversion of the cold air from the frigid lake sitting beneath a warmer layer creates weird images that hover on the horizon.

Now that we're well tucked up into the East Arm, Mike's job of navigating us down the lake is over. A Turbo Beaver buzzes overhead, and moments later the floatplane ties to our stern to pick him up.

Just before he leaves, I ask Mike what Yellowknife sailors do with their boats in winter. He chuckles and explains a long-standing tradition. "We store them on stands in the empty airplane hangar, but they are spaced a distance apart so each has a certain amount of privacy. It then becomes the major social gathering spot for the community on Saturday nights throughout the winter. Everyone cranks up their onboard barbecues and stoves to cook dinners, all the while welcoming crews from other yachts to walk over and climb aboard to share cocktails and appetizers."

"Later in the evening," he says, "things usually get out of hand when everyone decides to descend on a single boat (usually the largest and most comfortable). Then the party really takes off!"

We laugh as we say we'll be back some Saturday night next winter. Then we wave Mike off.

Anyone can be a Cartographer

For another week, we explore at leisure in a far more rugged setting than in the previous days. Sheer cliffs soar up 1,200 feet and drop another 3,000 feet below the surface. A common mooring technique beside these vertical faces is to hammer pitons into the rock and lie to fenders.

As we poke into uncharted fjords and coves, we recall Mike's encouragement to become cartographers. Any boater who gunkholes with a depth sounder and sketch pad can name points to be incorporated into the next edition of the guide.

After completing a clockwise loop of the region, we return to Devil's Channel where we drop anchor at Danforth Bay, named by a sailor who lost his Danforth anchor. At the appointed time a seaplane appears overhead and moments later sets down beside us. We exchange places with the return-delivery crew and soon are aloft.

Arctic Cruising—Sailing at the Edge

Having completed our journey through vast areas of stark beauty, simplicity, and, yes, danger, we head back to civilization. Our exploration of these Arctic wilds awoke in us a childlike excitement and sense of fun that we adults often forget. We had no need to set records on our venture; we needed only to travel slowly in one of Nature's remote realms and trust ourselves.

Thanks, Mike, for inviting us to check out this out-of-the-ordinary wilderness cruising challenge in the land of the midnight sun.

Arctic Charter Basics: What Makes Great Slave Lake Different

Season: Mid-June to late September (an ice-out determines the start).

Light: Twenty-four hours of daylight in early summer; no night sailing restrictions.

Water: Drinkable straight from the lake (untreated); onboard tanks used for washing.

Charts: Limited official charts; many soundings areobservational, not surveyed.

Navigation: Few aids, no marinas, no Coast Guard presence.

Communications: Minimal to none once beyond Yellowknife

Weather: Rapid shifts; cold water year-round; wind can build steep seas quickly.

Ice: Floating ice common early season—never far from your evening "ice supply."

Bottom line: This is expedition sailing, not resort cruising. Judgment matters more than gear.

~

Floatplane docks, Yellowknife

Misty Too at anchor

Moorage against cliff face requires pitons and fenders

Never run out of ice

Chapter 12

CROATIA - SAILING THE ADRIATIC WAR ZONE

When the Croatian National Tourist Board offers me a chartered sailing yacht to cruise the Dalmatian Coast for one week, I wonder if I will need a flak jacket and helmet. The timing surprises me because I thought Croatia was still at war for its independence following the breakup of the former Yugoslavia into a patchwork of newly independent successor countries. Only a few years earlier, newspapers were reporting on the Siege of Dubrovnik and the shelling of other southern Croatian towns on the Adriatic coast by Serbian forces.

As far as I knew, hostilities could flare again at any time. However, the Tourist Board assures me that the war in Croatia has been over for several years and that life has returned to normal with all tourist amenities fully restored. They invite me to see for myself that peace has returned, so I can assure readers in my magazine articles that it's safe to return to the beautiful coastal beaches and islands that have always been a popular vacation haven.

Lingering Doubts

Despite lingering doubts, several weeks later my wife Risa, an accomplished sailor, and I arrive at Split on the Adriatic coast, Croatia's second-largest city, to prepare for the 100-mile sail south to Dubrovnik. Although Serbian gunboats had blockaded the port years earlier in 1991 and forced the closure of many industries, no fighting had occurred in Split. Apart from a few brief sea skirmishes, Split emerged relatively unscathed.

As we walk around the town, life appears to be normal. Marketplaces are bustling, children are playing in the parks, and no military uniforms are anywhere in sight. Split seems to once again be a popular tourist destination. The Roman emperor Diocletian's third-century palace—the city's major tourist attraction and a UNESCO World Heritage Site—forms about half of the Old Town of Split. Although it is referred to as a "palace" because of its intended use as the retirement residence for Diocletian, the term is misleading. The massive structure more closely resembles a large fortress. About half of it was for Diocletian's personal use, and the rest housed a military garrison for his protection.

The port of Split is close to all the large Dalmatian islands—Brač, Šolta, Čiovo, Hvar, and Vis—that we plan to visit in the days ahead. Our Slovenian-built Elan 431 is provided by Atlas Sailing, Croatia's largest charter company. Atlas had recently acquired twelve of these boats to replace its previous charter fleet, which had been sunk in Dubrovnik Harbor by enemy shelling in 1991. Our provisions are already on board when we arrive, and the checkout and chart orientation are efficient and straightforward.

Docking Dalmatian Style

We are soon free of the docks and on our way out to the Adriatic Sea through the Strait of Split. As a light wind fills in from the north, we bear away onto a broad reach as we round the north shore of Šolta. Once in open waters, we practice "man-overboard" drills and put the boat through all its paces. We learn that it points very well at a high angle to windward, tacks easily, and responds quickly to the helm. Leaving Šolta behind, by mid-afternoon we are well on our way to Brač. Once past Brač, we change course to the southeast for Hvar, where we seek dockage for our first night.

At the morning checkout, we had been told that all marinas require "Mediterranean mooring" for docking, a technique that is not common in the States. Rather than coming alongside a slip or pier beam-to, boats tie stern-to at a right angle to the quay or dock. This requires some delicate maneuvering when entering the basins of the small harbors where we intend to dock overnight.

Before starting this maneuver at Hvar, we make sure that fenders are positioned on each side of the boat. At bare steerageway, I swing a U-turn in front of the designated docking space, and then, after Risa drops the bow anchor about seven or eight boat-lengths from the quay, I try to carefully back into my assigned slip. As the boat is backing, Risa gradually pays out the anchor chain, ensuring enough scope to keep the boat secure.

The docking space can be quite narrow with boats on each side. Skippers unfamiliar with backing a boat risk hitting one of the boats already moored in place. They quickly learn that once they put the engine into reverse, instead of going backward the first four or five seconds, the stern tends to "walk" sideways in one direction depending upon which way the propeller turns, suddenly putting the boat at an angle to the quay instead of perpendicular to it. The rudder bites only after the boat is underway.

Earlier in the day, when we were in open water, we had simulated the Mediterranean mooring maneuver several times. Nevertheless, we botch a couple of attempts, requiring me to try repeatedly until I get it right. After the boat is finally positioned in the slip, I continue to back until the stern is close to the dock. Then Risa takes the wheel while I move to the stern. Holding the two stern lines, with one end of each already secured to the aft-quarter cleats, I jump ashore, loop the lines around the bollards, hop back aboard, and secure the lines to the stern cleats. If the harbor master had seen us enter, which either he didn't or else pretends he didn't, he likely would have come out to help, in which case the maneuver would have been easier. I could have simply tossed him the lines and asked him to loop the bollards or thread them through the quay rings and then throw the lines back.

Once the anchor has been dropped and the stern lines attached to the quay, more maneuvering is necessary. First, I back down hard to set the hook, ensuring it has a good hold and will not skim along the bottom. Then we adjust the stern and bow lines so we can step ashore, while leaving enough slack so normal wave action will not push the boat into the quay or sideways into the adjacent boats.

Hvar

With the harbor directly on the city square, Hvar is a charming small town. Restaurants, cafés, shops, and the most impressive building in Hvar, the Cathedral of St. Stephen, line the square. On the eastern side, the cathedral, dedicated to St. Stephen—the pope, martyr, and patron saint of Hvar—was built on the remains of a fourteenth-century Gothic church. After embellishments over the years, it stands today as a typical example of Dalmatian baroque architecture. Inside the cathedral, we are pleasantly surprised to discover extensive religious art, with extravagant altarpieces lining both outer aisles.

As we walk around the town, we learn that the major economic activity is the cultivation of lavender, used for aromatic oils and soaps. Hvar is often called the "Island of Lavender." Hvar also claims one of Croatia's two most famous winemaking zones. Vineyards on the southern side of the island are acclaimed for red wines produced from the Plavac Mali grape, while the central plain of the island is famous for whites.

For dinner that evening, we select a table at a restaurant in the square directly opposite our boat with prime views of many elegant yachts moored stern-to along the quay. With a selection of glistening fresh fish caught earlier in the day, it's not difficult to decide what to order. We select gregada, which is the traditional food of Hvar. Hvarska gregada consists of white fish—typically conger, grouper, or monkfish—and peeled potatoes flavored with parsley, garlic, and onion. At the recommendation of our waiter, we order a bottle of one of the island's rare varietals of wine: a blend of Drnekuša and Bogdanuša, with a deep ruby color and aromas of strawberry and ripe cherry, that pairs well with the fish. Finishing the excellent meal, we order Hvar's famous paprenjak, traditional gingerbread cookies spiced with honey, black pepper, and aromatic herbs.

As darkness settles over the harbor and we return to our yacht, we suddenly hear sweet chorale voices from nearby Saint Stephen Cathedral. For the next several hours, we are treated to seven different settings of "Ave Maria" hymns for choir and organ—a wonderful conclusion to our first day as we drift off to sleep gently rocked in our berths by the Adriatic's calm waters.

Dalmatian Islands

The following day we decide to roam this small cluster of Dalmatian Islands with no particular itinerary in mind, just to explore this section of the archipelago. The Dalmatian coast is spectacular, with the glistening Adriatic Sea flanked by mountain peaks towering over the fractured islands. Steady winds, minimal tides, isolated anchorages, ancient medieval towns, well-marked charts, easy navigation, and lots of sun make it easy to understand why this region is such a popular sail cruising destination. Although the strong Sirocco and Bora winds can blow up quickly, weather reports are reliable and a safe harbor is never far away.

Most of the day we find ourselves in the Korčula Channel, a strait separating two offshore islands, and late in the afternoon we head for the harbor of the namesake town of Korčula. Although we don't do much better than the day before when backing into the quay, no one seems concerned that it takes us three attempts to enter our slip.

Korčula—Wine Island

Once the boat is secure, we venture ashore to explore this medieval town, developed mainly between the thirteenth and fifteenth centuries under Venetian rule. It still has stone walls and towers with both Gothic and Renaissance architecture, including the fifteenth-century Saint Mark's Cathedral. The old town sits on a small peninsula, giving it both strategic protection and a striking setting.

The town square, which faces the harbor, is lined with restaurants, tapas bars, cafés, and a traditional konoba, a simple tavern-like restaurant. Locals tell us their town resembles a little Dubrovnik stacked up in layers like a wedding cake. Because the economy of the island depends on tourism, most people speak English, so we have no trouble asking locals about their community.

As we stroll around, we learn that Korčula has a reputation for being the primary wine island in the Dalmatian archipelago. Home to varietals you can't find anywhere else, Korčula is most famous for Grk, a white wine that is produced only on this island and not exported due to limited production. This unique wine is considered to be the emblem of the island itself.

Inquiring about the many attractive stone walls we see throughout the town, we learn that dry-stonework is somewhat unusual in Croatia.

It's a very durable building method by which structures are constructed from stones without mortar to bind them together.

As we explore Korčula and the other islands, I ask everyone we meet—waiters, harbor workers, winemakers, shopkeepers, and bartenders—about the effects on their communities of the recent war for Croatia's independence. After all, assessing the post-war situation is the reason the Tourist Board brought me here in the first place. People speak freely about the Serbian blockade of all the ports along the Adriatic Coast and are dismissive of the few naval skirmishes as brief—each lasting only a day or two. They proudly tell us that there had been no war destruction in Korčula. They say that only the Old Town of Dubrovnik was damaged when under siege, but any damages have been completely repaired. The event seems to them now to be nothing more than an unpleasant test of wills that they prefer to forget.

Changing the subject, the townspeople are proud to show us their local wines, museums, walled cities, and historical monuments dating from the Middle Ages. The way they tell it, whereas Hvar is a party town, Korčula tends to be sedate and suited more for "grown-ups."

A Star at the Table

After walking around all day, Risa and I both have big appetites by evening, which prepares us to enjoy the main reason we have come to Korčula: to dine at LD Terrace. This high-end restaurant, located in the Old Town with beautiful views over the Adriatic, serves cutting-edge land and sea cuisine. One of the very few restaurants on the Dalmatian Coast with a Michelin star, LD Terrace offers a menu with ingredients sourced from nearby farms and local fishermen.

Upon our arrival, the hostess seats us at a table on the veranda only twenty feet from the shore. Sweeping views of the distant islands glow as they are slowly absorbed into the fading light of the setting sun behind them. Anxious to learn more about Dalmatian food culture, we ask our server for recommendations. At her suggestion, we begin with appetizers consisting of a mix of marinated anchovies, octopus salad, pršut (Croatia's version of prosciutto), cheeses, marinated shrimp, and varieties of local olives. Our entrée is local sea bass in yellow curry with cauliflower and quinoa, paired with the much-acclaimed local wine, Grk. For dessert, we end with another island favorite, an affogato—an espresso with vanilla ice cream. Discussing the wonderful flavors and spices we have enjoyed, as we depart the restaurant, we agree that LD Terrace certainly lives up to its Michelin acclaim.

Korčula's sword dances

Our stopover on this island coincides with the town's weekly Thursday night sword dance performance in the village square. Korčula's sword dances are a 400-year-old cultural heritage. Two types of sword dance groups have performed in festivals since the seventeenth century. One group's members dance in a linked unified group by holding each other's single long sword, while in Korčula's unique sword dance, the Moreška, members clash their weapons.

As we watch this evening's half-hour performance of the Moreška, two groups of quick-footed performers dressed in colorful, medieval-style military regalia—one representing Moors and the other representing Christian Croats—engage in a mock battle over a veiled woman. Guess who wins! After our excellent dinner followed by this program, we return to our boat feeling fully immersed in the local culture of Korčula.

The Backbone of Croatian Cruising

Throughout the week we visit the five major islands between Split and Dubrovnik—Brač, Hvar, Vis, Korčula, and Mljet—each offering a slightly different perspective of Dalmatian island culture. None of the islands show any damage from the recent war with Serbia. Each night we tie up at one of the Adriatic Croatia International Club's (ACI) twenty-one marinas that stretch the entire length of the coast from the Istrian Peninsula south to Dubrovnik. These ACI marinas, which make up about half the total number of coastal marinas, were established in the mid-1980s to provide up-to-date facilities for cruising sailors from Europe.

Each marina is built within a harbor and includes modern docks with full utilities, chandlery services, a sanitary block, and general amenities. Ranking among the best recreational marinas I have seen in the United States and Europe, they are clean and appear to have been undisturbed by the war. In addition, they are staffed by knowledgeable multilingual personnel. In particular, ACI Marina Korčula is located in a sheltered bay not far from the historic center of Korčula. It is an ideal starting point for sailing trips to the national parks of Lastovo and Mljet, both of which lie not far from the island.

Dubrovnik—Seven Centuries, One Siege

We conclude our cruise in Dubrovnik, where we find a 700-year-old seafaring port that bears virtually no remaining traces of war damage that had threatened to destroy the ancient city when it was under siege. In earlier centuries, rival powers, out of respect for the ancient city, had refrained from attacking Dubrovnik.

The Venetian and Ottoman empires took over Dubrovnik at different times, largely without a pitched battle inside the walls. In the 1800s, Dubrovnik was captured by Napoleon but without a fight. The Russian fleet of Admiral Senyavin came to attack Dubrovnik, but they lowered their guns and gave up on the attack. Not a single shell or bullet was fired at Dubrovnik. History indicates the level of respect afforded to Dubrovnik over the centuries.

Thus, this historic walled city, which symbolized the pinnacle of cosmopolitan Mediterranean life during the Renaissance, was remarkably well-preserved for seven centuries until October 1991, when Serbian gunners began intensive shelling. Positioned at the top of an overlooking hill, the attacking forces found an easy target as they lobbed countless aerial shells upon the defenseless city.

Boosted with an outpouring of world support, the people of Dubrovnik set out to rebuild the city's treasure-trove of architectural monuments, historic buildings, and artworks. All services, including water, electricity, communications, roads, tourist lodging, and a new airport, have now been restored. To ensure that the world will never forget the terrible destruction inflicted by the bombing, every damaged section of the black-walled city was repaired with white blocks of stone. Today, as visitors observe these white-stone sections, they know exactly how badly certain areas of the city had been destroyed.

Safe Harbors, Open Doors

Before making this trip, mention of Croatia evoked images I had seen on CNN of tanks stuck in mud and long lines of refugees. Instead, I find that the Old City has been totally rebuilt following the Balkan conflicts. Tourists who return today to coastal Croatia can expect to find beautiful beaches, welcoming people, and a coast offering outstanding wines, excellent restaurants, great sailing venues, and wonderful opportunities to explore the rich history and culture of the Dalmatian Coast—with little trace of what the locals consider a long-forgotten war, best left astern.

~

Cruising Adriatic coast

Dubrovnik

Island of Hvar

Island of Korčula

Chapter 13

DENMARK - FAIRYTALE SAILING

Thanks to an offer from United Airlines for a complimentary air ticket, I can accept an assignment from the editor of a national sailing magazine to write an article about charter sailing in the Baltic Sea. There is an implicit understanding that I will give credit in my article to the airline for my transportation, assuming that the credit is deserved. It would be a violation of journalistic ethics for United to require a favorable mention of their services in my articles, and likewise unethical for me to promise something in return.

I catch a flight from my home in Seattle to JFK and connect with a red-eye to Hamburg, Germany, where I had lived for almost a decade in the late 1970s. For several days, I visit friends I have not seen since I left more than twenty years earlier. When I mention that I'm looking for a crew to join me for a one-week sailing charter in Denmark, two good friends, Eric and Gerhard, agree to accompany me.

During the time I lived in Hamburg, I had taken my family on many sailing weekends in the waters of the Danish archipelago, so I am familiar with sailing conditions among these islands. Now I want an extended cruise to gather material for my assigned article, and for several other international sailing magazines with readerships beyond that of the assigning publication.

Nyborg to Valdemar's Castle

The three of us pile into Eric's car for the drive north from Hamburg up the Schleswig-Holstein peninsula to Kiel. From there, we board a ferry to Nyborg on the south Danish island of Funen. After provisioning at a local market, we check in with the yacht charter company where our yacht, which I had booked earlier, is ready for us.

The moment we hoist sail to head out of Nyborg Harbor on *Lido*, our chartered 31-foot Bianca sloop, we sense we've drawn a super boat for the week—small, speedy, and solid. This typical Scandinavian design, which is at peak performance while power-reaching, quickly takes us south between Funen's southeast coast and Langeland. Here we enter into a fairytale world that Hans Christian Andersen, who grew up here, used as the setting for his wonderful children's stories.

The wind is brisk, and the sea is ruffled with small whitecaps. All around, thatch-roofed houses clustered in pastoral villages, seascapes of bays and islands, quaint fishing harbors, and rolling fields combine to blend land, sea, and fantasy into a colorful, shimmering panorama.

After tacking up the well-buoyed channel to Svendborg Sound, we moor for the evening at Troense on tiny Tåsinge, an island known for its fifteenth-century castles and manors. After furling the sails, we hike about a mile to Valdemars Slot, an enormous castle beautifully situated on the sound that is surrounded by manicured lawns, deer parks, and a swan-dotted moat. We can't help but feel we have wandered into a child's picture book, perhaps Andersen's setting for "The Ugly Duckling." Our elegant dinner in the castle's restaurant is all the more intriguing because we are under the chapel and above the dungeon—a sort of fantasy limbo between heaven and hell.

Faaborg's Herring Boats

Our second day takes us along the winding passage past Svendborg, a relatively young 750-year-old seafaring town compared with nearby Odense, which dates back more than 1,000 years. We drink in the beauty of lush green island pastures, golden linseed fields, and vistas of rye and sugar beets rolling down to water's edge. Accenting the scene, dozens of Danish flags—a white cross on a red field claimed to be the world's oldest national standard—snap in the breeze.

Today is Valdemar's Day, equivalent to the U.S. Flag Day, commemorating King Valdemar's triumph in the Battle of Estonia 800 years ago. According to legend, the Danish flag was handed down from heaven to King Valdemar, thereby rallying the beleaguered troops to victory.

In the evening, we arrive at Funen's southwest coast town of Faaborg in time to watch the return of the herring boats. The silvery delicacies are unloaded from the holds of the overladen vessels into bushel baskets, then dumped into the bucket of a front-end loader, and carried off to an awaiting truck. This so whets our appetites that we seek out a seafood restaurant, of which there are many on the town square, and indulge in the herring plate—a selection of dilled, curried, spiced, and marinated renditions of this Baltic staple.

Danish children learn to sail at an early age in 8-foot Optimist prams. You can tell when school is out by the swarms of tiny, moth-like sails flying out onto the bays every afternoon. As teenagers, many Danes continue their sailing education aboard traditionally rigged sail training ships operated by local businessmen's clubs in every island hamlet. Shortly after our arrival, four of these vessels sail into Faaborg and moor near us, making for a rowdy but fun evening with everyone in the harbor invited to join their onboard parties.

The following morning, we head south to Ærø Sound. Sailing past tiny Lyø, Avernakø, and Drejø islands, we think of the children who live there and imagine their daily ferry commute to school on Funen. In winter the commute is more exciting because the children travel across the ice by bus. As a precaution, the vehicle is equipped with two enormous pontoons, one on each side as large as the bus itself, sufficient to keep the bus afloat in case the spring thaw comes earlier than expected.

Ærø's Medieval Village

That afternoon we arrive at the island of Ærø at Ærøskøbing—a carefully preserved town founded in the 1250s. As we explore, we understand why travel writers rank it among the top places in the world to visit. It breathes peace and calm. Tiny half-timbered houses painted in cheerful hues—gold with blue trim, pistachio with gray framing, reds paired with black—form a nostalgic backdrop. Beside the doors, embellished with brightly painted carved sailing ships, blooming roses and hollyhocks climb upward, reaching past the eaves of red-tile roofs. Everything is petite, tidy, and quaint. A maze of cobblestone streets tangles underfoot, while ornate cast-iron lamps throw connecting shadows across lace-draped windows. A bottle-ship collection of more than 500 models, crafted by retired sea cook "Bottle Peter," captures Ærø's proud maritime heritage.

The next day we rent bicycles to explore the island's interior. We're advised to ride west first, then enjoy an effortless return with the wind at our backs. Scattered across the countryside are remnants of ancient Viking culture—rock-strewn mounds, barrows, dolmens, and burial grounds. No one knows who heaved these giant boulders into such strange formations or why, and no one seems overly concerned. Their presence is simply accepted as part of a long-forgotten past.

Each hill is crowned by either a village church or a modern windmill. The island's name, appropriately suggestive of aerodynamics, feels fitting. Ærø has developed one of the most advanced wind-energy research programs in the world. This 750-year-old town became the first energy self-sufficient community in Europe—perhaps the world—by harnessing wind, biogas, solar energy, and straw-fired heating systems.

Breakwater at Marstal

The next morning, we sail the tricky, ten-mile channel to Marstal at the eastern tip of Ærø. The free-spirited, jolly townspeople of this seafaring hamlet love to tell stories about their 250-year-old jetty. The half-mile breakwater was built with huge granite blocks brought back long ago as ballast by the town's sea captains when Ærø was one of Europe's major ports. Construction was simple. In winter the granite blocks were pushed out onto the ice to predetermined locations. In spring, when the ice melted, the blocks sank into place.

The maritime pride of Ærø is further reflected in a joke about two sea captains from Marstal who happened to meet in Hong Kong.

"Which way did you come?" asks the first.

"This trip I came by Ærøskøbing," replies the second.

Pastries, Herring, and Beer

Our next day's sail takes us east to Rudkøbing on Langeland Island, our last stop before returning to Nyborg. By this time, we have our stopover routine down pat; pick a moorage near the toilet block, which is always clean and modern; pay the harbormaster his fee while inquiring about the weather; visit the local bakery to stock up with an assortment of pastries; and then check out the town's sightseeing attractions—museum, church, boatyard, castle, and old town. We also visit the Bianca boatyard, producers of our *Lido*.

As darkness settles, we like to seek out a choice restaurant where we order our by-now favorite herring appetizer followed by a main course of fresh cod, flatfish, or plaice. Fresh vegetables from the many island farms are always available, along with terrific desserts of freshly picked cherries, gooseberries, or whatever is in season. With more than 300 active breweries in Denmark, the beer is legendary, dominated, of course, by Tuborg and Carlsberg.

Returning to our boat in darkness each night, we collapse into our bunks, filled with the pleasures of sailing together on one of the finest cruising grounds in the world. What a delight to enjoy an unhurried interlude in the fairytale land that, as children, we foolishly believed was make-believe.

~

Reception house greets visitors to Valdamar's Castle, Tåsinge

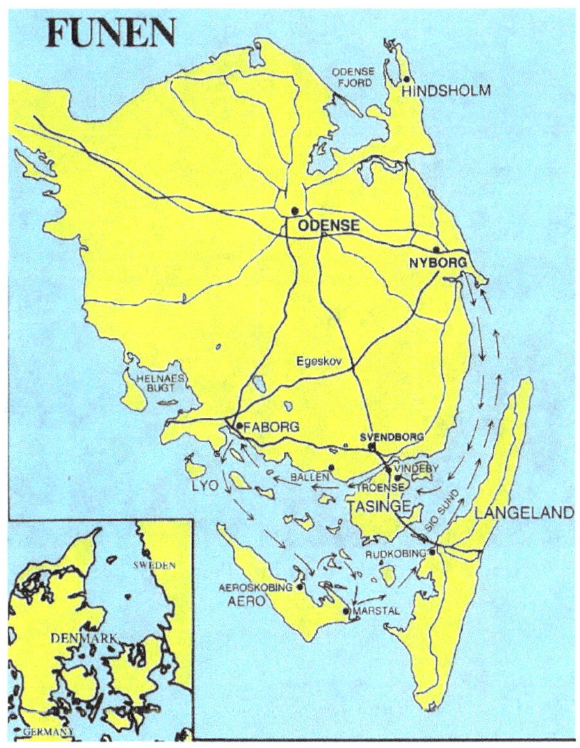

Map of Funen with itinerary

Homes in medieval Nyborg

National Maritime Training Tall Ship, Svendborg

Chapter 14

FRANCE - BY BIKE & BARGE

When Louis XVI and Marie Antoinette once rode through the great iron gates of Château de Fontainebleau, local villagers must have stared in awe. More than two centuries later, however, astonishment better describes the reactions of the crowds when our group of a dozen cyclists threads among tourists through the same grand entrance.

The royal palace is just one of the memorable stops during our weeklong bike-and-barge journey through north-central France, hosted by International Bicycle Tours. Our route winds through farmland, canals, and forests—a region where time flows at the gentle pace of a river current.

Arriving from across the U.S., our group of enthusiastic recreational cyclists—mostly edging into retirement but still fit and active—shares a love of the outdoors, boats, and travel that immerses us in local life. Having explored Europe's great cities earlier in life, we now crave its quiet corners: small villages, canals, countryside, and the rhythm of rural France. Friendship comes easily as we anticipate the week ahead.

Journey Through the Canals of France

Our six-day itinerary traces part of a series of historic canals that connect the great rivers of France—a network of 5,000 miles built between the seventeenth and nineteenth centuries as lifelines for trade. These waterways continue today to aid the transport of goods and carry tourists like us who prefer the slow, deliberate pleasures of discovery.

Each morning we depart from our barge to embark on a twenty- to forty-mile ride along country roads and lanes that link rural villages. Along the way, we plan to explore these small hamlets with their museums, sculpture gardens, and historical attractions. At each stopover we tour the attractions with local guides who explain the region's history. At midday, we stop at a prearranged café that serves a regional dish, and in late afternoon we drop down along the canal's shady banks and pedal to the rendezvous point with our barge.

Returning to our staterooms after each day's ride, we're assured that our cabins and belongings will be exactly as we left them that morning—and that hot showers and gourmet dinners await each evening.

The beauty of canal travel lies in its unhurried rhythm—the chance to absorb landscapes of vineyards, farmsteads, and stone bridges reflected in still water. Our route is one of many canal bike-and-barge journeys organized by International Bicycle Tours, a leader in luxury cycling across Europe.

Montargis—The Venice of the Gâtinais

Our journey begins in Montargis, a medieval town at the confluence of the Loing River and Briare Canal. Because of the many canals that thread through its streets, the town bills itself as the "Venice of the Gâtinais," a region in central France celebrated for its stunning natural landscapes, rich history, and charming towns. Numerous plaques dedicated to Joan of Arc commemorate her visit to the city after being wounded in her unsuccessful attack on Paris in 1429.

After our transatlantic flights, we gladly stretch our legs as we explore Montargis. Although modern in many ways, the town retains medieval charm in its downtown area. Our group meets in the late afternoon at a shop on Place Mirabeau. It is here, at this original location in the seventeenth century during the reign of Louis XIII, that pralines were invented. We sample the crunchy sweets and purchase enough of this confection—made from almonds (in the States, we use pecans) and cooked sugar—to ensure quick energy infusions during our daily rides. The scent of caramelized sugar clings to our fingers as we stroll back to the barge, already half in love with this way of travel.

Aboard *Fleur*

It's time now to board and stow our bags on *Fleur*, our home for the next seven days. Originally a working cargo barge, *Fleur* was transformed in 2001 into a boutique floating hotel. At 128 feet long and 17 feet wide, she offers plenty of room to spread out: ten cozy twin cabins below deck, each with private bath, and above, a dining salon, library, and shaded sundeck where we gather for wine and conversation. The vessel is fully air-conditioned and equipped with Wi-Fi.

Aboard are twenty sleek Gudereit bicycles equipped with state-of-the-art internal-hub gears—smooth, quiet, and reliable. Compared with derailleur bikes commonly used in the U.S., these Gudereits shift more easily, prevent the chain from slipping off the sprockets, and avoid rubbing chain grease on our legs.

Fleur's crew includes a captain, mate, housekeeper, and chef. Our guide Geoff, a genial Englishman fluent in French, leads the rides, while Gustav, the mechanic, follows in a support van. Ellen, our Dutch chef, creates meals that highlight the finesse of French cuisine in addition to the warmth of traditional Mediterranean dishes from Spain and Italy. Aromas of fresh bread, garlic, and herbs permeate the air, and Ellen's dishes—paired with regional wines—quickly become part of the day's rhythm.

The First Ride—Glass and Reflections

As our first morning begins, we enjoy a hearty breakfast accompanied by the clanging of bicycles as Gustav lifts them ashore. After breakfast, Geoff delivers a safety briefing and Gustav adjusts each bike for our personal comfort. Soon we set off on our inaugural ride, with Gustav trailing in the support van stocked with spare parts.

Twenty miles later, we reach Dordives, a quiet village with a surprising legacy. At its Museum of Glass, we learn that due to the fine silica sand found in the region, the town once supported hundreds of glassmakers and has been the center of glass manufacturing in Europe dating back to the Mesopotamian era. For years, the famous sand was shipped throughout Europe and used almost exclusively by the Venetian glass fabricators on the island of Murano.

To meet the needs of America's nineteenth-century railroad industry for heat-resistant glass needed in signal lanterns, Dordives developed and supplied a special borosilicate "thermal glass" made by adding borax to silica. Because lead was removed, this was the first glass used for cookware. Today Dordives and the neighboring towns continue to be a major center for the manufacture of Pyrex cookware, crystal, and fiber-optic cables. The museum here glitters with centuries of craftsmanship—a reminder of how even the humblest villages once shaped the world.

After lunch, our ride continues along country roads through shady woods and onto open farmland. In the late afternoon, we turn onto a dirt trail that leads us back to the Loing Canal, where *Fleur* is moored beneath overhanging trees near the hamlet of Néronville. We arrive as the light is turning honey-gold. After hot showers and a change of clothes, we reconvene on the forward deck to enjoy cocktails while the sun sinks over the bow. A perfect conclusion to a perfect first day.

Sculptures and Systems

Our route is designed to stop at little-known museum gems, and the next day offers a good example. At 8:15 a.m., we are back in our saddles riding to the town of Égreville, home to the Bourdelle Garden-Museum. Sculptor and painter Antoine Bourdelle, together with his protégé and friend Auguste Rodin, was one of the pioneers of twentieth-century monumental sculpture. Trees, shrubs, and flowering beds lining meandering pathways harmonize with Bourdelle's fifty-seven sculptures, placed strategically throughout the gardens.

Heads tilt back as we gaze upward to admire the larger-than-life bronze statues—*Hercules the Archer*, *The Dying Centaur*, *Adam and Eve in The Garden of Eden*, and numerous Art Deco–style allegorical figures. Winding our way among them feels like wandering through myth.

This short visit prompts several of our group, at the end of the trip, to visit the Musée Bourdelle in Paris, which contains more than 500 of his works.

By now we've mastered IBT's clever "corner system," which ensures no one takes a wrong turn and gets lost. Whenever we approach a turn on our route, Geoff points to the corner—a signal that the rider directly behind him should stop, dismount, point the way for the following riders, and then rejoin once the last rider—called "the sweep"—arrives. Often when we ride through a medieval village with many twists and turns, more than half our group stand guard at corners, waving others through, before regrouping. Only after we exit the town do we reunite.

Following our visit to Bourdelle's Garden-Museum, we pedal past fields of wheat, barley, and canola to the industrial town of Nemours. Not coincidentally, Nemours is the sister town of Wilmington, Delaware, home of DuPont de Nemours & Company, commonly known as DuPont Corporation. The town is the ancestral home of the du Pont de Nemours family, members of which became prosperous chemical manufacturers in the United States when they founded DuPont in 1802. Shortly thereafter, the company went into the gunpowder business at the urging of Thomas Jefferson.

Completing our twenty-five-mile ride for the day, we return to *Fleur*, which is peacefully moored just beyond Nemours, nestled beside a small forest. Keeping with different national themes for our dinner, tonight is Italian Night on board. Chef Ellen, having purchased fresh vegetables earlier that day, prepares a crisp Italian salad, lasagna, and tiramisu for dessert—a meal sufficient both to please our taste buds and replenish calories burned on the day's ride.

Art and History Along the Loing

The following day we pedal to the medieval town of Moret-sur-Loing, where our canal, which begins at the Loing River, ends at the Seine. A local guide leads us through narrow lanes immortalized by the British-born Impressionist painter Alfred Sisley, who made this riverside village his home while capturing its bridges and river views. Sisley, along with Monet, Renoir, and other French greats, helped found the Impressionist movement. Standing where he once set up his easel, it's easy to see why he loved this town—the soft light, the arched bridges, the river slipping quietly under willows.

The nearby bicycle museum, Musée du Vélo, houses a collection of antique bicycles—wooden frames, solid tires, and contraptions that make our sleek eleven-gear bikes feel miraculous by comparison. We also learn how Europe's cycling culture differs from America's. In Europe, bicyclists—who are part of daily life—tend to be either competitive athletes training for races or local residents riding to the market, whereas in the U.S., we ride mostly for recreation. Perhaps that explains the curious stares we sometimes receive from villagers watching our Lycra-clad procession and wondering what we are doing as we pedal through their villages.

Fontainebleau and Beyond

History buffs in the group are delighted to learn that Moret is the site of one of Napoleon's last victories in 1814 before abdicating at Château de Fontainebleau and being banished to the island of Elba. The next morning, we follow Napoleon's journey to Fontainebleau—though our arrival at the palace is less dramatic than Napoleon's and far more cheerful. We enter not as a disgraced leader, but as eager tourists.

At Château de Fontainebleau, a guide leads us through salons once graced by Louis XIV, the "Sun King." The palace later served as Nazi headquarters during World War II and, after liberation, as NATO's European base. Its gilded rooms and echoing corridors hold centuries of stories.

Much as we enjoy the grandiosity of Louis XIV, we're happy to escape the crowds of tourists to return to the simple pleasure of our bikes as we roll through the forests of Fontainebleau. Now the largest remaining woodland in France, the Forest of Fontainebleau stretches for miles. Sunlight filters through the canopy of oak and beech as we ride, the air cool and earthy. We end the day in Melun, a quiet suburb of Paris, where *Fleur* awaits beside a peaceful wharf.

Paris by River and Foot

The next day's ride is short—just to Évry, where we rejoin *Fleur* for lunch and then cruise the Seine toward Paris. Woodlands and pastoral scenery along the riverbanks give way to quays, bridges, factories, commercial buildings, and finally the unmistakable skyline of the great city itself.

Legs strengthened from several hundred miles of pedaling across the French countryside, we're ready to explore Paris on foot. We begin at Père-Lachaise Cemetery, visiting the graves of such greats as Oscar Wilde, Jim Morrison, Chopin, Molière, and Yves Montand. From there we wander to Notre-Dame, the Louvre, and finally just amble along the banks of the Seine, savoring the feeling of belonging, however briefly, to this timeless city.

That evening, at our farewell dinner aboard *Fleur*, we raise our glasses to the week behind us. Addresses are exchanged, and then, rather than indulging in farewells, we begin planning to get together next year for another bike-and-barge cruise down another quiet canal.

Fleur

Loing Canal at sunset

Mid-Morning Break

Setting up for morning ride

Chapter 15

MARSHALL ISLANDS - MEDICAL MERCY SHIP

While driving around Seattle's Union Bay one day, I do a double take. What catches my eye is the incongruous sight of three towering masts of a square-rigged ship rising above dozens of commercial fishing boats undergoing repairs and retrofits before returning to Alaska's rich fishing grounds. I park and scurry down the docks for a closer look. Sure enough, a topsail schooner sits there, the likes of which haven't been seen in Pacific Northwest waters for more than a hundred years.

Tole Mour—Gift of Life and Health

As I stand there dumbfounded, I hear someone on board call my name. My old friend John Guzzwell, one of the country's great sailing legends and a lifelong sailor and boatbuilder, waves me aboard. At age twenty-nine, John built *Trekka*, a 21-foot wooden yawl, and completed a circumnavigation in what was then the smallest boat to do so. A veteran of many ocean voyages, he chronicled his experiences in numerous books. As a boatbuilder, he pioneered innovative techniques such as cold-molded construction.

While we chat over a cup of coffee in one of the ship's staterooms, John fills me in. He is the construction manager responsible for outfitting this 150-foot steel-hulled schooner as a medical mercy ship for the Honolulu-based Marimed (Maritime Medicine) Foundation to be operated in the Marshall Islands of Micronesia. The $2.4 million vessel is owned by the government of the sovereign Republic of the Marshall Islands. The foundation was created three years earlier by David and Dr. Lonnie Higgins to provide education and health and disease-screening clinics in Micronesia. Marshallese schoolchildren selected the ship's name, *Tole Mour*, meaning "gift of life and health."

Under John's guidance, craftsmen busy themselves installing basic systems and tanks, generators, shafting and propeller, a rudder assembly, three mast sections, and a 600-hp eight-cylinder diesel engine. Its final configuration will include examination rooms, a diagnostic laboratory, a pharmacy, an eye clinic, a dental clinic, X-ray equipment, and an operating room. After the ship is launched and delivered to the Marshall Islands, twelve medical personnel will serve on rotating tours.

John recounts an amusing anecdote: the ship's designer, New Zealander Ted Eubank, recently visited and was shocked to find her sitting three inches deeper than called for in his design. He was greatly relieved, however, to learn that she was being constructed in freshwater rather than in seawater, for which she was designed.

The sailing-ship concept, according to John, dates back to 1852, when specially designed *Morning Star* sailing ships operated out of Boston to provide health and educational services in Micronesia. The tall ship approach to outer-island support remains the most cost-effective method of getting health care to the islanders. Fuel costs are minimal, and maintenance is low.

In the Marshall Islands, because the outer islands have no hotels, restaurants, running water, or electricity, a sailing ship provides low-cost infrastructure for delivering health care to the 38,000 inhabitants. The country's seventy square miles of land are scattered among twenty-nine atolls and five mountaintop islands spread across half a million square miles of ocean.

The population faces serious health problems, including malnutrition, high infant mortality, diabetes, tuberculosis, leprosy, high adolescent suicide rates, alcoholism, and radiation illnesses resulting from nuclear tests following WWII.

I am particularly interested in learning more about this program—not because of my love for classic sailing vessels, but because of my familiarity with the Marshall Islands, where I worked in my first career as an engineer–physicist in Sandia National Laboratories' atmospheric nuclear testing program. I knew firsthand of the devastation to these people inflicted by our country's nuclear tests conducted on their land.

Marimed Foundation

A few days after my discussion with John, I telephone the Higginses in Honolulu. After explaining my connection with the Marshall Islands and expressing my interest in the *Tole Mour*, I tell them I'm keen to write an article about their foundation.

They inform me that the ship won't be ready for another year, but in the interim the Marimed Foundation will continue to operate clinics in the outer islands using small aircraft. These efforts, however, are subject to space and weight restrictions imposed by air and boat services—limitations that severely curtail the supplies, medications, and equipment the medical teams can carry to these remote areas.

After several more telephone calls, and perceiving my strong interest, Lonnie and David invite me to the Marshall Islands to see how the tall ship—currently being built and outfitted in the Pacific Northwest—will serve the health needs of this island nation. Naturally, I jump at the opportunity.

Arriving in Honolulu from Seattle a few weeks later, I briefly visit Marimed's headquarters before connecting to Continental's Air Micronesia service, which provides regular flights to the Marshall Islands and other island nations of the central Pacific.

At the country's capital, Majuro, I am met by Lonnie and David, both in their forties—a disarmingly charming duo who could easily be mistaken for the ultimate high-pressure yuppie couple. Instead, they have committed themselves to building a successful health-care program in the Pacific.

As I get to know them, I recognize that Lonnie easily wins the hearts of the people she serves with her infectious sense of humor. She is balanced by the quiet, no-nonsense presence of David, a corporate lawyer and first-class yachtsman in his own right. She makes any situation light. He keeps things grounded. Together they've mustered forces to make their dream of significantly improving health-care delivery in Micronesia their life's work.

In the afternoon, Lonnie and the dozen volunteers who make up the Marimed health team—dentists, physicians, nurses, and medical technicians recruited from throughout the country—join other health-care professionals from the nation's Health Services Ministry. Together they board a chartered plane to Jaluit, one of the outer islands. By working in concert with the government's social-services and health-agency personnel at these outer-island field clinics, and by including Marshallese on its staff, Marimed has earned the support of the people and the endorsement of government officials of the Marshall Islands.

David explains that this contrasts with other well-meaning groups that arrive with their staff and equipment for a short stopover in Majuro, then travel independently to the outer islands without coordinating with government health authorities. They often go about their work unaware of the problems they create—introducing new drugs unsuited to the area, antagonizing government-appointed health assistants by bypassing them, showing insensitivity to the cultural mores of these traditional matriarchal societies, and leaving the people with false hopes by failing to follow up after initial visits.

Although the Marimed health team carries minimal equipment and supplies, the aircraft is overweight, so David and I are bumped. We must wait two days for the next commercial flight.

One of those days, I spend hours perusing old newspapers in the town's library to learn more about the culture of the Marshallese. A whimsical column about unemployment in an old newspaper catches my eye. Here's an excerpt:

"There is no unemployment problem, for everyone is unemployed most of the time. Work is an unnecessary luxury. A simple thatched cottage and perhaps an outrigger canoe are a native's capital. Nature does the rest. Only three things to do: eating, sleeping, and loving. For the first, Nature provides bountifully; the second follows as a natural consequence; so all energies remain for the last."

On the second day, when I meet with local health officials and devote more time to research in the library, I learn that life in the Marshall Islands is not as idyllic as it may seem.

Atmospheric Nuclear Testing

The United States conducted sixty-seven nuclear tests in the Marshall Islands between 1946 and 1958—the equivalent of detonating 1.5 Hiroshima-sized bombs every day for those twelve years. The largest test, called Castle Bravo, led to the radiation poisoning of many Marshallese citizens and contamination of atolls that are still unusable to this day. The resettlement attempts proved catastrophic, especially for the people of Rongelap, who often had to be relocated a second time.

Incidents of cancer, thyroid disorders, miscarriages, and deformities multiplied. Residents were often not warned in advance of the tests and were directly exposed to radiation that caused alopecia, skin lesions, leukemia, and cancers. It is estimated that Marshallese female population has cervical cancer mortality sixty times higher than that of a comparable population in the U.S.—a legacy of nuclear radiation.

While living in the islands, I heard of many so-called "monster births," which are infants born covered with hair and bearing little resemblance to human form. The midwives would quietly end the infants' lives and later inform the mother that the child had been stillborn.

In addition to rendering much of the land uninhabitable and harming the people, contamination has damaged the coral reefs and underwater ecosystems of those vulnerable atolls.

The medical problems faced by the Marshallese are overwhelming. Simple statistics I find tell the story. In 1987, the islands had the highest adolescent male suicide rate in the world; rampant drug and alcohol abuse; infant mortality four times greater than in the U.S.; diabetes in forty percent of adults; chronic night blindness caused by vitamin A deficiency among children; widespread infant malnutrition; two polio outbreaks within the previous two decades with more than half the deaths among children; leprosy… and the list goes on. Compounding these problems: a birthrate that's among the highest in the world and a population that is fifty percent under fourteen years old.

U.S. Mandate—Relocation and Ruin

The country's history as a U.S. mandate adds another ugly dimension to the picture. In the 1950s, when nuclear tests were conducted at Enewetak and Bikini atolls, entire communities were relocated to other islands—some before the tests because they risked radiation exposure, and others afterward, when both the people and their land had been contaminated. These relocations stand as testimonies to the insensitivity of the U.S. military.

Islanders who had been living on breadfruit diets practically starved when they were moved to atolls with only coconut palms and no breadfruit. Fishing canoes suited for protected lagoons inside atoll reefs were useless to islanders relocated to mountaintop islands with no lagoons. In addition, a large segment of the population suffered from radiation-related medical complications while many in younger generations were born with radiation-induced genetic defects.

Intending to help the Marshallese, the U.S. government attempted to make amends by flooding the tiny islands with dollars, refined foods, and western goods. But these measures further disrupted the local culture. Complications arise when the government makes cash compensation to radiation victims and displaced landowners. In a cashless society, the money frequently finds its way to alcohol and drugs. Even worse, in many respects, it is spent on imported refined foods, candy, and soft drinks, which lead to more diabetes, hypertension, and obesity. Because Western dental hygiene is foreign to the Marshallese, sugar causes rapid deterioration of teeth and gums—something I later witness when I rejoin the medical team. The introduction of Western goods such as electrical appliances not only disrupts the culture but also proves of little use in a country spread across dozens of islands with a limited power grid.

Field Medicine and Barefoot Dentistry

Two days after David and I were bumped, we fly to the outer islands. As I look down on tiny strands of paradise, studded with reefs and edged by glistening white beaches, it seems as though only cruise ships would belong in this idyllic setting. Knowing the truth about the ravages of disease and poor health on these islands, I see the reality behind the mirage and understand why Marimed considers *Tole Mour* essential for carrying out disease-screening and health-education programs the Marshall Islands government has cited as top priorities.

For two weeks, I travel among the outer islands accompanying the medical team as it spends two or three days in each village and then moves on. Sometimes there's a school building or dispensary where the field clinics are set up by day and the team sleeps at night. Otherwise, it's a matter of constructing a makeshift structure, often with coral sand as a floor and the overhead canopy of palm leaves as a ceiling. Portable generators power the mobile dental units and charge batteries for the medical instruments.

This is the ultimate in field medicine and barefoot dentistry: six clinics—pediatric, dental, immunization, hypertension, and two separate health education sessions for men and women—are each handicapped in their own way. Nevertheless, the team members remain optimistic, often repeating, "When the ship is here, we won't have these problems."

Working non-stop throughout the day, the three-man dental team fills cavities, extracts teeth, and applies sealants to healthy teeth. At night they distribute toothbrushes to all the children and conduct classes on how to use them—items otherwise foreign to Marshallese culture. The children all giggle when the instructors put the brushes in their own mouths to demonstrate the proper brushing technique. Sadly, by morning the toothbrushes lie scattered throughout the grounds, where the children have haphazardly discarded them.

Candy and soft drinks, prevalent in villages with greater Western exposure, are devastating young teeth. I see case after case of teenagers with half their teeth rotted away. A seventeen-year-old girl needs five fillings and two extractions, and a twenty-four-year-old woman needs ten extractions. Often the baby teeth of younger children are so badly deteriorated that the dentists pull them simply to rid the mouth of potential infection. In many cases, teeth have already completely decayed, leaving behind just the root.

The biggest handicap for the dentists is the lack of X-ray equipment. In one year, when *Tole Mour* is scheduled to arrive, she will be equipped with an X-ray unit and other sophisticated dental instruments to perform root canals, place crowns, fix bridges, and perform surgical extractions.

In conducting physical exams, the doctors look for heart murmurs, cleft palates, intestinal parasites, physical deformities, ear infections, perforated eardrums, night blindness, and skin infections. They treat patients as best they can with their limited supplies and equipment.

A fearful young mother carrying her baby in her arms appears at the door of one makeshift dispensary. Although she had likely prepared herself for weeks for this day, knowing she must bring her infant for vaccinations, she nevertheless hesitates. Lonnie looks up, flashes a smile, then walks to the door, takes the woman's hand, and leads her to a chair by the long table covered with vaccine bottles, disinfectants, medical cards, and a box of syringes. Lonnie's gentle, friendly grip eases the woman's fear.

The baby is first. Lonnie moves carefully and quickly yet conveys a sense of casual reassurance. The needle pricks the baby's arm, just as the first cry escapes the infant's lips. The mother is next. With one hand she strokes her child while she offers her other arm to Lonnie. Lonnie pauses a moment, glances into the mother's uncertain eyes, then turns again to the infant. Now the mother appears almost impatient for her injection. Lonnie complies, and then it is over. Mother and child leave the dispensary, and two more medical charts receive checks in the columns indicating they have both been vaccinated against tuberculosis.

The goal of the immunization clinic is to vaccinate children against the usual childhood diseases, but keeping the vaccine chilled is a problem. Health officials estimate that as much as half the serum brought to the Marshall Islands is ineffective due to improper storage and handling. Again, this problem will be solved when the ship arrives, because medication will be stored in cooling units in *Tole Mour's* pharmacy until just before use.

Pap smears and tissue samples from the women's clinic must be sent to Majuro for analysis, a cumbersome process involving delicate handling of sensitive specimen trays. When *Tole Mour* arrives, she will be equipped with a diagnostic lab where pathology can be determined within hours while the medical team is still at the same village.

Mejrirok—The Moment That Matters

One Sunday morning, when the team arrives at Mejrirok, an island in Jaluit Atoll, we are surprised to find the village deserted. Then, hearing singing in the distance, we realize everyone is at church. Not wanting to disturb anyone, we quietly meander around the village while waiting for the service to end. As I wander off by myself, I happen to glance into the open door of a hut. A small child is lying still. All alone.

Concerned that this might be a problem, I call Lonnie to take a look. Without hesitation, she runs into the hut and, recognizing that the child is lethargic, grabs him and races along the path. Breathless, she reaches the improvised health dispensary beside the lagoon. "If we only had the ship now," she utters desperately.

Other members of the medical team scatter to gather IV serum, medication, and packets of rehydration solution to treat the malnourished, dehydrated infant—at ten pounds, he weighs less than half of what he should. In this case, the child is fortunate. The health team has brought emergency medical supplies, and within thirty-six hours, Robby is transported by boat, jeep, and plane to the hospital in Majuro.

In deference to the cultural traditions of the Marshallese, our medical team does not bring food on our trip. In fact, it would be disrespectful to our hosts to prepare our own meals. Every evening around 10:00 p.m., as we sit in our temporary lodging—usually a schoolhouse or community center—we begin to hear in the distance the gradually increasing sound of women singing. Their gentle strains suit the sweet, soft setting. The village women enter our building and place gifts of food in the center of the room—all carefully wrapped in pandanus leaves and woven frond dishes. We are seated in chairs in a semicircle, and the women sit on the floor. The eldest woman then stands to deliver a long speech welcoming us to their village and presents the offerings, which she says are not much but are all they have and come from their hearts.

Then we introduce ourselves to the applause of our hosts. Despite the elder's comments, the women have brought an enormous amount of food—enough to fill both them and us—but they leave before we begin our feast. We have three times more than we can eat—fish, octopus, crabs, shellfish, breadfruit, coconut, jack-a-roo (fermented sap of the coconut palm), bananas, rice, chicken, pork, and an assortment of vegetables. A buffet to remember!

Developing Health from Within

When I later ask Lonnie why she and David created Marimed, to which they now devote themselves full time, she explains it grew out of a passing idea during a five-year cruise with their two children on their 96-foot schooner, *Deliverance*. "When we came near land, I would offer my services as a doctor to local medical representatives." Lonnie treated patients first in Saint Lucia, then in Antigua, Roatán in the Bay Islands of Honduras, the Marquesas, and elsewhere in the western Pacific. Though trained as an obstetrician, she learned other types of medicine this way and, through donations from pharmaceutical and medical supply companies, built up *Deliverance's* medical inventory.

The couple gradually devoted more time to maritime medicine during their island stopovers, culminating three years ago when they decided to work full time on Marimed.

"We especially wanted to help the people of Micronesia because of the shame we feel for what the U.S. government has done," explained Lonnie, in reference to the legacy of America's nuclear testing activities in the region. "It is terrible how the government has fostered a dependency of the Marshallese people on the United States. We want to show that they can develop a quality health-care program themselves."

~

Lateen rig outrigger sailing canoe

Tole Mour can set four headsails

Tole Mour escorted by U.S. Coast Guard

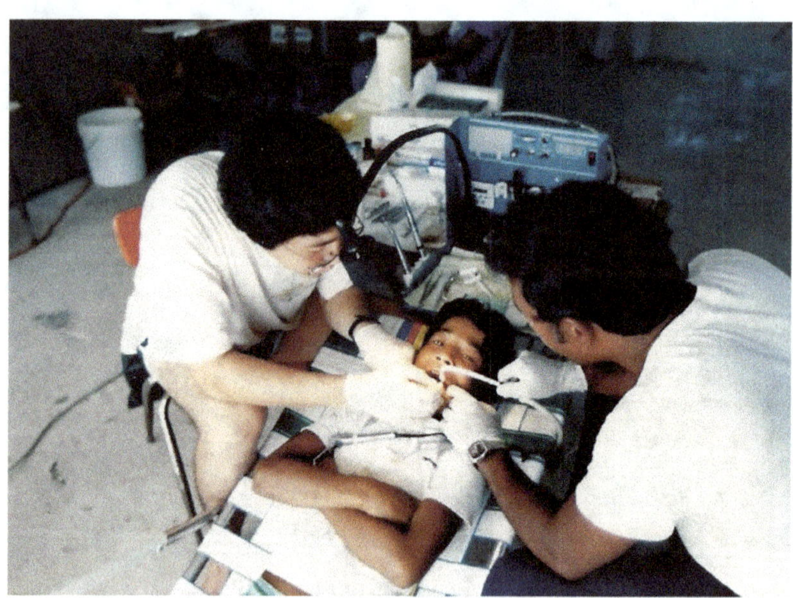

Dr. Jerry Hino and Marshallese dental assistant perform oral exam

Dr. Lonnie Higgins with malnourished child

Marshallese children proudly displaying their new toothbrushes

Chapter 16

NEW CALEDONIA - TREES OF ÎLE DES PINS

Trees!

It's the trees!

To see the legendary trees on Isle of Pines—that's why we are traveling a third of the way around the world to this isolated speck in the southwest Pacific.

As our Air New Zealand jet circles 5,000-foot peaks on approach, we eagerly scan the sailing paradise below. Where are the famous pine trees? We don't see any.

We see the turquoise waters of the world's largest lagoon glistening against the dark blue ocean. We see ribbons of golden sand broken by mangrove forests fringing the coastline. We see coconut trees and stands of eucalyptus, kaori, and banyan trees marching from the lower foothills up to jagged volcanic pinnacles. But where is the island with the trees we have come all this way to see?

Within an 800-mile coral-reef necklace of whitewater pearls floats New Caledonia's long, slender main island, Grande Terre. The Isle of Pines (Île des Pins), the dot below this angled exclamation mark, is our destination. But as we are to learn, Nature has set up numerous barriers to keep people away from this semi-sacred spot.

Paris of the Pacific

We are four long-time sailor friends looking forward to a ten-day charter in New Caledonia. We start at the charter-company base in New Caledonia's capital city Nouméa, which lies along a ten-mile peninsula at the southwestern end of Grande Terre. Known as the "Paris of the Pacific," Nouméa cultivates "la vie à la française," offering the amenities of a Parisian shopping boulevard. To maintain its hold on this valuable overseas territory, which started as a garrison, France supplies New Caledonia with a steady flow of export goods: wines, cheeses, perfumes, fashion clothing, and automobiles. In addition to being home to a rich French-influenced culture, New Caledonia is also home to a rich diversity of reefs and ecosystems that are designated UNESCO World Heritage Sites.

Tucked along the waterfront among luxury yachts (few foreign cruising boats here), Nouméa Yacht Charters harbors a small sailing fleet at Port Plaisance. Here, elegant French-designed keel boats and catamarans are available for bareboat, crewed, and flotilla charters. The base manager, a French-speaking Australian, supplies us with fresh pastries, fragrant cheeses, and bottles of French wine. The checkout is thorough, the provisioning easy, and the briefing detailed. Although she doesn't try to dissuade us from going there, she informs us that none of her charter clients has ever sailed to the Isle of Pines. (Gulp!)

Blight of the Pacific

Armed with the charterers' guidebook *Cruising in New Caledonia*, we are soon under sail on an Oceanis 390, *Kunie II*, with our compass bearing southeast to Isle of Pines, just over sixty miles away. The city's waterfront of vast white beaches and charming marinas glows against a backdrop of commercial buildings framed by brilliant flame trees, orchids, and bougainvillea before it all fades away in our wake.

Only now does the blight of this paradise become all too evident. Ugly scars and deep cuts slash the 250-mile-long spine of Grande Terre. Open-pit mining operations, which date back more than 150 years and still continue today, testify to New Caledonia's rich ore deposits. The world's largest known nickel reserves lie here, and the territory is the fourth-largest producer of nickel ore, a major component in the production of stainless steel. New Caledonia also supports thriving cobalt, gold, chromium, manganese, and iron mining operations.

Leaving the blight behind us, we focus on the unexplored islands, isolated beaches, and fair winds that lie ahead. The 185-foot lighthouse on Amédée Islet twelve miles due south beckons, marking the main passage through the outer reef.

We tuck into a protected cove for the night and depart early the next morning for Île Ouen, known for its turtles and jade mines. Water visibility is excellent, making it easy to see the many coral heads in the area. We sail without trouble through Woodin Canal, a deep-water marine channel cut through an area once strewn with patch reefs and bommies (columns or pinnacles of coral rising from the seabed to—or near—the surface). The patchwork and random distribution of these hard-to-spot hazards cause us to reconsider our itinerary, particularly since our guidebook describes these underwater threats as far more extensive on the approach to Isle of Pines. But having come this far, we're determined not to be deterred, so we continue on as planned.

Entering Prony Bay, we discover New Caledonia's renowned red and white beaches. Beautiful as the red beaches are to behold, the guidebook warns against walking on the red sand and informs us that unless anchor chains are thoroughly cleaned, they can discolor the deck. Created by run-off from extensive mining in the area, the ocher clays leave a deep stain that is almost impossible to wash out.

Avoiding the red sands, we anchor in a quiet setting called Bonne Anse, then explore by dinghy and foot the hidden coves and twisted shoreline. Narrow paths lead us to a deserted mine and an abandoned ore crushing plant. We see no evidence of any attempt to clean up this environmental disaster site where high concentrations of iron and chromium lend the soil a bizarre red and green cast. Mountain streams, tinted these same weird hues, meander through pine forests and cut into the sea.

Hazardous Passages

Days earlier, with perseverance, we had overcome the initial challenge of complicated travel logistics required simply to find flights from the western U.S. to New Caledonia. Now we must overcome another major deterrent to reach our destination. Our course to Isle of Pines leads southeast through a thirty-mile, coral-infested passage, crossing the strong westerly currents of Havannah and Sarchelle Pass. With warnings to keep a close lookout for the numerous reefs that often pop up unexpectedly, the cruising guide devotes many pages to the intricacies of this passage. Depth sounders, we are told, are of little use here since coral heads rise directly from the bottom. Moreover, the passage should be made between 9:00 a.m. and 3:00 p.m. when the sun is high, because spotting the coral hazards at other times would be extremely difficult.

With no way to predict the current set, we anxiously watch for every light-brown patch. Adding to our unease are suspect soundings dating to the French Admiralty charts from the 1800s. We cautiously feel our way along, relying upon sharp eyes, dead reckoning, and triangulated position fixes from the islets and 800-foot Nga Peak, the highest point on distant Isle of Pines. At one point, we change course to avoid a slightly submerged coral head, only to have a bommie appear directly ahead. With no alternative, at the last moment we make the risky decision to pass between the two, fortunately missing them both. Admittedly, our nerves are frazzled, but by day's end we rejoice in our success in crossing safely into Gadji Bay on the northwest coast of our destination.

To See the Trees

To cartographers, it's just another tiny island speck in the southwestern Pacific, but for us Isle of Pines holds an otherworldly fascination bordering on the mystical. We have traveled a great distance and overcome significant challenges to see the famous pines.

Suddenly, they loom before us in all their majestic grandeur. Vibrant flowers, turquoise waters, and snow-white beaches—spectacular in their own right—all fade into the background as we gaze in awe upon the stunning Cook pines (Araucaria columnaris) rising up before us. Elongated shafts of dark green tower to 200 feet, five to six times taller than the coconut palms bordering the beaches. If we weren't seeing for ourselves, it would be hard to imagine trunks four feet in diameter tapering to pointed tips that reach to the sky, filled in with branches laden with thick tufts of needles. Each tree reveals a splendor of its own. Seen together, a stand of these giants is indeed awe-inspiring.

Unlike many neighboring Pacific islands, the Isle of Pines has survived the ravages of the modern world's extractive industries and is preserved today in its natural state. Although sandalwood and rosewood across the island were harvested by Europeans in the 1800s, the ancient pines, regarded as sacred by the native Melanesians, have never been cut. The pines remain today much as they did when Captain James Cook sailed by in 1774. Wary of reefs, Cook did not land on Kunie—the island's Melanesian name. However, for the benefit of the European world, Cook renamed Kunie in honor of the trees.

In addition to the natural coral reef deterrent, Isle of Pines was further protected when it became a French penal colony, home to thousands of political deportees from France in 1872. From that time on, European settlement on the island was forbidden. Although the prison has long been closed, as we explore the island, we discover the ruined remains of several monuments, gravestones, plaques, and buildings from that era.

Gardens Below the Surface

Our remaining days are filled with exploring small nearby islands where we bathe in natural pools, snorkel in shallow-water reefs, and meet Melanesian villagers. To admire the trees from every vantage, we shift anchorages daily, moving among small bays named Ouaméo, Kanumera, and Kuto, though most of the smaller bays are unnamed.

The reefs rest on the world's oldest known platform for coral formation, an important factor explaining the region's great variety of marine flora and fauna. Fluorescent corals were first discovered right here. We never miss an opportunity at each anchorage to grab face masks and snorkels, and plunge overboard to view the fascinating marine life and unusual corals.

Endless schools of fish with all the colors of a child's paintbox are always on the move—parrotfish, angelfish, clownfish, butterflyfish, triggerfish, damselfish, and more—either seeking food or avoiding predators. Tiny fish dart in and out of crevasses in the coral or seek protection in the tentacles of sea anemones. Stingrays, manta rays, and eagle rays glide by gracefully and effortlessly.

We keep a respectful distance from reef sharks and eels—said to be harmless—and sea snakes, less so. Turtles and lobsters seem to be everywhere while underwater middens, the remains of discarded prey, help us locate octopus lairs. Deeply crevassed brain coral, waving sea fans, and other hard- and soft-coral species create colorful coral gardens, each trying to attract the attention of various marine creatures. Who needs television when a living world of wonders waits just below the surface?

As we relax in the evening after a day of sailing, snorkeling, and exploring, we reflect that we have overcome three main obstacles to reach this remote destination. First, we had to negotiate complicated travel logistics to arrive at Nouméa on the main island of New Caledonia. Second, over several days sailing on our own in unfamiliar and unusual conditions, we had to navigate on old charts while on constant lookout for coral hazards. We had more than our share of close calls making that final passage! Third, once here, we are entirely on our own—no ports or harbors, no marine supplies or fuel, and only a small convenience store for basic provisioning. There's no one to help if we have a medical emergency or a breakdown aboard. But thanks to careful planning (and good luck), we've suffered no mishaps.

On our final evening on Isle of Pines, we ascend a hill rising high above the main village, Vao, to a cemetery amidst an old pine grove. For a long time, we sit in silence, absorbing the scene before us. No wonder the Melanesians regard these trees as sacred. Although we will be departing soon, we will carry with us—and always cherish—the memory of this remarkable place. Here, along with at all other locations on the island, the ever-present, silent, towering pines dominate the view, holding us, like all who have made this pilgrimage, under their spell.

~

200-foot pine trees, Isle of Pines

Church at Vao

Kunie inhabitants, Isle of Pines

Penal colony prison ruins

Chapter 17

PALAU - AT RAINBOW'S END

Amazement—that describes the initial reaction of cruising sailors Tova and Navot Bornovski when they first arrived at Palau in 1986. All around the turquoise expanse of protected waters they saw luxuriant vegetation and white-sand beaches on hundreds of small, jungle-cloaked, uninhabited islands, where the fragrance of ginger, jasmine, and plumeria scented the air.

Their second reaction was one of surprise. Where were the other boats? Across the vast lagoon, not another sail appeared. In fact, they saw no other boats of any kind at all. Intrigued by both what they saw and what they did not see, the couple decided to interrupt their four-year around-the-world sailing trip for a few days to explore this little-known island group at the far western edge of Micronesia.

"As we cruised into Nikko Bay, a labyrinth of emerald Rock Islands in a turquoise-blue lagoon," Tova recalls, "our minds were spinning. We were amazed by the richness of the marine environment.

When we saw the lifestyle, the beauty of the place, and the opportunities, we decided to make this our permanent home."

The scene that the Bornovskis saw four decades ago has changed little today. The remoteness of this tiny island-nation, composed of 340 jungle islands and atolls, has prevented it from catching on as a destination for cruising yachtsmen. Located 4,600 miles southwest of Honolulu and 200 miles from Yap, its nearest neighbor in Micronesia, and just seven degrees north of the equator, this isolated archipelago is truly a place apart. Although the Palauans' ancestors ranked among the greatest sailors and navigators in history, most of the islanders today—except those who work in the commercial fishing and dive industries—don't go near the water.

Rainbow's End

Many Pacific Island legends refer to a gigantic rainbow that extends east to west across the ocean. These myths recount how this graceful arc protects the thousands of miles of scattered islands along the equator. The people of Palau claim that their land represents the pot of gold where the legendary rainbow touches down. The proof: the riches of their land, the bounty of their waters, and their multimillennial-old traditions. "Welcome to Palau—The Rainbow's End," proclaims the immigration form.

Palau, part of the Caroline Islands chain, has been inhabited for more than 3,000 years, settled by people of Polynesian, Malayan, and Melanesian lineage. In modern times, the Republic of Palau came under Spanish, German, and then Japanese rule, culminating in Japanese administration from 1919 through the end of World War II. The archipelago was a U.S. trust territory for nearly fifty years before becoming independent in 1994.

Today Palau offers internet, satellite TV, and other modern amenities. English and Palauan are the official languages, and the currency is the American dollar. Though appearing Americanized, Palauans have preserved their culture, ceremonies, exchanges, and councils—both on land and at sea.

Cruising Among the Rock Islands

Once the Bornovskis, originally from Israel, settled into their new home, they joined the dive community, taking jobs with Fish 'n Fins, the country's first dive center. For several years they worked on Palau's first live-aboard dive boat, *San Tamarin*, a 50-foot sloop. With Navot as dive master and Tova serving as chef, they helped pioneer the evolving dive tourism business.

In the late 1990s, the Bornovskis purchased Fish 'n Fins and began to include multi-day tours of Palau's unique cruising grounds. Now they offer both diving and cruising charters on their two live-aboard vessels: *Ocean Hunter I*, a 60-foot steel-hulled motorsailer, and *Ocean Hunter III*, a 90-foot motor yacht, formerly a research vessel.

Barrier reefs protect the many lagoons from the Philippine Sea to the west and the North Pacific Ocean to the east. Inside the main lagoon, hundreds of small limestone islets, the Rock Islands, await exploration. Wave action and freshwater runoff have eroded the base of the soft limestone pinnacles, giving the islets a mushroom-like overhang. Around their shores, the isles offer stunning corals, natural arches, colorful fish, marine lakes, white-sand beaches, and countless anchorages and coves with remarkably few visitors. Some of the last untouched tropical jungle of the Pacific covers the islets' interiors. A particular favorite is Ulong Island, where Season 10 of the TV series *Survivor* was filmed.

Other popular anchorages are the islands with "jellyfish lakes." Changes in sea level millions of years ago formed these marine lakes, which are inhabited by stingless jellyfish. Visitors can snorkel among nebulae of the translucent pink creatures that gently bob like tiny balloons. Propelled by ghostly parasols opening and shutting in a gentle pulsing rhythm, the gelatinous flotilla resembles a slow-motion ballet.

During World War II, Palau was a major Japanese military base. In March 1944, U.S. Navy bombers and fighter planes raided the Japanese fleet and sank more than sixty ships—dubbed the "Lost Fleet of the Rock Islands"—in the area's shallow waters. Boaters can anchor nearby and explore these wrecks, which are protected by law from souvenir hunters. In 2000, Navot and a dive team discovered the remains of the only U.S. warship found to date in these waters, the Navy destroyer USS *Perry*.

In 2002, the Bornovskis established the Micronesian Shark Foundation (MSF) to study the region's declining shark population. With support from the National Geographic Society and researchers at Boston University, they organize Shark Weeks every year. Researchers count and tag sharks during the gray reef shark mating season. The studies confirm a population decline of fifty percent in just two decades, mainly because of the demand for shark fin soup, a delicacy prized by the wealthy in Asia. To protect these sought-after sharks, Palau created the world's first shark sanctuary in 2009, banning all commercial shark fishing in its waters.

Life Above the Reefs

Palau holds more attractions than just those of the sea. The government, to ease pressure on its fragile coral reefs while at the same time appealing to a broader spectrum of vacationers, has begun promoting its ecotourism and cultural attractions—stone monoliths,

World War II relics, waterfalls, historical sites, ancient burial caves, and untouched golden beaches. Most dive operators also now include land tours to acquaint visitors with this country's rich heritage.

"There's so much more to show visitors than just what's in and on the water," explains Tova, who supports the government initiative as vice president of the Palau Tourism Association. "To develop our local tourism, we have organized many community events and built the first school of hospitality and tourism."

In this matrilineal nation, women choose tribal chiefs, own the land, and control traditional riches. As currency, in addition to the American dollar, Palauans use money beads—*udoud*—made from glass paste. Beads are exchanged at childbirth and marriage ceremonies.

Tradition also means graciousness to guests, including a unique way to wave goodbye. The hosts raise hands high up and sway in an exaggerated manner back and forth from the waist for as long as the departing visitors are in sight.

Centuries-old *bai*, men's meeting houses, still stand, painted with motifs of sharks denoting bravery and money birds, a symbol of prosperity. Ancient stone money wheels dot the fields and gardens. And, like the stone statues found on Easter Island, mysterious, massive four-foot-high monoliths (carved from basalt, a non-native stone) rise up on Babeldaob, Palau's largest island. No one knows how or why they came to be there.

Laced with numerous rivers, Babeldaob is also known for its waterfalls, where waters rush over twenty-foot drops before coursing smoothly down to the sea. Grottos and natural whirlpools along the rivers' courses offer sites where visitors can enjoy refreshing swims.

Koror

Quirky and charming, Koror is Palau's main commercial center and home to three-fourths of the country's 20,000 inhabitants. The town stretches four miles across four islands connected by bridges and causeways. Shops and neighborhoods line its two-lane road, but because municipal regulations, which are quite strict, remain in the hands of the locals, no hotel or restaurant chains are allowed.

The Etpison Museum and the Belau National Museum give visitors insight into the country's arts, crafts, traditions, and culture. Exhibits explain the history behind the legends carved onto wooden storyboards. Designs often incorporate fish, turtles, manta rays, and other ocean motifs. The Palau International Coral Reef Center houses an aquarium and a mariculture project featuring a nursery of giant clams.

A Taste of the Rainbow

With culinary influences from Japan, the Philippines, the United States, Malaysia, and Indonesia, Palau's cuisine is a Pacific fusion of seafood, spices, and fresh fruits and vegetables. Locavores eat the fish they catch, taro from their patch, and almonds from the trees in their yards. Islanders also have a taste for the unusual: soup made with sand crab, kangkung (like watercress), and coconut crab with sweet flesh that takes on the taste of its namesake.

Drawing from her years as a chef on charter boats and in her restaurant, Barracuda, in Koror, Tova has written a cookbook, *Taste of Rainbow's End*. "Rain and sun—the creators of the rainbow—with the right balance, will produce an abundance of vegetables and fruits," Tova reads from her book. "The tropical fruits of Palau have a taste long forgotten: a pineapple that is the pure essence of sweetness, a papaya whose deep orange color reflects its richness, and a taste of banana you cannot eat elsewhere."

Palau's most notorious nosh is fruit bat, served in a steamer basket and wrapped in its wings as though dressed for Halloween. Pair your bat with local taro wine, which, at thirty-eight proof, resembles brandy. Because of its sharp burn, locals drink it mixed with grape-flavored Tang—definitely an acquired taste.

But then, aren't these the unique kinds of experiences that attract us to out-of-the-way cruising ports-of-call all around the world? Here in Palau, in case we don't find that legendary pot of gold at the rainbow's end, we can at least find a basket of bat and a vat of taro-and-Tang wine!

~

Rock Islands

Long house interior

Men's long house

Ocean Hunter I liveaboard dive boat

Palauan wood carver

Petting dolphins

Chapter 18

TAHITI - SAILING INTO PARADISE

Two slab-sided peaks jut above the tropical sea's horizon. Their silhouettes, softened by the trade-wind haze, push into billowy clouds tinged with pale green reflections from emerald slopes. No wonder sailors describe their approach to shrine-like Bora Bora as a pilgrimage.

Bora Bora is just one of 121 islands and atolls that make up French Polynesia, an overseas collectivity of France. Politically, it is part of France, which oversees its foreign affairs, but it enjoys broad autonomy in internal matters.

Many people refer to this tropical paradise as Tahiti, after the largest island in the archipelago. Topography ranges from soaring "high islands" like Bora Bora, crowned with dragon-tooth peaks, to tiny motus (islets) and coral atolls that encircle blue lagoons. Located about 2,500 miles south of Hawaii, the islands are surprisingly easy to reach, just an eight-hour nonstop flight from Los Angeles or San Francisco.

French Polynesia's Leeward Islands

Our cruising grounds are the Leeward Islands, the westernmost group of the Society Islands, clustered around 17° south latitude and 151° west longitude. The Leewards comprise four main islands: Raiatea and Taha'a together in the middle; Huahine twenty-five miles to the east; and Bora Bora thirty-five miles to the northwest. All are volcanic island-atolls that erupted from the sea some ten million years ago. They have since partially subsided, leaving surrounding barrier reefs that enclose crystal-clear lagoons ranging from half a mile to two miles wide.

For our ten-day sailing adventure, my four friends and I—longtime sailing buddies who have often chartered together—first fly into Papeete, the capital of French Polynesia. From the air, the island resembles an ancient castle, its keep protected by the ramparts of mottled motu islets and a barrier reef girdling a turquoise moat.

Raiatea to Taha'a

Air Tahiti connects Papeete to Raiatea, the center of French Polynesia's cruising grounds in the Leeward Islands and home of several yacht charter companies. Upon arriving at the airport, we are met by the operations manager of Moorings Yacht Charters. While driving us to the charter base on Raiatea's east coast at Marina Apooiti, he extols the cruising attractions of Polynesia and gives tips on finding the best anchorages.

With the week's provisions already stowed on board, we slip the dock lines of our Jeanneau 44 and sail out of the shadows of 3,400-foot Mount Tefatoaiti, Raiatea's highest peak, into the sunny lagoon. A beam reach carries us north past several villages, including the island's commercial center, Uturoa. The shoreline here is flat—no white-sand beaches. Coastal hills, carpeted in lush greenery, give way to sprawling coconut plantations on the upper slopes, while even higher up wild tropical vegetation clings to soaring peaks.

Along the north coast, we carefully navigate a minefield of fringe coral to reach Taha'a, a sister atoll that shares a common reef with Raiatea. The slightest brush with coral could be disastrous, but our charts are excellent, and buoys marking the reefs are easy to spot. Marina Iti in Apu Bay near Pai-pai Pass is our first night's anchorage and the departure point for Bora Bora the next day.

Bora Bora

Although Pai-pai Pass is well defined with range markers, the following morning we wait out an approaching squall before entering the natural channel through the reefs. Ten minutes later we're out on the open sea where a steady rhythm of soft trades and gentle swells pushes us toward Bora Bora, beckoning from the western horizon.

Most of the fourteen islands in the Society Group have several entrances. Raiatea, for example, has eight. Bora Bora has only one, and therein lies its charm for those who approach by sea. For thousands of years, the driving force of the easterly trade winds blowing through the twin peaks, plus the gullies on the slopes, have funneled rainwater runoff into the lagoon at the center of the west coast. Spilling in a narrow band toward the sea, the fresh water inhibits coral growth of the barrier reef, creating the single entry.

As we swing around the south coast of our destined island, the two 2,000-foot peaks brighten and dim as they throw shadows at each other in a dramatic interplay of light and dark. Once clear of the southwest corner, marked by a forty-foot tower, we reach along the reef, standing clear of the local fishermen trolling precariously on the crests of giant swells that crash upon the coral ramparts.

Inside the World's Most Famous Lagoon

Inside Teavanui Pass on the glassy lagoon, white-sand motus nestle behind the outer reef like pearls strung together by the thin line of breaking surf. This first glimpse of Bora Bora is little changed since Captain James Cook landed in 1769. The sense of discovery is not lost today, even by tourists traveling in by air who must traverse from the airport landing strip across the island's lagoon by boat.

Eager for a swim and a walk along the gleaming beaches, my friends and I anchor at Motu Tevairoa and dive into cool, transparent waters. Later that afternoon, we sail to the southwest end of the lagoon where, relaxing at anchor with cans of local Hinano beer in hand, we quietly absorb the beauty of the setting. Purple shadows creep down fractured peaks, darkening aquamarine lagoon waters, then spread across white-sand motu beaches to the east of the island. The fragrance of tropical flowers drifts across the waters; then, minutes later, a rain squall breaks loose from the dark horizon and sweeps through the lagoon, chased by a glistening rainbow.

Swimming with Sharks

The following morning my friends and I ride with a dozen other visitors in a small launch to the inner edge of the reef. Equipped with fins and snorkels, we swim behind our Tahitian guide through a labyrinth of reef formations to a yellow polypropylene rope secured between two coral heads—our line of demarcation. We hope the blacktip reef sharks know the rules too!

Gripping the rope, we wait while our young leader throws several dead fish to the opposite side of the line. Within minutes a five-foot shark snaps them up. More sharks arrive until there are perhaps twenty slicing back and forth, combing the water for remnants. Several times the menacing predators come within a few feet, fix us with icy stares, and then decide not to challenge the protective powers of our "magic" yellow cord. After they have their fill and depart, sighs of relief bubble from our snorkels as we swim back to scramble into the launch.

Island Time, Ashore

The rest of the day we snorkel on our own in the shallows of the lagoon. The marine life here is incredible—hundreds of colonies of abstract-patterned, brilliantly colored fish dart in and out of magnificent coral formations covered with invertebrates of every color: purple, orange, green, and whatever other colors one can imagine and countless shades between.

The two centers for boaters cruising the South Pacific are the Oa Oa Lodge and Bora Bora Yacht Club. Both locations are mail pick-up points. Messages are left for those yet to arrive, who in turn leave notes for those coming behind.

Cuisine at BB Yacht Club, said by locals to be the best on the island, is Polynesian with a French twist featuring fresh, succulent seafood delivered straight from the fishing boats to the yacht club's wharf. The proprietors of Oa Oa welcome visitors with mooring buoys off their docks and a lagoon bar serving hamburgers and hotdogs, making it a magnet for Americans seeking a change from French cuisine. We couldn't make up our minds, so we alternated between the two each night.

Everyday Bora Bora

Most Bora Borans live in Vaitape, a one-street, waterfront collection of pastel clapboard buildings with metal corrugated roofs jumbled along the quay facing the commercial wharf. We quietly observe the Polynesians going about their daily lives, speaking softly to one another and punctuating their conversations with gestures and laughter. Many young girls and women wear flowers in their hair—garlands, crowns, and tiaras of frangipani, bird-of-paradise, hibiscus, and the indigenous six-petaled white tiare. For clothing, most wear colorful pareus, two-yard lengths of floral cloth wrapped according to the wearer's taste.

Children are playing everywhere. Several young boys poke long sticks at fruit high in a tree while others hold blankets beneath. When the prize plums fall, greedy hands snatch them up and pop into eager mouths. Two boys on bicycles pedal by with freshly speared fish swinging from their handlebars. A grandmother rides past on a bicycle, its baskets full of groceries. With a hibiscus behind one ear and a big smile stretched across her wrinkled face, she maneuvers patiently among the children and stray dogs. A young mother drives past on a motor scooter—the equivalent of the family Chevy. On the footrest two children, protected from falling out by the mother's legs, are planted among assorted shopping bundles.

Paradise Still Awaits

At a small bay, a young, bare-breasted woman wades into thigh-deep water. Standing motionless as her eyes search the water, she holds a fishnet on her shoulder ready to be thrown at the first glint. We pause briefly to admire her—a living Gauguin canvas—then move on, embarrassed to have disturbed her silence.

The following days, as we move to different anchorages, we witness similar scenes many times over. These islanders possess the level of leisure so coveted by the developed world, with no wish to take on any degree of industrialization. They remind us that paradise still awaits—quietly—beneath the twin peaks of Bora Bora.

Bora Bora— straight ahead into paradise

Bora Bora looms closer

Colorful pareus drying in the wind

Outrigger sailing canoe

Pedaling home from market

Chapter 19

TONGA - FIRST TO GREET THE NEW DAY

It is said that every island nation in the South Pacific has been environmentally despoiled by the influence of European explorers and settlers—every island except one— the Kingdom of Tonga. This island nation successfully kept American and European intruders at bay through the astute diplomacy of its kings for several hundred years. Furthermore, in-the-know cruising sailors report that the northern islands of this kingdom offer some of the best sailing waters to be found anywhere. Why not go there to see for myself?

Together with three friends from my hometown of Seattle, I spend days trying to arrange the logistics, which prove complicated. It takes two or three days, with connections through either Fiji or New Zealand, to fly to the capital of Nuku'alofa on the main island of Tongatapu. From there we have to schedule another flight to Neiafu, a principal town in the Vava'u group of islands and home to The Moorings charter base, where we will pick up our yacht.

Once air tickets are in hand and other logistics are settled, we are on our way. We allow ourselves to spend two days in the capital before going on to begin the charter. Here we visit the museum and library, and learn about Tonga's history and culture. We make forays to the abode of the flying foxes, the dozens of blow holes along the west coast, the ancient burial temples, and the king's palace. As we travel around this main island, we hear singing everywhere. The Tongan people—even taxi drivers—think nothing of breaking into "sweet song," a blend of street-corner hymn and rich tropical melody.

Timeless Tonga

First impression: There is no fast-forward button on the timeline of this South Pacific nation, Polynesia's last remaining monarchy. The kingdom dates its 2,500-year origins not by chronicles but by mythology. Apart from adopting unobtrusive comforts that take the edge off the harshness of living, the Polynesian kingdom has steadfastly held to a way of life little changed since Captain Cook chanced upon the "Friendly Islands" in 1773.

The only instance when Tongans, now members of the British Commonwealth, concerned themselves with time was more than 100 years ago when they were asked which side of the International Date Line they wanted to be on. Even though the deeply religious nation lies slightly east of the 180-degree meridian, the king chose the western side, reasoning that the prayers of his people would be the first to reach God's ears each morning. Indeed, the 170-island constitutional monarchy of just over 100,000 inhabitants, spreading from 15° to 23° south latitude and 173° to 177° west longitude, is the first nation in the world to greet the new day.

Vava'u—The Cruising Heart of Tonga

Time now to get on with the charter. A short flight brings us to Vava'u and the string of tropical island gems that constitute the cruising grounds of the northernmost of Tonga's three island groups. After a quick provisioning trip to the local supermarket in Neiafu and a checkout of our chartered Beneteau 432 at The Moorings base, we are on our way down the six-mile channel.

The magic of Tonga immediately begins to take us under its spell. The crystal-clear water is barely ruffled by the warm 8-knot trade winds that veer and shift around the 300-foot-high mountaintop islands of this drowned continent. With the wind on our beam, we thread our way south, surprised that the scattering of sixty lush, tropical islands that comprise the Vava'u group provides complete protection from the big South Pacific rollers. Fishing boats are few, and with only a handful of the islands inhabited, the area has a feel of total isolation. It's a blend of Australia's Whitsunday Islands and the British Virgin Islands, but without the crowds. Dozens of tiny islands ringed with white-sand beaches and countless secluded anchorages are all within easy cruising distance of each other. Constant balmy trade winds make for perfect sailing, and year-round air and sea temperatures in the 70°s guarantee comfort in or out of the water. Consequently, no one place is better than any other. Everywhere is perfect.

Feast at Aisea's Beach—A Tongan Welcome

Late in the afternoon we drop anchor at Aisea's Beach, our only must-do stop of the week. Here we join the crews of a dozen other charter boats in this palm-fringed cove for a Tongan feast. By the time we row ashore, the beach is alive with activity as Tongan women lay out pandanus mats piled high with guavas, yams, breadfruit, mangoes, custard apples, and other local fruits. Men tend the umus, or pit fires, that give off delectable aromas of roasting chicken, pig, and fish, heightened by the fragrance of island spices thrown into the mix.

The preparations take time, but we're content to wait. Other "*papalangis*" on charter, mostly from the U.S. West Coast, come ashore, and together we enjoy watching the Tongans as they sing and play while readying the feast. We're mindful of the advice given by The Moorings manager that Tongans do their socializing and talking before food is served. Once the meal is served, conversation stops and eating begins, so if you have anything to say, say it before you sit down.

Finally all is ready, and with lighthearted ceremony, we are led to our places. Sitting on mats around the mountain of food, we're amazed that everything before us is so readily available. I can understand a comment once made by the king that a person would have to be a fool to starve in Tonga.

Dancers and singers perform while we're served tasty, mostly sweet, dishes from polas, or long-runner trays made of palm fronds. Profuse displays of frangipani, jasmine, shell ginger, and richly colored tropical blossoms garnish the servings. We attempt to follow the Tongan custom of eating with our fingers and scraping with shell spoons from our banana-leaf plates, but frustrated by awkward efforts to maintain decorum, we soon abandon our attempts and simply dig in.

The food, music, and cordiality of our carefree hosts break any lingering connections with the stresses of tension-packed living back home and subtly draw us into the spirit of Tongan life. All too soon the evening twilight is upon us, yielding to a pitch-black sky punctuated by millions of twinkling jewels. Under the *Southern Cross*, time stands still for us, as it has for all eternity in this Polynesian paradise. We have shifted into Tonga time.

Mariner's Cave—An Underwater Threshold

The next day's sail is to a destination I had dreamed of as a child, one that has found its way into adventure books around the world. After sailing around the northern tip of Nuapapu, we motor down the west coast. As groves of coconut palms on the ridge open to a clearing, we recognize the telltale landmark of a single prominent tree standing alone above a white stain on the cliff's face. Directly below is the famous Mariner's Cave, not so much an underwater cave as a cave with an underwater entrance. The underwater entry opens into an above-water chamber deep within the cliff.

Legends tell of the innocent finding secret refuge while villainous pursuers searched the island in vain. Although stories say it takes exceptional stamina and swimming ability to enter the cave, The Moorings' manager assured us at our briefing that we could do it.

Somewhat apprehensive, two of us don snorkeling gear and, leaving the timid behind to tend the boat, swim to the cliff. Sure enough, below us the vast cave opens up amidst a dazzling array of coral reefs and colorful tropical fish. We attempt several practice dives to see how far under the ledge we can swim and still get back before our lungs explode. The depth of the entrance is only eight feet and the passage fifteen feet long, comparable to swimming under the boat's keel; nevertheless, the intimidating black tunnel erodes our confidence.

Finally, after mustering up all our courage, we dive furiously down into the tunnel. Then, feeling along the rock and coral ledge above us until locating an opening, we surface into a black void gasping for air. Our lungs suck in fresh, cool air until after a few breaths, we relax. Moments later, as our eyes adjust to the blue-white hue reflected up from outside, we gaze up at a fifty-foot-high vault with features that seem to be sculpted of a luminous sapphire rock. Every craggy ledge glows in vivid detail made clear by the eerie crystal light.

Suddenly, everything disappears in a blotch of green fog. We blink, but no film over our eyes distorts our vision. Seconds later, the crystal clarity returns. This pattern repeats with fog returning as every heaving wave compresses the air, causing the moisture to condense, only to disappear when the water level again drops.

The swim into and out of the cave turns out to be so easy that we return several times, laughing at our initial intimidation. So much for the stamina theory!

Marble Diplomacy

That night we anchor at Port Maurelle, named for a Spaniard, the first European to see Vava'u, when he stopped briefly in 1781 to take on water. Tonga was fortunate never to be colonized or subdued during the eighteenth-century European push for expansion into the Pacific. Dutch, English, French, and Spanish explorers all passed through Tonga, but none stayed. Even Captain Cook, who wrote in his journal glorious praises of Tonga and its people, was dissuaded through subterfuge from traveling to Vava'u. While at the Ha'apai group, Cook wanted to visit Vava'u but changed his mind when told there was no safe harbor and coral reefs made the area hazardous. He never learned that Vava'u has one of the finest natural harbors in the Pacific, with deep open channels throughout the islands.

At Port Maurelle, young boys greet us as they fish on an unseen reef where they walk with no hesitation, their feet long accustomed to the rough and jagged coral edges. Standing in a foot of water at the edge of the underwater formation, they let their lines, weighed down by Coca-Cola bottles, sink to the bottom.

We row our dinghy near and command their attention with a universal lure for small boys all over the world—a bag of marbles. Instantly they start running a zigzag path through the water toward us, following the underwater reefs that, to our eyes, are invisible. When they come as close as their coral path will allow, we row to them and give each a shiny new shooter, prizes that make them forget their fishing and run back to the village to share their new treasures.

"Blackbirding"—The Reason Villages Moved Inland

A sad chapter in the history of Tonga occurred in the nineteenth century when European traders made a practice of "blackbirding," swooping down on small villages to kidnap the inhabitants to sell into the slave trade. Many Tongans were forcibly taken from their homes and sent to South America to work the mines. To guard against this, the king decreed no inhabitants would be allowed to live on the smaller outlying islands, and all villages should be moved safely away from the coast to protected lagoons where large ships would have difficult access. Consequently, many smaller villages were consolidated in Hunga, the destination of our next day's sail. This westernmost island has a large lagoon, with an entrance that can be navigated only at high tide, without current, and with good sunlight.

Hunga Village—Life Inland

After negotiating this tricky fifty-foot-wide pass, we cross the lagoon to a lake-like anchorage near the village fishing boats. Once ashore, we follow a swept path through citrus groves, up a hill, to a cluster of neat buildings on a large grassy plateau. As in all Tongan villages, pigs, dogs, and chickens roam freely except in the fenced-off flower gardens surrounding every *fale*, or home. Some buildings are of block construction, but most are open, covered on both sides and the floor with finely woven pandanus mats and roofed with thick thatched reeds.

At first, our presence sends the children scurrying to hide, peeping cautiously from behind the buildings. But all shyness disappears when we open bags of trinkets and toys. They swarm around us, eager to check our collection of yo-yos, paddle balls, party favors, whistles, and goofy glasses. My friends and I become instant family and are taken in tow by little hands of children eager to show us their village. We had checked at the charter base before our trip to ask whether these gifts would be culturally insensitive to the villagers. The base manager assured us they would be appropriate and much appreciated because they don't introduce items of Western culture that would detract from their lifestyle.

Just as we wonder how to extricate ourselves from our playful young hosts, we hear the peal of a church bell from the center of the village. The children immediately scamper away as their parents, dressed in their finest clothes, walk to the simple wooden church for evening vespers. Women wear tunic-like dresses, and men are clad in the traditional ankle-length skirts. Both have soft mats tied around their waists, the customary sign of respect and formality.

Mainstay of Tongan Culture

Only now do I realize how enormous these handsome people are. Without appearing fat, most Tongan women stand close to six feet tall and exceed 200 pounds. The men tower well over the women and average fifty pounds heavier. Despite their size, Tongans are extremely gentle and so soft-spoken that it's often difficult to hear them when they speak.

As the service begins, the strains of choral voices from the church break the late-afternoon silence with an alluring, plaintive beauty. Singing is a mainstay of their culture, and most Tongans are born with perfect pitch. Hymns brought to Tonga by Christian missionaries years ago have been transformed with native rhythms and Polynesian lyrics to create music that is uniquely Tongan. Although Tongan singing is well-known around the world, hearing it in a simple village on one of the remote islands imbues it with a mystical quality that sends shivers down our spines.

Timed Out

On our remaining days in Tonga, we unhurriedly explore other islands as one sunny day slips imperceptibly into the next. Navigating the islands is straightforward when we rely on the only detailed chart created by The Moorings. The use of numbers to identify more than fifty anchorages eliminates the need to learn the long, complicated island names.

Our leisurely one-week cruise affords us plenty of time to snorkel, sail, fish, and collect shells. We lose ourselves in the enchantment of these Vava'u waters that sparkle over jewel-covered reefs and then darken in black-blue depths. We explore twisted inlets, hidden anchorages, and golden-sand beaches to our hearts' content.

Then, on our last day with pockets laden with shells and unforgettable memories, it is time to re-enter the world of "Time."

King of Tonga's Royal Palace

Anchorage, Aisea's Beach

Feast on Aisea's Beach

Tongan banana harvest

Underwater entrance to Mariner's Cave at Nuapapu

Entrance to Hunga Lagoon

Chapter 20

HARMONY ON THE *BOUNTY*

The mutiny on the *Bounty*—perhaps the most infamous mutiny in history—seems to have found a harmonious ending.

The story begins on the 200th anniversary of the mutiny. This was when Captain Ron Bligh-Ware of Australia, a sixth-generation descendant of Captain William Bligh, took command of the three-masted, fully rigged ship *Child of Bounty* as it caught the trade winds after setting out from Toaroa Harbor in Tahiti.

In 1789, the original tall ship, on a mission to bring breadfruit to the Caribbean, set sail on the same course, laden with 1,015 tropical plants. The breadfruit (or *uru,* as Polynesians call it) was intended as food for enslaved workers on sugar plantations in the British West Indies. It was an ideal source of nourishment because breadfruit trees were fast-growing, required little care, and produced ample quantities of carbohydrate-rich fruit. But the infamous mutiny on April 28 of that year led to the mission's failure and subsequent historical events surrounding it.

Once Around the Ship

Bligh-Ware's first mate on this commemorative voyage to the Polynesian Kingdom of Tonga was thirty-year-old Lieutenant Commander Gerald Christian of the Royal Australian Navy, a seventh-generation descendant of William Bligh's first mate, Fletcher Christian, who led the mutiny.

Following the carefully scripted plan, while the ship lay off Tofua Island in Tonga's Ha'apai Group, Christian and the "mutinous" crew looked on as Bligh-Ware, a retired merchant marine officer, and a band of "loyal" followers were lowered over the side in a 23-foot wooden longboat, closely duplicating the original bloodless mutiny.

This time, however, the deposed captain did not set out on a 3,600-mile voyage to Timor in Indonesia, as his forebear had done. Instead, he instructed his crew to row once around the mother ship before being brought back aboard. The two crew factions then made peace and agreed to put aside—once and for all—hostile feelings that had lingered for more than two centuries.

The joke among the crew was that everyone made amends because longboats are so expensive that no one was willing to let such a valuable craft sail off on an epic voyage. Yet six years earlier, Bligh-Ware did exactly that.

Showing the same daring and seamanship as his distant ancestor, he re-enacted the open-boat voyage from Tonga to Indonesia. In a twenty-three-foot longboat with an eight-person crew, he sailed and rowed from Tofua to Timor, passing Fiji, which his ancestor charted on that same journey. The voyage was just as extraordinary and perilous in modern times as it had been two centuries earlier.

Twenty-nine-year-old Karlene Christian previously ran a dive shop on Norfolk Island, was exuberant about taking part in the reenactment. "Not only was it great to be part of this reenactment, but crewing on a tall ship was a terrific way to see the South Pacific," said the seventh-generation descendant of the *Bounty's* first mate.

Another descendant of Fletcher Christian, Jodie Brown of Sydney, Australia, agreed: "It was a real adventure climbing in the rigging and struggling with the rest of the crew when we had to furl the ship's fifteen sails. It was especially exciting knowing we were doing the same thing the original *Bounty* crew did more than two centuries earlier."

Replica Not to be Sunk

The replica ship, a two-million-dollar duplicate of the original British armed transport in her exterior lines and rigging, was built in New Zealand in 1984 for the film *The Bounty,* starring Mel Gibson and Anthony Hopkins. Below decks, however, the replica was outfitted with air conditioning, modern navigation equipment, well-appointed cabins, auxiliary engines, hot-water showers, and sufficient amenities—all helping to ensure there wouldn't be a repeat mutiny among the thirteen permanent crew members and twenty-five paying voyage crew.

The mutiny reenactment in 1989 was only one part of the commemoration of the original *Bounty's* voyage. The following year Lieutenant Commander Gerald Christian took over command and sailed from Tahiti to Pitcairn Island in the eastern Pacific, arriving at the original landing site of the mutineers. Just as the longboat replica was not allowed to set out for Indonesia, similarly, the *Bounty* replica did not suffer the fate of its namesake, which was burned and scuttled in Bounty Bay.

Instead of a burning at Pitcairn, a reunion celebration took place between the crew and the islanders, most of whom were descendants of the mutineers. Pitcairn, which has no harbor or ship landing, is perhaps the most remote permanent settlement in the world and was the last British colony in the Pacific.

Most Photographed Ship

For much of her early life, the 133-foot steel-hulled *Bounty* replica was laid up at Long Beach, California. She was later purchased by Bounty Voyages of Sydney, Australia, and put into charter service with berths available for adventurous passengers. Since then, the tall ship has sailed around the world, appeared in the television miniseries *Captain James Cook*, and sailed to Vancouver for the 1986 World Expo.

In 1987, she was in Fremantle, Western Australia, for the America's Cup season, returning to England to participate in the Australian Bicentennial First Fleet reenactment and other tall ship parades. Afterward, the *Bounty* was once again put into service for charter voyages among the island groups of the South Pacific, including the commemorative voyage in April 1989.

Underway with 7,000 square feet of sail and her distinctive bowsprit sail configuration, she became one of the most photographed tall ships in the world.

Tragically, on October 29, 2012, while ninety miles off Cape Hatteras, North Carolina, the square-rigged sailing ship encountered high seas brought on by Hurricane Sandy and sank. The Coast Guard rescued fourteen of the sixteen crew members, but Captain Robin Walbridge and Claudene Christian, a descendant of Fletcher Christian, were not found.

Breadfruit Finally Arrives

As for the breadfruit, two years after completing his longboat voyage and returning to England, Captain Bligh—undaunted by his ordeal—remained dedicated to his original goal of collecting and transporting breadfruit and set sail again. In 1793, he docked HMS *Providence* in Kingstown, Saint Vincent and the Grenadines, a small island nation in the Caribbean Sea, delivering a cargo of several hundred breadfruit saplings. Today, the Caribbean is one of the world's largest producers of breadfruit.

~

Fletcher Christian descendants Karlene Christian and Jodie Brown

Replica of 23-foot longboat sailed by Captain Bligh and outcast crew

Chapter 21

AUSTRALIA - SAILING THE WHITSUNDAYS

When the organizers of Hamilton Island Race Week invite me to attend what has come to be known as Australia's premier, good-time yachting event, I am at first suspicious. Why would they want to yank a 'Yank' journalist into their midst?

The official reason is that they feel this well-established annual event warrants international media exposure. My hunch is that they want to refute the image conveyed to the American press that Aussies are just a bunch of kangaroo-lovin', crocodile-huntin', beer-bustin' renegades whose only redeeming feature is they know how to throw great parties. This latter consideration is good enough for me, so I accept the invitation.

Two weeks later, I receive round-trip air tickets by mail for my wife and me, covering flights from Seattle to Sydney, connecting through Brisbane to Queensland's Hamilton Island. With a bit of further negotiation, the race organizers agree to provide one of their sailing charter yachts at the end of the regatta, allowing us to take a one-week cruise of the Whitsunday Islands.

Captain Cook Unimpressed

Hamilton Island sits smack in the middle of the seventy-four-island archipelago that Captain (then Lieutenant) James Cook named the Whitsundays after grounding his ship, *Endeavour*, on Whit Sunday in June 1770. He was so unimpressed with the surrounding islands that he gave them a dismissive label—simply the "Whitsundays." The archipelago was unworthy of a name in honor of royalty or friends, as was his usual custom. Stopping only long enough to make repairs and drop off a few goats for marooned sailors, he sailed away to chart lands more worthy of his attention.

Two hundred and fifty years later, these Robinson Crusoe islands in the Coral Sea, sandwiched between Australia's northeast coast and the 1,200-mile-long Great Barrier Reef, are the heart of Australia's booming vacation trade and one of the world's foremost yacht-cruising regions.

The goats, meanwhile, multiplied and ravaged the delicate island ecology until the 1960s, when they were exterminated. Now the land has recovered. Today, scattered off the Queensland coast on the same latitude south as Hawaii is north, the islands mesmerize visitors with the beauty of their deep-green tropical vegetation and somber gray-blue gum trees.

Until the middle of the past century, the islands were marginal sheep and cattle grazing lands with only a handful of family-operated hotels and camping resorts. In the early 1960s, land developers turned their attention to this region, with plans to cover these pristine jewels with condos, hotels, and resort facilities for vacationers.

Fortunately, the National Park authorities intervened and absorbed the islands into the national park system, effectively stopping all development. Ever since, tourist growth has been limited to the seven small, original resorts tucked out of sight in protected anchorages on six islands. The remaining sixty-eight islands are, by government decree, unpopulated. This guarantees that the rolling hills covered with natural gum-tree vegetation, the hidden coves, and the lovely, unspoiled beaches will remain as they are now, untouched for future generations.

Regatta Format

Things begin to go crazy the moment my flight touches down on Hamilton Island's coral-built jet airstrip. Suddenly, a figure on a motorcycle comes out of nowhere, racing our jet down the runway. "Oh, that's just Keith Williams," my seatmate remarks, as though that explains everything. It turns out that Williams owns the island and everything that's on it. The eccentric, monocled multimillionaire has a collection of motorcycles, reportedly the largest in Australia, that he keeps in his own museum on the island. Screaming down the airstrip at 120 miles per hour on a rare, limited-production Suzuki model, the benevolent monarch races alongside our plane as a promotion stunt for a film about Hamilton Island Resort. It seems to me that this stunt reaffirms just about everything we in the U.S. hear about Aussies.

Moments after landing, I'm whisked to the marina by a golf cart, hurried onto a press boat, and zoomed out to the course, where the yachts are preparing for the start of the first race. Hardly a wisp of wind stirs, inauspicious for the regatta, but great for me to see who is in the fleet. This year's event has attracted a record 108 competitors—keelboats, catamarans, and trimarans—divided into five classes, each racing on different courses but returning at night to the Hamilton Island marina for the parties that typically run all night into early dawn.

For the next week, I divide my time between on-land interviews with skippers about their new yachts and forays out on the water in a chase boat, photographing the tight racing while the competitors jostle for position as they round the windward and leeward marks. Although the winds during the week range from fickle to near gale-force, the race committee completes each day's events as planned.

Regatta Controversy

Only one controversy arises that casts a blemish on the week's events. Unfortunately, it involves a New Zealand entry. (New Zealanders are traditional rivals of the Aussies.) The New Zealand yacht owner is accused of deceiving the race committee by cheating on his vessel's handicap rating. Every entrant is required to complete a rating sheet disclosing pertinent information and measurements used to determine a boat's handicap rating.

One question asks whether the boat has an engine with a propeller and shaft attached to the hull. If yes, due to the appendage drag, the boat is awarded additional minutes when computing its final standings. This Kiwi owner confirmed his boat had a propeller and shaft, but during the races the race committee observed that his boat was faster than expected.

In the evening back at the marina, a diver photographed the bottom of the boat, revealing a trapdoor that allowed the propeller and shaft to be retracted, thus accounting for the boat's superior performance. When confronted with this evidence at the race committee hearing, the owner, looking a bit guilty, responds that he answered honestly: he had an underwater appendage. But because the handicap rating form did not ask whether it could be retracted, he did not volunteer the information.

Although he could have been thrown out of the regatta for alleged cheating, the race committee allows him to continue racing with his handicap rating adjusted to show a clean bottom. The shame felt by the owner and his crew is deemed punishment enough.

Whitehaven Beach Party

The racing highlight of the week is the overnight Coral Sea Race, where old rivalries and new scores are traditionally settled. This endurance event begins with light south-easterly winds and predictable sunny skies, making for picture-postcard viewing from spectator boats. The entire Whitsunday chain is blanketed with white sails as five fleets scatter in all directions.

After all racers return safely the next day, no one seems to care about winners, losers, handicap adjustments, protests, or disqualifications. Everyone's attention is focused on the week's real highlight: the next day's party on Whitehaven Beach.

In the morning, a flotilla of several hundred yachts sails across to neighboring Whitsunday Island and anchors in the lee of this fabled beach. The day becomes a combination of a Gallipoli landing and a bacchanalian fest as hundreds of sailors shuttle from their yachts to the big yellow XXXX (pronounced "four-X") beer tent, all the while celebrating what may be the world's biggest beer party.

As I step from my dinghy onto this four-mile crescent shoreline, I'm struck by a novel sensation. Between my toes, I feel the sugary texture not of sand, but of pure white silica. The tiny white crystals refract the sun's rays into sparkles, creating a tropical snowy wonderland with light shimmering as if it were a sunny, frosty winter morning. For many Australians, a trip to this gift from the geologic past, lapped by dazzling blue waters and bathed in continuous sunshine, represents nothing less than a pilgrimage. Such beauty carries a touch of sacredness. Among all the splendors I discover in the Whitsundays, Whitehaven Beach places second to none.

This sparkling crescent of white silica sand has become something of a national symbol for the Australians ever since the Japanese, who tend to view Australia as a harvest bed for raw materials, tried to buy it several decades earlier. Their intent was to ship the silica to Japan to stoke their industrial furnaces. The Aussie reply was swift and emphatic. "Hands off! It's one of our national treasures," asserts a veteran of previous Race Weeks, "and we come here each year to make sure it stays that way." The outcry not only stopped the sale of the silica but galvanized the government to protect the beach as a National Trust property.

The annual XXXX cricket match turns into a rout, and the tug-of-war games prove nothing except that you can't pull a rope while holding a can of beer. The wet T-shirt contest, conducted in the same three divisions as the racing yachts—maxi, cruising, and handicap—leaves nothing to the imagination, again consistent with the American perception of the good-time, partying spirit of the people down under.

Proving Grounds

Hamilton Island Race Week is more than just a single event. It's a proving ground for all the new Australian and New Zealand yachts, which, if they do well in this series, will be shipped to the northern hemisphere to compete on the international circuit of the world's major regattas: the Kenwood Cup in Hawaii, the Big Boat Series on San Francisco Bay, the Admiral's Cup in England, and numerous sailing world championships held throughout North America and Europe.

Following the awards dinner, where winners collect their trophies and losers nurse their hurt egos, the fleet disbands, some returning to their home ports and others loading onto cargo ships for the journey to the wintry north where they will wait a few months for the start of the racing season. As for me, this is the time I have been waiting for—time to join my sailing partner, my wife, who has just flown into Hamilton Island, and time to begin a cruise of this wondrous Virgin Islands–sized chain of islands.

Realizing a Far-Off Dream

Sailing in Australia's Whitsunday Islands has long been a far-off dream, now about to become reality. Moments after my wife's plane from Brisbane lands on Hamilton Island, an open-air coach whisks us up the hill to my room overlooking Catseye Beach, the half-mile crescent around which the resort's half-dozen buildings are pleasingly situated. To allow my wife a day to recover from jet lag before sailing, we set out to explore this tropical setting that Australians consider their showcase resort destination.

Hamilton Island offers a variety of tropical gardens, nature trails, mountaintop fauna parks, and countless hidden sandy beaches. The well-planned, 2,000-guest resort complex comprises numerous restaurants, nightclubs, waterfront shops, and a modern marina. After a day exploring these attractions, we cap the evening with a beachside dinner of Moreton Bay bugs (a locally renowned crayfish) and a bottle of crisp Hunter Valley Sauvignon Blanc.

Down at the marina the next morning, we board a high-speed catamaran to Shute Harbour on the coast; then a twenty-minute ride takes us to the operations base of Queensland Yacht Charters at Airlie Beach, the region's vacation center and gateway to the islands. The charter base manager welcomes us aboard our Australian-built Cavalier 37, a comfortable Laurie Davidson–designed sloop, already provisioned for our week's cruise.

During the following days, I learn that cruising in the Whitsundays opens up two different worlds: solitude enjoyed on isolated beaches and hidden coves, or social indulgences at holiday resorts ranging from five-star super-elegant accommodations to rustically simple ones. We mix a little of each.

As we cross Molle Channel in a 15-knot breeze, we put the boat through every point of sail and are pleased with her performance. Navigating by the guidebook and detailed charts, we take a bearing from the tower on Daydream Island to negotiate Unsafe Passage (safe for cruising boats despite the name) into Whitsunday Channel and the heart of the islands.

Our first impressions remind us of the Caribbean. Mountaintop islands jut up through a dark sea ruffled by southeast trade winds, stretching across the horizon. Green hills slope down to little inlets, sheltered coves, and outstretched beaches. Fringing coral reefs lighten the water surrounding the shoreline of alternating white sand and lush undergrowth.

South Molle and Nara Inlet

Our first day's sail takes us past Daydream Island to South Molle Island, where we anchor at the village-style resort set on the beachfront among swaying coconut palms and brilliant bougainvillea. In the dining room, we savor a lunch of Queensland tropical fruit and a mixed seafood plate of grilled barramundi, prawns, calamari, and mussels, all freshly caught in local waters. Afterward, we hike through gum-tree forests, following a bush trail along the far side of South Molle to a hilltop lookout with a spectacular view down Whitsunday Passage. Pleasantly distracting is the flurry of reds and greens as tropical lorikeets flock around us in anticipation of the usual tourist breadcrumb feedings.

Opting for a quiet anchorage that night instead of the resort's disco nightlife, we raise the anchor and sail to three-mile-long Nara Inlet on Hook Island two hours away. We carefully navigate the shifting sandbar at the mouth and then, as the surrounding hills kill the wind, motor the final half mile to the head of the bay.

At the end of this otherwise pristine cove, we are shocked by what we see. Graffiti—bold, bright, and dazzling—smears the jumbled boulders rimming the shore for perhaps half a mile. Boaters have spray-painted their signatures, names of boats, and dates of visits, some dating back more than a century, using every color in a child's paintbox.

This sight is a jarring contrast to the untouched beauty of the hundreds of other coves throughout the region. Possibly, this display serves as a modern response to the 2,000-year-old Aboriginal rock paintings in the caves beneath the overhanging bluffs. The paintings are the work of the Ngaro people, seafarers who sailed iron-bark canoes sewn fore-and-aft with vines made watertight by natural gum from eucalyptus trees. These ancient artistic expressions, now protected by government authority, along with a view down Nara Inlet, are well worth the twenty-minute hike through gum trees and Cook pines up the steep slope to the overlook.

Hook Island

A kookaburra's jungle-like laugh floats across the water, awakening us in our berths early the next morning. Today's sail continues north along the east coast of Whitsunday Island to the region's major dive center, Hook Island Wilderness Resort. "Resort" is something of a misnomer for this small, camp-like facility on the beach, which attracts backpackers and budget-conscious travelers. Because it's farthest from the mainland in an outpost setting, Hook Island offers the Whitsundays in their most pristine state. The water is exceptionally clear, and the region's best dive sites are concentrated on the east side of the island.

Nearby is the Hook Island Underwater Observatory, an observation platform thirty feet beneath the water's surface, which brings non-divers face to face with the marine world surrounding the fringe reefs. We view the coral through the glass, then make a closer inspection by snorkeling the coral gardens surrounding nearby reefs.

Sadly, cyclones later destroyed all the Hook Island facilities, but new owners plan a complete restoration and a major eco-resort.

Great Barrier Reef

At noon the next day, a prearranged Turbo-Beaver floatplane lands at our anchorage to shuttle us thirty miles out to the edge of the Great Barrier Reef. After landing at the Reef World floating platform beside Hardy Reef, we don scuba gear and for the next two hours explore the wondrous world of hard and soft corals, giant clams, sea stars, colorful reef fish, and other underwater marvels.

Composed of more than 2,900 individual reefs and 900 islands, the Great Barrier Reef is the world's largest living organism, larger than Great Britain. Astronauts have reported that the 1,200-mile-long formation is the only living entity visible from space. There are 400 types of coral, 4,000 mollusks, 1,500 species of fish, and countless thousands of sponges, worms, crustaceans, and sea cucumbers, all choreographed in an underwater Eden. In addition, the reef is a breeding area for humpback whales and six of the world's seven species of marine turtles.

The reefs and surrounding waters are assured of protection into the future because they are within the largest marine park in the world, Great Barrier Reef Marine Park, which also includes the Whitsunday

Islands National Park. But ocean acidification driven by pollution and climate change is causing coral bleaching and extensive damage to the reef.

A Perfect Day

The next day's sail brings us to the top of Hook Island in Cateran Bay at Border Island. The cruising guide notes that we are near Cid Harbour, on the western side of Whitsunday Island. This harbor played a significant role for the Allied Navy ships in World War II. Naval vessels involved in the Battle of the Coral Sea crowded together in this hidden natural harbor while Japanese planes searched the entire South Pacific in vain.

Here at Border Island, we enjoy one of those all-too-few gems of a lifetime—a timeless interval of sailing, gunkholing, swimming, and boat lounging. Passing countless small sandy beaches with warm winds driving the sails, our spirited sloop takes on a life of her own, showing us the soul of the island. In passing, we encounter *Gretel* and *Southern Cross*, the famous 12-Metre America's Cup challengers of 1962 and 1974, now in regular day-charter service in the Whitsundays.

The day is also one of gourmet pleasures, as my wife employs her culinary talents to prepare dishes made with ingredients she acquired along the way. We start our day with Eggs Provençal, made with fresh tomatoes and parmesan and fresh tropical fruits of the region. For lunch, we enjoy milky oysters from Cid Harbour and the renowned Moreton Bay bugs. The evening's appetizer of calamari salad is followed by coral trout, our pleasure heightened by a fine bottle of Hunter Valley Chardonnay.

No weight-loss program here—just lots of fun, great eating, and idyllic sailing, all fading into soft memories as the *Southern Cross* rises in a dome of blazing stars that evening. When we slip into the water for a late-night swim, millions of bioluminescent creatures glow all around us in the sea. We are the center of the universe—diamonds above, diamonds below.

Hayman Island

The next day we sail to the northern limit of the Whitsundays to reach Hayman Island, site of a luxurious five-star resort, a stunning contrast to the wild beauty of the reef. As we motor into the marina, we find ourselves surrounded by opulence. Not only are we by far the smallest boat, but we're also the only yacht without a uniformed crew aboard. This place is definitely off-limits for the shoestring sailor. I'm sure we're allowed entry only because of my credentials as a yachting journalist.

Once we recover our balance, not just from being on land but from the jolt of being in this incomparable setting, the resort hostess takes us on a tour of what is reputed to be the most luxurious resort in all of Australia. The collection of guest rooms, suites, and villas are spread across three distinct wings, each artfully integrated with acres of spectacular swimming pools (both saltwater and fresh), panoramic seascapes, tropical rainforest gardens, and treasured art collections.

Works of art ranging from Grecian urns to modern sculptures are displayed throughout the series of connected indoor/outdoor buildings, with vases of flowers placed in every nook. After the tour, we're treated to a tropical fruit and mixed-seafood lunch beside a glaringly white beach edged with graceful palms and brilliant bougainvillea.

No beach activity has been invented that isn't offered at Hayman. Everything from parasailing to diving at its own privately owned island at the Great Barrier Reef is available to guests. For the evening hours, guests may choose from five restaurants and bars, several lounges, game rooms, libraries, and a nightclub featuring internationally acclaimed performing artists. If you wish, there's a valet service to unpack and press your clothes. All the details are carefully arranged, down to a sprig of Australian wildflowers placed on the pillow when evening maids turn down pure linen sheets for you each night.

We indulge ourselves for one night, love it, and then move on.

Lindeman Island

A long day's sail takes us from northernmost Hayman Island to the southernmost extent of the Whitsundays, Lindeman Island, once Australia's only Club Med resort. Lindeman is known for its golden beaches and unusually bold birds. Thousands of green-and-red lorikeets have taken over the island. The birds land on everything—including the heads, hands, and shoulders of tourists who arm themselves with birdseed and assume a scarecrow stance!

Unfortunately, following our visit, the resort was completely destroyed by a cyclone that swept over the island. Restoration is now underway to build a new eco-resort. The proposed five-star resort will feature swimming pools, a golf course, restaurants and bars, a spa and gym, a solar farm, an event venue, staff accommodations, more than 200 rooms, and a new jetty.

Captain Cook's Mistake

Our final day's sail brings us back to the Queensland Yacht Charters base at Airlie Beach; a high-speed catamaran returns us to Hamilton Island where we spend our final night in a luxurious suite close to where Beatle George Harrison once had a home on the island.

The next morning's flight from Hamilton Island to Sydney affords views of the Whitsunday Islands standing like sentinel outposts beside undulating stretches of the Great Barrier Reef. Seen from above, the coral appears to twist upon itself like a multicolored snake, protecting these perfect cruising waters from the South Pacific's unleashed fury. The reef is as stunning seen from the air as it is from the water.

Reflecting on our week's cruise, I conclude that Captain Cook made a grave mistake. How could anyone not appreciate all the loveliness of the Whitsundays? After his ship *Endeavour* ran aground, Captain Cook should have stayed ashore and sent the goats back out to sea!

~

2,000-year-old Aboriginal rock paintings, Nara Inlet

Float plant shuttles us thirty miles from our anchorage to Great Barrier Reef

Gallipoli-like landing, Whitehaven Beach

South Molle Island

Swarming rainbow lorikeets, Lindeman Island

Tight competition, Hamilton Island Race Week

Chapter 22

AUSTRALIA - DIVING IN OZ

Co-written with Risa Wyatt

"They're coming!" Coop, our divemaster, points toward shadows emerging from the watery blue yonder. Our group of ten divers kneels motionless on the sandy bottom, thirty feet beneath the surface. Soon we are surrounded by a dozen potato cod—gigantic groupers measuring five feet long and weighing about 200 pounds. Friendly and inquisitive, the fish swim right up to us. Suddenly, another massive shape appears, streaking toward a piece of bait Coop holds in his outstretched hand. A 400-pound Maori wrasse, spectacular in its green-and-purple coloration and hump-headed profile, swoops from above.

"It makes you realize we are in their element," Coop observes after we surface.

Marine Garden of Eden

The Great Barrier Reef (GBR) constantly awes and amazes. Extending 1,500 miles into the Coral Sea parallel to Australia's northeast coast, it ranks as the world's largest living organism—often cited as the only life form on Earth visible from outer space. As the largest reef system in the world, it also encompasses the planet's largest protected marine ecosystem. Its domain takes in creatures as fantastic as giant clams four feet across; tiny nudibranchs daubed in neon blue and orange; and dugongs, manatee-like marine mammals that early sailors mistook for mermaids.

Despite its name, the Great Barrier Reef does not form a solid blockade but instead consists of 2,900 reefs, 900 islands, and countless cays woven together like a tapestry. Packing more life per square yard than almost any other locale on the planet, it serves as home for 400 types of coral, 1,500 species of fish, 4,000 varieties of mollusks, and 500 species of seaweed. And the list goes on: 16 species of sea snakes, 215 species of birds, 30 species of whales and dolphins, 136 species of sharks and rays, 2,500 species of sponges, thousands of invertebrates, and countless numbers of migratory birds.

Australia's Aboriginal people living along the coast once found rich sustenance in the sea, fishing and gathering shells along the reefs and cays, then weaving these images into their Dreamtime myths and rock art. All that changed with the arrival of early European settlers. Viewing the reef as a resource to be plundered, settlers set up turtle canneries and mined guano, phosphate, and other minerals from the islands. With little regard for the reef's well-being, bulldozers carved freighter-loading terminals and airstrips into coral and fragile vegetation.

Fortunately, by the mid-twentieth century, that thoughtlessness started to change. In 1975, Australia established the Great Barrier Reef Marine Park Authority to manage the reef. In 1981, the GBR was declared a World Heritage Site, and in 1983, it became a national marine park, putting it under government protection. The park, roughly the size of California, takes in 133,000 square miles.

Considered one of the world's leading marine planning groups, the Marine Park Authority has established controls that protect the reef while still allowing the public—sailors, scuba divers, snorkelers, and birders—to experience this wonder where Nature still rules.

From Shore to Sea

Pods of dolphins, frigate birds, cays shaped like beach-rimmed Valentines—these are just some of the sights that visitors enjoy when traveling from the Australian mainland to the reef. Trips depart by sea or air from coastal towns in Queensland, Australia's northeastern state, known for its beaches and rainforests.

Traveling at forty miles per hour, high-speed catamarans carrying up to 300 passengers make day trips to the reef from major coastal gateways: Port Douglas, Cairns, Townsville, Gladstone, and Bundaberg. The vessels dock either at man-made dive platforms at the reef's edge or at islands on the reef itself. Several cruise operators offer guests the opportunity to observe or participate in research projects. Alternatively, visitors can fly to the reef by helicopter or floatplane.

Once at the reef, most visitors choose to snorkel—or those who are scuba-certified, to tank-dive—along the coral shelf. "Every time you dive, you see something new—a school of baitfish or some barracuda," remarks our PADI dive instructor.

Most of the dives are shallow—thirty to sixty feet. People who don't want to get wet can embark in a semi-submersible vessel to enjoy a fish-eye perspective of coral gardens and marine life.

For serious scuba enthusiasts, live-aboard dive vessels are the top choice. Based in Cairns, Mike Ball Dive Expeditions operates three catamarans. "The service was outrageous. Since staff members always dive with guests, it creates a real feeling of camaraderie," comments

Andy Alpine from California, who took trips on the *Spoilsport* and *Supersport.* "I did the Scuba Zoo dive, a shark-feed that delivers views from the safety of a cage. We saw several bronze whaler sharks."

Visitors can also explore the tide pools on a naturalist-led reef-walk in a designated area. "Stay on sand channels, or stand in the center of dead coral boulders," our guide instructs us. "Touching living coral can destroy it, as well as the creatures burrowed within its crevices."

Satiate the Predators

Estimated to be up to 500,000 years old in some sections, the GBR is made up of undersea mountains upon which coral reefs have developed. The coral forms from polyps, small primitive animals resembling sea anemones that join together in colonies. Most polyps feed at night, extending tentacles to capture prey ranging from plankton to small fish. Each polyp produces a hard surface by secreting calcium carbonate. When a polyp dies, it leaves behind its hard skeleton, so skeleton upon skeleton upon skeleton gradually builds up the reef. While the coral polyp acts as the builder, the sea serves as architect. Broken into sand by pounding waves, skeletons and shells of sea life that once lived in the reef community help form cays and islands.

The reef grows and reproduces in sync with the moon and tide. During the Australian spring in late November or early December—and always after the full moon—vast numbers of coral polyps spawn at the same time, releasing sperm and egg bundles that float to the surface, then mesh like keys in locks before sinking to the bottom. Scientists describe this mass spawning as a strategy to "satiate the predators." Although hungry fish swarm in to gorge on this bounty, a few fertilized eggs survive to create the next generation of coral.

Observers say diving during a coral spawn feels like being caught in an underwater blizzard—you're surrounded by swirling, surging egg bundles. The bloom can cut underwater visibility on the reef to 30 feet rather than the usual 100, but what a thrill to witness such a powerful phenomenon! An inside joke among scientists refers to this phenomenon as "the world's greatest orgasm by the world's greatest organism!"

Survival in the Food Chain

Life in the fast lane is a snap compared with life in the food chain. "Let Nature Take its Course," read signs at several island eco-resorts. Easier said than done. At Heron Island, we find it difficult not to intervene while we watch seagulls gobble an entire hatch of 100 baby green turtles, unfortunate to have been born during daylight hours. On another nature walk, we witness noddy terns flailing on the ground, unable to fly because burrs from the Pisonia tree are entangled in their wings. "It's all part of Nature's design," explains our guide. "Since reef birds don't eat seed pods, Pisonia can colonize only by having their seeds enmesh with a bird's feathers. The bird's carcass creates nutrients for the seed to germinate."

Darwin's rules also apply below the waterline. The vivid beauty of the reef contrasts with the ferocity of its denizens. Color on the reef becomes a strategy for survival. Fish and mollusks must match the coral color palette so they can hunt unseen—or hide camouflaged from predators. For defense, Nature has equipped many creatures that lack speed or strength with alternative weaponry: corals sting and paralyze, starfish bristle with poisonous spines, shell dwellers bore into each other, and sea snakes pack more venom than any rattler.

Far Northern Section

Although the reef sits close to the coast in northern Queensland—just nine miles from Port Douglas and Cairns—the southern portion lies nearly 100 miles offshore. The GBR divides into four sections, or management areas, each with unique attractions.

Seldom visited because the lack of roads and resort accommodations on the coast makes it practically inaccessible, the 440-mile stretch from Cape York to just north of Lizard Island remains the most unspoiled part of the reef. Specialist cruises and liveaboard dive boats based in Cairns and Port Douglas cater to divers and tourists interested in visiting this band of reefs. Highlights include Raine Island, a rookery for brown and masked boobies, along with a nesting area for marine turtles.

Cairns Section

A siesta-paced, sun-washed city, Cairns serves as Queensland's adventure central with enough treks, tracks, climbs, and dives to occupy the most adventurous traveler full time. Since the reef lies close to the coast here, this ranks as the most accessible area for visitors. From both Cairns and Port Douglas, day trippers to the reef depart aboard high-speed catamarans, such as *Quicksilver* to Agincourt Reef, or *Reef Rocket* to Green Island. Especially popular, Green Island attracts hundreds of visitors daily to its white-sand beaches for snorkeling, beaching, and walkabouts.

Located near the famous Cod Hole dive site, Lizard Island encompasses 2,500 acres of the national park. The Lizard Island Research Station offers tours explaining its studies of tropical reefs and fish. In addition, the island draws scuba enthusiasts because of the giant clams in the offshore waters. When the light-sensitive spots on the clam's brown mantle sense danger, the double shells clamp shut like a bank vault. (Contrary to the goofy cartoons, divers can't get caught inside.)

Central Section

From Lizard Island to the southern part of the Whitsunday Islands, the reef swings farther from the mainland. Principal gateways include Townsville, Proserpine, and Hamilton Island. Visiting Townsville Reef HQ Aquarium, which houses the planet's largest living-coral aquarium, feels just like diving. Visitors walk through a sixty-five-foot-long acrylic tunnel surrounded by soft and hard corals, sponges, and fish—including sharks. Operated by the Great Barrier Reef Marine Park Authority, it's one of only a few facilities in the world where coral has spawned.

Out on the reef, divers will want to explore the wreck of the SS *Yongala*, a 346-foot-long steamer that sank in a cyclone in 1911. Resting seventy-five percent intact at forty to ninety feet down, the ship slumbers encrusted by corals and sponges. "The amount of fish life is amazing—I saw large trevally jacks and a squadron of rays," Alpine enthuses.

MacKay/Capricorn Section

Of the world's seven sea turtle species, six—all listed as either endangered or vulnerable—make their home in Australian waters. Straddling the Tropic of Capricorn, the region from the Whitsundays to the seas off Bundaberg serves as one of the world's major breeding grounds for green, hawksbill, and loggerhead turtles. A microcosm for the entire reef section, the waters surrounding Heron Island shelter sixty percent of the species of fish and seventy-five percent of the types of corals found in the GBR. Here, divers enjoy Wistari Reef, with its forests of staghorn coral and creatures ranging from angelfish to wobbegong sharks. Anchoring the southern tip of the GBR, Lady Elliott Island features giant manta rays.

Fragile Giant

The GBR reigns as a fragile giant as efforts continue to protect its coral and marine life. In July 2004, the Australian government banned commercial fishing from one-third of the reef, thus helping ensure healthier corals and bigger fish for tourists to see.

Further challenges remain. Outbreaks of crown-of-thorns starfish, which devour living coral, have increased in frequency and severity. Agricultural development and tree clearing on the Australian mainland have increased runoff of sediment and fertilizer into offshore waters, boosting algae growth. Global warming looms as another menace: coral flourishes best between temperatures of 77° and 84° Fahrenheit; higher temperatures cause coral bleaching, which can eventually kill the reef.

"Take only photos—Leave only bubbles" remains the golden guideline for all visitors. The intent is that those words won't become the hollow hope of a lost cause, but will instead promise the chance to save this underwater Eden forever.

Float planes deliver guests to Great Barrier Reef dive platforms

Giant clams can exceed four-feet-wide and 450 pounds

Naturalists instruct guests to walk in sand channels or on dead coral boulders

Snorkeling on Great Barrier Reef

Chapter 23

NEW ZEALAND - SAILING THE LEVIATHAN *KZ1*

"Your name has been put on the list of authorized personnel. Be here at 5:30 a.m. tomorrow. And, by the way, come dressed in white."

With these cryptic words, I am invited by a syndicate spokesman, who telephones my Auckland hotel room late in the evening, to sail the following morning aboard New Zealand's *KZ1* challenger for the America's Cup. This will be the final day of sea trials in Auckland before the boat is shipped to San Diego to face San Diego Yacht Club's defender, *Stars and Stripes 88,* in the 1988 America's Cup.

Pre-Sunrise Activity

Hours later, after clearing two checkpoints at the Devonport Naval Yard, I arrive just before sunrise at the dockside security compound: a jumble of trailers, workshops, storage lockers, and a communications nerve center. Ignoring my presence, dozens of white-clad crew members bustle about in the half-lit shadows, consulting posted computer printouts before scurrying off to perform assigned tasks. Down the ramp and across the floating dock, the white leviathan sleeps, half hidden in the predawn gloom. Several crew members are busy washing the enormous overhanging decks, obviously an important matter.

Heading the boat-wash roster is the notice, "The Boat looks Bad when it's Dirty, which makes us Look Bad." Beside the roster is the crew sheet listing fifty-six names with functions and responsibilities. The terms are imaginative: "speed team," "concept sailmakers," "rail crew" (which includes syndicate head Michael Fay), "thrust team," and "illness coordinator."

When I hear another American accent, I turn to meet the sail master for the *New Zealand* challenger, Rod Davis, whose Kiwi allegiance is cemented by his marriage to sail designer Tom Schnackenberg's sister. On this eighteenth and last day of sea trials since the launch a month earlier, Davis expresses disappointment not to have the 8-knot winds needed to complete the performance analysis program. Despite the plan for a predawn departure, the winds are strengthening faster than anticipated.

"Talk with the crew about anything, take all the photos you want, wander anywhere on the boat—but don't go below deck to the computer center," Davis tells me. Pretty lenient conditions for an American journalist, I think. For all he knows, I could be a spy for the American syndicate! After addressing me, Davis gives the general command to load up and prepare for cast-off.

Into the Blackness of Waitematā Harbour

Only as I join the throng moving toward the boat do I really see *New Zealand.* My impression is that this leviathan looks more like an extension of the floating dock than the winged wonder itself. As I step onto the gleaming white, moonlit deck, I notice that the boat doesn't tip in the slightest, even as forty crew members scamper over the starboard rail. After shore hands drop the docking lines, chase boats gingerly nudge us away from shore, and the tender pulls us into the blackness of Waitematā Harbour.

As crew members tend to their routine jobs, I survey the tennis-court-size deck with those long, sweeping wings glistening in the early dawn light. The clean sweep of the deck, with only minimal hardware and fittings, is interrupted by four open hatches, each glowing with blue-white light from video tubes, TV monitors, and terminal displays below. The faint whirr of disc drives confirms the presence of elaborate electronics and banks of computers. The sound makes me aware of how silently we are moving through the water under tow at 10 knots.

Exactly what is below deck, anyway? Three sophisticated computer systems, I am told. One monitors the stress load on the hull and rigging; another interprets photos of the sails taken at one-third-of-a-second intervals by cameras mounted at the top of the 154-foot mast; the third compares actual with target boat speed based on wind conditions and sail angle. This is clearly stratospheric technology that, along with the keel design and mast construction, is kept very secret.

Utter Exhilaration, Unrestrained Glee

As the sun's early rays illuminate the super-tall, spindly mast and rigging, we arrive at the outer reaches of the harbor at Rangitoto Channel, an area of the Hauraki Gulf deep enough to pose no risk to *New Zealand's* 21-foot keel. The crew comes to life as Davis, transmitting by handheld radio to stations throughout the boat and to the three chase launches, issues commands. Up goes the giant mainsail. I peer through the forward hatches where I glimpse the flailing arms of eight laboring crew bent over coffee-grinder winches. The tow line is dropped, and moments later the number three jib is hoisted as we fall away on a starboard tack under sail, close-hauled in 18 knots of wind.

Beforehand, I had tried to imagine how going under sail in this overscaled planing dinghy would feel, but nothing I imagined could have prepared me for the utter exhilaration of the next few minutes.

As the sails harvest the breeze, this white leviathan suddenly awakens from its sleep and leaps to life. Heeling slightly to port, it accelerates with a steady rush like a bullet train. There is no sensation of sound or speed—only the feel of the apparent wind on my face as it builds and shifts to the bow while we pick up speed. Spray explodes from the hull as if, somewhere below us, firehoses have been unleashed, blasting in every direction. But strangely, we leave no wake. I gain some sense of our speed only when I glance at the foaming stern waves of the twin-outboard chase boats trying to keep up with us.

Digital displays on deck also spring to life. Three banks of deck-mounted readouts begin a dance of their own, ticking off tenths of a knot of boat speed: 8…9…10…11…11.6 knots… heel angle twenty-three–twenty-four degrees. Despite the knot meter's elevated readout, the boat seems to be standing still, because I hear no sound, see no wake, notice no reaction to the waves. Looking up, I see an exaggerated twist in the mainsail with the top quarter still luffing, an indication that the boat is far from optimal trim, even with this unbelievable speed. Designer Bruce Farr's press release, boasting that the boat would achieve 12 knots on the wind, is clearly an understatement!

As all heads turn toward the digital readouts, a look of unrestrained glee replaces the crew's nonchalant expressions. The boat's sudden burst of speed elicits a surge of adrenaline in everyone aboard. While thirteen bodies remain fixed on the windward rail, others spring into action as quiet commands rise up from below: "Ease the Cunningham." "More twist in the main." "Slack the jib…." All familiar commands with one notable difference: with each order, instead of one crewmember responding, four or more jump into action. Most positions throughout the boat likewise require triple or quadruple the typical manpower.

We are an impressive sight with white hull, white sails, and crew decked out in all white. I wonder if our lack of color is an attempt to camouflage our numbers, or maybe it is simply to create a sharp, nautical look mandated by syndicate leader Michael Fay as a hallmark of his challenge. Perhaps everyone wears white, blending in with the white hull, to conceal the insignificance of the human element on this giant of a boat. I wonder if they would have taken me along if I had shown up all in red?

Everything is Oversized

Everything about this winged messenger from Mercury Bay Boating Club begs for comparison. Its 126-foot length and 26-foot-wide deck could accommodate four 12-meter yachts with room to spare. The towering sixteen-story mast looks fragile and spindly, supported by tapered spreaders extending sixteen feet outboard from the stick. One of the mast men, who had previously been hoisted to the top of the mast, told me he had looked down upon a helicopter that had come near for close-up photos. I smile inwardly as I recall that my first sailboat, a 12-foot Penguin, was only three-quarters the length of a single *New Zealand* spreader.

The deck hardware on this oversized boat no longer seems exaggerated as I realize the enormous power of the forces transferred from the wind to the rig. Blocks, shackles, cleats, sheaves—all the usual hardware—appear normal until I touch them and realize that, by comparison, I have hands the size of a two-year-old's. Indeed, the entire crew also seems too small.

"Prepare to come about," calls helmsman David Barnes. In the next few moments, the rail crew and I (not knowing quite what I'm doing as I follow along) lie flat on our stomachs as a dinosaur's tail sweeps across the deck with only two feet of clearance. If I had simply stood there like a deer in the headlights and been swept by the boom into the sea, I'm sure the crew would have had to mobilize a "Man Overboard" drill.

No Sounds, Just Unstoppable Power

Again, there is no sound—nothing like the thunderclap heard on the old J-Class boats of comparable size. With not a moment's hesitation, the boat comes about like a planing dinghy—its motion seems unstoppable. The rail crew quickly hustles to the windward hiking wing, clamoring up the canted deck to provide ballast. The boat heels to twenty-three degrees, but no farther, preventing the lower wing from touching the water and slowing boat speed.

As the jib is trimmed, it then occurs to me there are no coffee-grinder winches on deck, just two covered pedestal mounts in the foredeck. "It's another first," explains one of the crew in response to my question. "We took them off the deck shortly after launching and instead re-positioned the halyard and jib sheet coffee-grinders below deck. It lightens the load, reduces wind resistance, gives us more deck area, and lowers our center of gravity." He adds that television monitors are being added below deck so the "sewer" crew can follow top-deck action.

"Let's get a reef in the main," shouts Davis, as the wind builds to 23 knots. Thirty seconds later, after ten crew members shorten the mainsail to the first line of reef points, we fall off onto a broad reach, and boat speed increases to 16 knots. Three deck-mounted displays show that the heel angle has decreased four degrees.

Forty pairs of anxious eyes look up to see how much flex is in the rig. From below decks, information gleaned from video screens is called up to Davis, who decides the wind is building too fast. He's concerned about the potential for overstressing the boat while it's still being tuned. As the wind gusts to 25 knots, remote readouts from the mast-mounted cells show increasing forces on the rigging. After consulting with helmsman David Barnes, Davis calls for a starboard takedown, another precision performance, and waits for calmer conditions.

Turning to me, Barnes explains, "We've sailed these conditions before and have nothing to prove. It's not worth the risk to the rig just before we leave."

Once the tow line is again secured, Davis relaxes and chats openly with me about the sea trial program, comparing the role of the crew to that of test pilots. "We're still dealing with fairly basic things like keel position, rig design, and sail plan," explains the former skipper of the 12-meter Eagle campaign for the '86/'87 Cup. "We have most of the rough data except for very light wind conditions. Refinements won't come until we're in San Diego where we'll have two major differences—more wind shear and larger swells. We're still trying to understand exactly what the boat can do."

Half an hour later the wind subsides and again we're under sail. As we go through different headings, the dialogue is unbroken between those below deck gathering data for the computers, the boat's afterguard, and the several video crews on the chase boats recording the different sail profiles. Davis and Barnes resume the trials, putting the graceful superboat through a series of data-collecting maneuvers.

Last Day of Sea Trials

Finally satisfied with the day's program, Davis calls for the tow line, and an hour later we're back at the docks. The crew still has the better part of the day ahead to complete new work assignments already posted for them when they step ashore.

Back on land, I meet with Peter Wilson, shore manager for the New Zealand challenge. "One day I went out as part of the rail crew, and my first reaction was, 'Wow!'" says the transplanted Englishman, who was shore manager for the Canadian True North 12-Meter Challenge in 1986. "The second time we were saying, 'It's quite a boat.' Now our reaction is simply, 'Let's get on with sailing.'"

Before I depart, I take one final long look at this graceful giant of a boat. What, I wonder, will others feel when they see it berthed at San Diego's Terminal 10? I have no doubt that whatever the outcome of the America's Cup in September off Point Loma, Americans will have witnessed a truly extraordinary winged leviathan.

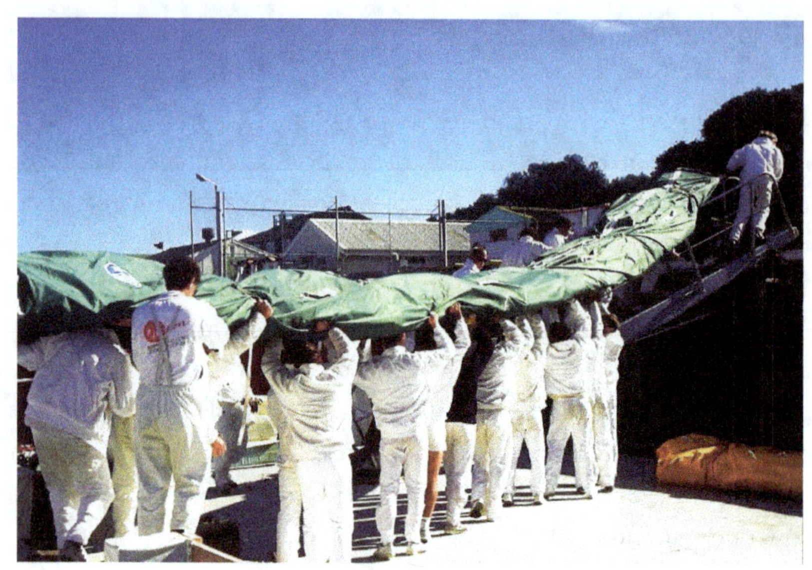

Carrying furled mainsail ashore

Dropping the mainsail

Halfway up the sixteen-story mast

Rail Meat

Chapter 24

JAPAN - SAVE THE SEA

If you ride a subway during Tokyo's rush hour, it's highly unlikely you'll see carelessly discarded trash. Walk around the streets of Japanese cities, and you'll be impressed by how clean and neat the surroundings are. But take a hike to any beach or along an inland waterway, and you'll think you've stumbled into a garbage dump—at least that's the way it was before the start of the country's first campaign to clean up its coastline.

Westerners are often mystified at this striking contrast in the Japanese lifestyle. The explanation is to be found by looking back into the country's history. For 200 years during the Edo period, the Japanese weren't allowed to travel offshore or welcome foreigners from abroad. Because the sea was the link to the forbidden outside world, it became isolated from their culture; consequently, it was not considered deserving of care or respect.

Mark Morita

Nevertheless, in a country which had been lax about dealing with environmental issues, some years ago a Japanese yachting group founded the nation's first environmental organization dedicated to stopping pollution of the oceans. Credit goes to a prominent Japanese businessman, Masatoshi Mark Morita, once the country's most active competitor in international yacht racing, as he campaigned his 50-foot yacht *Champosa* on the U.S. and European yacht racing circuits.

What impelled him to create a coastal clean-up organization? When Morita watched television coverage of trapped birds dying in an oil spill slick, the ardent yacht racer was so stunned at the tragedy that he decided to do something about it. Speaking through an interpreter, Morita explains, "Seeing the dying, oiled birds really shocked me. Suddenly, I realized how awful this could become for the next generation if we continue polluting the sea."

The International 50-Foot Yacht Association holds a yearly series of five regattas at venues throughout Europe, the United States, and Japan on its World Cup race circuit. Under the leadership of Morita, the association established a precedent among yachting federations to stop pollution of the seas by adopting a no-litter provision in its association bylaws. Any violating boat would be subject to race disqualification.

Save the Sea

Morita hammered out a vision for a national campaign to make the Japanese more conscious about not littering beaches and polluting the oceans, an effort he hopes eventually to spread to the rest of the world. Thus, "Save the Sea" was born, the first environmental effort in Japan directed toward cleaning up the sea.

Launched at the Japan 50-Foot World Cup Regatta some years ago in Miura City, the Save the Sea campaign, managed by independent directors who have taken over for Morita and organized a grassroots movement, called on sailors and all other sea-loving people throughout the world to commit to preserving the purity of the world's oceans.

To ensure the movement remains free of political influence and business interests, bylaws prevent politicians and businessmen from holding positions on the governing board. According to Morita, the campaign can remain a grassroots effort only if the leadership is free of potential conflicts of interest. Therefore, the board is composed of artists, journalists, teachers, and professionals from specialized environmental fields.

One of Japan's foremost artists, Kiyoshi Awanzu, whose work is exhibited at the New York Modern Art Gallery, designed the movement's logo. It depicts a weeping sea turtle laying her eggs on a beach threatened by toxic air and water pollutants spewed from a nearby industrial city. A sprawling mountain of garbage dominates the background. According to the artist, Japanese culture honors the turtle as a sacred symbol of the continuity of life; her tears indicate that all living creatures are in danger, and continuity of existence is by no means assured. The same theme is captured in a new song, "Save the Sea," which is taught in schools throughout the country.

Student Poster Contest

Within Japan, the goal of Save the Sea has been to awaken the country to the importance of treating the sea with respect. The first step was a poster contest among elementary and high school students, a project immediately endorsed by government organizations including the Ministries of Education, Foreign Affairs, and Environment, and promoted nationally by the country's largest newspapers. In the first year the response yielded more than 5,300 submissions, each reflecting a child's view of the impact of pollution and human carelessness on the ocean.

"The poster contest was intended to see what children thought of the ocean, and the results were magnificent," says Morita. "They portrayed massive destruction to the marine life due to practices of throwing waste into the sea, a very strong message that has made a significant impact on older generations."

The category finalists from different age groups traveled to Miura, host for the 50-Foot World Cup, and received national commendation when the posters were put on display. The exhibit circulated within Japan before being sent to New York, where the posters were hung in the lobby of the United Nations building. Proceeds from the sale of the campaign's T-shirts, buttons, and posters used to publicize this environmental cause were given to the United Nations Environment Program (UNEP), headquartered in Nairobi, Kenya.

The children's poster competition, an annual event, was conceived as a non-threatening way to work at the family level by bringing parents a sense of awareness about respecting the sea while distancing the movement from politics and business interests.

Morita explains that coastal recreation is not part of the Japanese culture. Consequently, Save the Sea seeks to overturn a long-held view, similar to the Japanese view of a rice field or the American view of a cornfield, that the ocean is nothing more than a large watery field whose purpose is simply to provide a harvest of seafood. What is needed, Morita says, is consensus-building, not confrontation.

Environmental Alarm Clocks

The second step of the program reached beyond the family into regional communities with a series of "Environmental Alarm Clock" campaigns. Information was disseminated to the public, outlining the sources of ocean pollution. Many Japanese beaches were heavily littered with plastic refuse and discarded trash; coral surrounding the coast was dying; and Osaka Bay, Sagami Sea, and other coastal waters were heavily polluted with industrial waste. Morita explains, "We can't ask people to clean up until they wake up, which is why we used the image of an alarm clock in this second phase of the campaign."

Challenge to Society

By the third phase, Save the Sea organizers felt that the media exposure had raised the awareness levels enough to generate widespread concern, and it was time for action. Every sector of society was challenged to eliminate their particular polluting practices.

Morita is confident that Japanese people now understand the harm being done to the sea and will take corrective action. "It does no good to attack companies, because they will just become angry. This is a new problem for us, and we only began monitoring water purity some years ago when the first environmental laws were passed. Industries have been criticized by the public, so now they must do something. The Japanese way of thinking is to change what is wrong immediately. But first we have to help people see what is wrong."

~

Finalists in Save the Sea student poster contest

Save the Sea, founder, Mark Morita, aboard his 50-foot sailing yacht

Chapter 25

ABACOS - SAILING THE ABC'S

Squall Approaching

Lazing under sail in a gentle breeze in calm waters aboard *Bethkaren*, our chartered Moorings 352, we don't have a worry in the world. We're at ease under blue skies in paradise until… what are those gray clouds to the north?

A squall line over Great Abaco Island is swiftly sweeping down upon us. We spring into action: chug the drinks, muscle a double reef in the mainsail, furl the jib, break out our foul-weather gear, and prepare safety harnesse's in case we need to go on deck in rough seas. Next, we plot a new course to ensure enough sea room to safely ride out the blow that will likely cut our visibility to practically zero.

Setting an anchor anywhere in the Sea of Abaco is straightforward because the water is typically less than fifteen feet deep. So, we lower the anchor, pay out generous scope, and cleat the mainsheet down tight, which will offer some stability.

Just as the first drops begin to assault us, we duck into the cabin and secure the hatches below. Wild winds, breaking seas, and pelting rain create pandemonium all around as the squall hits, but we remain comfortable and dry below deck. When all calms down half an hour later, we raise the anchor. The sun dries the last droplets from the cleansed deck and rigging as gentle trade winds once again fill our sails. We're now back to where we were before. Today is just another typical day in the amazing Abacos.

The ease with which we weather the sudden squall reflects the laid-back spirit of our cruise. Our family crew consists of three generations of sailors, each with different goals: two sprightly grandparents in their seventies wanting to read and relax in isolated anchorages, their twin seventeen-year-old grandsons eager to push the boat to her limits, and my wife and I, who prefer a mix of gentle sailing and leisurely gunkholing.

In the Abacos, we find plenty of opportunities to accommodate our differing aims. Dozens of islands and cays, mostly uninhabited, offer miles of forgotten, sugar-sand beaches fringed with swaying casuarina trees and coconut palms. In the evenings, countless snug coves and quiet little harbors offer a welcoming choice of secure overnight anchorages.

Off-Season Cruising

Best of all, there are no crowds here now. When winter storms send sun-seeking northerners fleeing south to crowded Florida beaches, it's off-season in the Abacos, less than an hour's flight from Miami. The throngs won't arrive until spring, when armadas of Floridian sportfishing yachts cross the Gulf Stream in search of gamefish. In winter, however, these islands belong to those of us who prefer quiet, off-the-track, subtropical beauty and fair sailing winds.

After a short flight from Miami the previous day, we begin our trip by clearing customs in Marsh Harbour. Then a quick taxi ride takes us to The Moorings charter base. The manager is most diligent in reviewing *Bethkaren's* equipment, rigging, and inventory with us. He then spreads out a chart of the cruising area and suggests a mix of isolated anchorages and quaint settlement harbors.

The cruising waters of the Abacos, a boomerang-shaped cluster of islands and cays sheltered in the Sea of Abaco, extend more than fifty nautical miles from Little Abaco Island in the northwest to Little Harbour in the southeast. In contrast to the smooth coastline of Great Abaco Island on the southwestern edge, the northwest border consists of fragmented barrier islands protected from the pounding Atlantic rollers by the country's 130-mile barrier reef.

After picking up a week's provisions at the nearby Ample Hamper market, we're ready to cast off. With a full afternoon sail ahead of us, we set course up the coast of Great Abaco Island, putting *Bethkaren* through all points of sail. She responds easily to the helm as we tack among the Fish Cays, giving us confidence that we can handle her in tight quarters.

Concerned that shoals might appear at any moment and that an abrupt depth change could bring us to a jolting stop, for the first hour we keep alert to listen for the depth sounder alarm. While it's unnerving to see straight down to the seafloor, which seems so close, we soon learn the seabed along our course is more or less flat with minimal changes, so we eventually forget our worries about depth.

Lazing Among the Cays

As the afternoon sun sinks lower in the west, we set course for Great Guana Cay, one of the smallest settlements of the Out Islands. With fewer than 100 inhabitants, Great Guana is famous for golden-pink beaches, colorful nearshore coral, craggy rocks, and the Guana Beach Resort and Marina. With hammocks (claimed to be a Bahamian invention) strung in a beachfront palm grove, Guana Beach has continued as a rustic barefoot-and-T-shirt stopover for cruising yachtsmen since its founding in the 1950s.

The resort's reputation is built on its signature rum drink, the "Guana Grabber," and its distinguished kitchen, highly regarded throughout the area. The restaurant serves lobster tails, the ubiquitous conch cooked in any one of countless ways, and a selection of freshly caught fish—an eclectic menu ranging from Cajun to Asian. Our family group orders a little of everything, then passes the platters around so everyone shares.

Treasure Cay, the second stop on our cruise, claims to be the site of the original American settlement. In 1783, 600 British Loyalists settled at Carleton Point after the Revolutionary War, preferring to live in the British-controlled Bahamas rather than in the newly independent States.

In summer the docks and anchorages of this marina are packed with sportfishing motor yachts. But because fishing season has not yet kicked into gear, we have the premises virtually to ourselves, prompting the staff to fall all over themselves in making us feel at home. Our service at dinner has never been so good.

From Treasure Cay we alternate between quiet isolated anchorages and settlement harbors. In some villages we can buy the daily *New York Times*, while in others the mailboat stops only once a week. Snorkeling highlights our lunch stopovers at Fowl Cay Reef and Sandy Cay Reef, both underwater national parks.

We dive on the Civil War gunboat USS *Adirondack*, which lies on the sandy bottom near Man-O-War Cay, a Cape Cod–style settlement where boatbuilding is still an art. Man-O-War is best known for its Abaco-built "smacks," native sailing sloops with oversized booms, protruding bowsprits, and shallow drafts designed for stability and work.

Hope Town

Perched high on Elbow Cay, a landmark red-and-white candy-striped lighthouse built in 1863 rises above the settlement of Hope Town. To preserve the charm of this colorful eighteenth-century New England–style seafaring village, the local government limits the number of automobile trips per day through town.

By dinghy we explore the shops, colonial harbor-front cottages, and restaurants built on stilts over the marina basin. After tying to the dinghy dock, we walk to the historic downtown section and the Wyannie Malone Historical Museum, which documents the town's founding in 1783 by British Loyalists from South Carolina. As we continue through town, we find open market stalls offering local fruit, conch, crawfish, and grouper. Flavoring the back roads of the settlement are the lime greens, sherbet lemons, and rose pinks of small sandbox homes, each stylishly decorated with white gingerbread trim adorning the entryways and white picket fences surrounding small fruit and vegetable gardens.

Planting Gardens

The soil is so rich in the Abacos that the act of eating a tomato sandwich outside can result in a tomato garden springing up soon after. People claim they farm by tossing cantaloupe and watermelon seeds and vegetable peels out the front door. Then they take credit for these accidental, bountiful fruit and vegetable gardens as though they are the result of many hours of labor.

Eager to continue sampling the local foods, we consume familiar fruits like bananas, pineapples, limes, and papayas. Then we tantalize our taste buds with akee, mammee, jujube, sugar apple, tamarind, breadfruit, soursop, sapodilla, and the islands' most popular fruit, the guinep. Heeding local advice to let the seeds fall on the ground, we may well have "planted" more gardens ourselves!

Jewel of the Bahamas

Five miles south of Hope Town, Abaco Inn, on the easternmost point of land in the Abacos, located high on a coral outcrop of Elbow Cay, commands views westward to its marina in White Sound and to the Atlantic rollers coming in from the east. The inn welcomes cruising yachtsmen to tie up to its docks free of charge and enjoy gourmet cuisine in an away-from-it-all atmosphere.

After a wonderful meal of fresh grouper and sand dabs, we stroll along the ocean beach, dazzled by the full moon sending golden beams streaking across the breaking surf. Then we cross the narrow strip of land back to *Bethkaren* and fall into our bunks, rocked to sleep by the sound of gentle waves lapping against the hull.

We rise early the next morning, wanting to put in a full day of activity before returning *Bethkaren* to The Moorings charter base late that afternoon. With snorkels and masks in hand, we start the day with a morning ocean swim.

The marine life doesn't disappoint as we patrol around the numerous coral outcroppings, watching schools of colorful fish weave majestic patterns as they swim by. Snorkeling in these tropical waters is a delight, surrounded by vibrant coral reefs teeming with marine life and dazzling fish shimmering in the sunlight. In every crevice in the rocks, we find a pair of eyes guarding a home or perhaps waiting for an unsuspecting meal to swim by.

Drying ourselves off as we go but still in bathing suits, we meander along the beach and then up the gentle slope to the veranda of Abaco Inn. Awaiting us is a memorable breakfast buffet offering all the fresh fruits we sampled throughout our week's cruise.

But we don't linger, because we want to get in a full day's sail. After quick showers and then back into shorts and T-shirts, we cast off the mooring lines and, once clear of the docks, raise the sails.

With the winds holding steady, we arrive back at Fish Cays, which was our destination on the first day. Upon arriving, we drop the anchor, enjoy a final quick swim in the crystal-clear waters, eat the last of our sandwich fixings, then hoist the sail and, on a downwind run, deliver *Bethkaren* home to her charter base.

The Moorings base manager is quick to review the boat's inventory and check us out—nothing missing, nothing broken. Off the boat in no time, we taxi to the Great Abaco Beach Resort and Boat Harbour Marina where we spend the late afternoon walking the grounds to reclaim our land legs. This plush resort eases us back to the modern world, yet allows us one final lingering evening steeped in the natural beauty and friendly hospitality of what Abaconians understandably call the "Jewel of the Bahamas."

~

Gazebo at Elbow Cay's Abaco Inn

Hope Town's candy-striped lighthouse

Nipper's on Great Guana Cay, party central in the Abacos

White picket fences surround Hope Town homes

Chapter 26

BELIZE - REEFS AND RAINFORESTS

Hoping to learn the local waters from a professional captain well enough to return one day and cruise on my own under sail, I visit Belize aboard the 163-foot crewed charter yacht *Temptress Adventurer*, operated by Temptress Cruises. The journey begins in Belize City, the gateway to the country, only two hours' flying time from Miami, Houston, and New Orleans.

Within minutes of the yacht's departure from the municipal dock, we are out of sight of civilization. I stand beside the young Belizean captain as we cruise south along the coast in the Inner Channel, the long, narrow stretch of water between the reef and the mainland, and pay close attention as he reviews the nautical charts with me and points out landmarks along the way. After several hours underway, we arrive at our evening's anchorage, an isolated, mango-fringed island opposite the village of Gales Point.

Guardians of Gales Point

Gales Point was an early Maroon community settled in this isolated location by escaped slaves who resisted enslavement by fleeing the colonial authorities. Today the local Creole villagers in Gales Point are the guardians of the protected feeding and nesting grounds of two of Belize's most endangered animals: the Caribbean manatee and the hawksbill sea turtle.

Early the next morning, our group—birdwatchers, amateur archaeologists, scuba divers, environmentalists, and cruising yachtsmen such as myself who aren't quite ready to tackle the region on our own—dinghies cautiously into the muddy shallows of Manatee Lagoon, one of the world's largest playgrounds for manatees. Suddenly, the turbid waters around us erupt with life, enthralling us with the playful antics of these ten-foot sea cows that seem totally oblivious to our presence. Protective regulations of the Gales Point Wildlife Sanctuary—a mix of brackish shallows, mudflats, creeks, and mangrove swamps—prohibit disturbing the mangroves, which create the fragile wetlands habitat critical to manatees.

Later in the morning, our captain raises anchor and we proceed to Rendezvous Caye fifteen miles offshore beside the immense coral barrier reef, the marine counterpart to Belize's extensive tropical rainforest. Here the muddy coastal water gives way to a crystal-clear sea teeming with colorful fish and exotic marine creatures living amid delicate coral structures. The mangrove wetlands and rainforests of the interior mainland are replaced by glittering white beaches fringed with palm trees. After returning to the mainland, we anchor for the night at the mouth of the Sittee River.

Garifuna Culture

Keeping to a birdwatcher's schedule, in the predawn we tumble, half asleep, into our Zodiac inflatable to motor upriver, searching the shoreline for toucans, howler monkeys, flowering bromeliads, and the deadly fer-de-lance snake. At each stopover, the cruise company organizers engage boatmen and naturalists from nearby villages to show us the wildlife. This firsthand knowledge, coming directly from the native peoples—Creole, Maya, Mestizo, and Garifuna—leaves an unforgettable impression as we learn about their deep reverence for the land and their concern for keeping it unspoiled.

After the river excursion and return to *Temptress Adventurer*, we continue a short distance south to the small fishing village of Hopkins, which offers the first insight into the culture of the Garifuna, an ethnic group of mixed West African and Caribbean Indian ancestry. Our arrival touches off a holiday, and the entire community turns out to greet us. School is dismissed so the children can tell us about their lives and perform traditional folk dances for us. Once again, face-to-face contact with villagers impresses upon us how knowledgeable they are about their natural environment and how deeply they care about protecting it. They live every day close to the earth, depending on it for food, shelter, and their entire livelihoods.

Following our visit, we cruise away from the mainland to remote sections of the reef that are virtually untouched by humans. During the next few days, we explore southern sections of the reef. Wild King Caye turns out to be most intriguing. Here we find remnants of the only offshore settlement of the Mayan empire. Crabs on Wild King have become little archaeologists, dredging up fragments of pottery and remains of Maya coral architecture.

Mayan Culture—The Ancient Interior

Continuing back along the mainland coast, we alternate between shore excursions to isolated villages and inland treks to steamy rainforests. Our final stop is the country's southernmost town, Punta Gorda, located on the mainland near the Guatemalan border and was once the heart of the Mayan culture. Today the descendants of those early Mayans account for only ten percent of the country's population. Recent excavations have shown that Caracol, the largest of the country's several hundred Maya sites, is even larger than Tikal, long considered the most significant Maya restoration. Within Belize, 730 jungle-covered ancient cities have been discovered, along with 1,400 minor sites—dramatic proof of a once-flourishing civilization.

Contrary to popular belief, the Mayan culture is still very much alive, particularly in rural areas of southern Belize. Several Mayan villages have opened simple thatch-roof guest houses for travelers who want a firsthand look at a subsistence farming culture that has persisted for centuries.

Reef and Rainforest Preserved

Located on the east coast of Central America in the heart of the Caribbean Basin, Belize borders Mexico to the north, Guatemala to the west and south, and is flanked by the Caribbean Sea to the east. Belize is a two-part country: One half is the mainland, dominated by vast mountainous tracts of tropical rainforest; the other consists of islands along the country's renowned barrier reef. Because the country has only six major roads crisscrossing its rugged terrain, road travel is definitely not the way to go.

Running the entire length of the country's coastline and sheltering one of the richest ecosystems on the planet, the Mesoamerican Barrier Reef System, which includes the Belize Barrier Reef, is second in size only to Australia's Great Barrier Reef. Speckled with more than 200 islets and dozens of islands, the Belize Reef encompasses three of the Caribbean's four atolls.

To protect the fragile marine ecosystem and reverse degradation of the reef caused by escalating tourism, the Belize government has established many reserves and sanctuaries. Half Moon Caye Natural Monument was the first reserve to be established. Nearby, the Blue Hole, a 1,000-foot-diameter, 400-foot-deep limestone sinkhole popularized by Jacques Cousteau, has become Belize's most renowned dive site.

In 1987, when fish stocks in the area began to dwindle, the Hol Chan Marine Reserve became the first underwater sanctuary established in Central America. The country's newest national park is Laughing Bird Caye, a UNESCO World Heritage Site named for the laughing gulls that once gathered there in large numbers and have now nearly disappeared.

In recent years, the government has taken steps to protect the mainland rainforests and animal habitat in the same way it is preserving the reef. In Crooked Tree Wildlife Sanctuary, one can find tapirs, pumas, peccaries, and many of the country's 500 bird species, including the endangered jabiru stork, which has a wingspan of up to twelve feet. Because of the protection afforded by the Belize River Community Baboon Sanctuary, black howler monkeys have recovered from near extinction. Belizeans are particularly proud of their 125,000-acre Cockscomb Basin Wildlife Sanctuary, the only preserve in the world dedicated to protecting the jaguar.

Reef as Defender

Belize's history is inextricably tied to the reef, which shielded the region from the onslaught of early European colonization. Spanish and

Portuguese explorers settled every inch of the New World's coastline from Brazil to Mexico, but they were unwilling to risk the tricky crossing of the Belize Reef to set up a permanent outpost.

Consequently, English pirates and buccaneers used the area as a haven from which they launched attacks on the heavily laden Spanish galleons carrying New World riches back to Spain. During the next 150 years, more English settlers moved into the area, thereby giving Belize its national language, English, and an Anglican culture.

In 1871, Great Britain assumed administrative control of the region and named it British Honduras. In 1973, the British Parliament changed the name of the region to Belize. British ties to Belize ended when independence was declared in 1981.

Today Belize remains a small, unobtrusive—almost shy—country that seems out of step, if not lost, among many of the world's developing countries. Other countries in the same stage of development are determined to exploit their natural resources and are willing to trade the cultural values of community-style villages in exchange for modernization of their cities. Belize, instead, is taking a different approach, one calculated to raise the national standard of living while preserving its natural and cultural heritage.

For example, eighty percent of Belize's landmass is still covered with forests. This is mainly due to its low population of 423,000, making this country the most sparsely populated nation in Central America. In contrast, slightly smaller El Salvador is bursting with more than 6.3 million people and retains only twenty-five percent of its forests.

Thanks to its century-old democratic traditions, Belize is the only Latin American country that has never experienced the war-torn strife that has ravaged its neighbors. The Massachusetts-size nation enjoys relative prosperity, adequate health services, good public schools (it has one of the highest literacy rates in the world), and a government committed to preserving its environmental and cultural richness.

Discovering the Wonders

Each year, more and more tourists discover the wonders and beauty of Belize. Cruising yachtsmen, however, have been slower to recognize Belize's attractions. They have yet to discover the calm sailing waters, protected reef anchorages, and mainland coves ideal for gunkholing. Although several small cruise operators and a few crewed charter yachts are operating in Belize today, bareboating has been slower to take hold. Nevertheless, companies such as Sunsail Yacht Charters and The Moorings have established charter bases in the lagoon on the Placencia peninsula.

With the potential to rank among the world's great venues for cruising under sail, Belize, its coastline resplendent with quiet, mangrove-fringed bays, will draw sailors who yearn for adventure and a close-up encounter with a beautiful, practically untouched country.

~

2000-year-old Mayan temple at Caracol

Mayan weaver

Early-morning birdwatchers

Hand-carved mahogany canoe

Chapter 27

COSTA RICA - PURA VIDA

"Pura Vida!" Pure Life, indeed. This familiar greeting among Costa Ricans reflects their love for a life lived in harmony with the natural world. The very essence of clean, simple, outdoorsy Tico life rings clearly in this famous expression, which has become a rallying cry for environmental law and order throughout the world.

Paradise for Gunkholing

Vast stretches of pristine beaches often draw sailors cruising the Pacific coast to or from the Panama Canal to the deserted shores of Costa Rica. Those who stop over here will quickly discover the country's rich biodiversity. All 775 miles of its coastline on both the Pacific Ocean and the Caribbean Sea are accessible to the public and protected from development. The national parks, wildlife sanctuaries, quiet anchorages, and occasional full-service marinas dotting the rugged Pacific coastline make it a natural paradise for gunkholing.

When sailing from the north on the Pacific side, the first landfall is the marina at Flamingo Beach. The Gulf of Papagayo along the dry, northwest coast of Guanacaste Province also offers protected anchorages. There is plenty to see in the nearby savanna and tropical forest of Santa Rosa National Park, which protects 600 species of birds and mammals, and 2,000 species of moths. Those who stop over here in the fall may be lucky enough to witness the arrival of some of the more than 200,000 olive ridley turtles that come each year to nest on its sandy beach.

International developers are understandably attracted by the miles of sugar-sand beaches along the coastline. But the coastline itself is protected, and such development as is permitted is severely restricted: No structures may be built within 150 feet of the coast, and the adjacent 300 feet inland can be leased to, but not owned by, foreigners. The result is that developers, operating in accordance with the guidelines, have turned the area into an environmentally sensitive mega-resort destination.

Puntarenas—Where Jungle and Marina Converge

Sailors continuing south along the Pacific coast can gunkhole through an ecological preserve containing white-sand islands and the Guayabo National Park Sanctuary. The port city of Puntarenas in the Gulf of Nicoya offers boat repair services, a secure moorage at the Costa Rica Yacht Club, and a base from which to explore the beauties of Tortuga Island.

The next anchorage south is Manuel Antonio National Park, known for its stunning, electric-blue morpho butterflies. Jungle limbs stretching across sandy beaches and dipping into the Pacific swells create yet another bit of Eden. In accordance with the Costa Rican philosophy that Nature's terms—not man's—prevail, access to the park is possible only by wading barefoot across a shallow stream.

Unlike national parks in the U.S., where many amenities are provided, Costa Rica's rustic reserves and parks lack interpretive centers, plumbing, electricity, accommodations, tours, brochures, groomed trails, and permanent staff. Entry is often by tractor, ox cart, horse, or foot. Upkeep (usually minimal) is contracted out to local villagers.

Corcovado National Park—Costa Rica's Ecological Core

The final stop along the coast for southbound boaters is the banana port of Golfito in the Dulce Gulf. Nearby Corcovado National Park on the Osa Peninsula, considered the jewel of Costa Rica's park system, includes eight environmental habitats and is one of the most complex ecological regions in the world. This 100,000-acre coastal park contains more species of trees, insects, and birds than the entire U.S.

Although Costa Rica is slightly smaller than West Virginia and home to about five million inhabitants, the country has created some of the most innovative ecological preserves in the world. It boasts more than thirty national parks, fifty-one wildlife refuges, thirteen nature preserves, and the world's only two international biological reserves—one shared with Panama to the south, the other with Nicaragua to the north.

Land Bridge—Spine of the Americas

Located between 8° and 11° north latitude, Costa Rica is the land bridge between two continents. A monument in the central mountains marks the exact center between the land masses of North and South America. Four mountain ranges rise from both seacoasts to create a series of spines that divide the country into patterns of highlands and central valleys. Each is composed of a variety of habitats that include beaches, riversides, mangrove swamps, tropical dry forests, rainforests, cloud forests, and oak forests, along with cultivated lands and city parks.

This Central American isthmus nation has developed seven mega-conservation districts, each linking clusters of nature preserves, national parks, and forest reserves with adjacent private lands. Its twelve ecological zones contain 2,300 tree species, more than double the number (900) of species found in the United States. Costa Rica is home to 12,000 varieties of plants, 200 species of fruit, and 1,500 orchid varieties. No wonder this country has been compared to the Garden of Eden!

Noah's Ark May Have Disgorged Here

A quick inventory of wildlife suggests that Noah's Ark may have disgorged its cargo here. With 360 species of amphibians and reptiles—including all seven of the world's sea turtles—Costa Rica has greater wildlife diversity than all of Africa. Mammal species in the country include the ocelot, jaguar, anteater, armadillo, and others that many Americans may have never heard of: tapirs, peccaries, kinkajous, agoutis, coatimundis, and tamanduas. In addition, eighteen percent of the world's butterflies can be found here. With its location at the terminus of four North American flyways, this little country is home to 900 species of avian life, more than in the U.S. and Canada combined.

The underwater environment on both the Pacific and Caribbean coasts is no less rich. Scuba divers from around the world throng to marine preserves such as Cocos Island National Park (said to be the largest uninhabited island in the world), Caño Island Biological Reserve (reputed to be the most complex land-sea ecosystem on the planet), and the fringe reefs of Cahuita National Park on the Caribbean side. When Cocos and Caño Islands were declared off-limits to the producers of the 1993 movie *Jurassic Park*, film crews were sent instead to the raw jungle setting of the Carara Biological Reserve on the mainland.

Disarmed Democracy—The Peace Dividend

Costa Rica's pervading cultural ideology creates a unique national character in which twenty-five percent of the land is preserved by law, public education is the top national priority, and the standing military was abolished by a constitutional amendment. The budget previously allocated to the military has been dedicated to providing health care services and education.

Costa Rica's disarmed democracy seems almost too good to be true: the flora and fauna are exotic, the politics enlightened, the society nonviolent, and the natural environment protected. The population consists largely of a middle-class society with only a sprinkling of the very rich and very poor. Clearly, here are people who love their land. Pura Vida!

~

Chapter 28

ST. KITTS AND NEVIS - LITTLE NATION FIGHTS BACK

No part of the New World has suffered more brutal environmental change than the Lesser Antilles, the 400-mile island chain stretching from the Virgin Islands to Barbados.

So says environmentalist and sailor Roger Stone, a senior fellow of the World Wildlife Fund and the Conservation Foundation. During a nine-month cruise in the Caribbean, Stone poked his 38-foot Alden-designed sailboat, *Sanderling*, into polluted bays and blighted coves throughout the islands to document the devastating effects of human interference with nature.

Colonial Destruction

Stone observed that for 300 years during the colonial period, land on the islands was clear-cut and overstressed by the cultivation of tobacco, cotton, and sugarcane. Furthermore, transatlantic arrivals introduced dogs, cats, goats, and monkeys that competed with native wildlife, while exotic European plants pushed aside indigenous vegetation.

Beginning in the 1950s, another environmental onslaught was led by developers whose indiscriminate bulldozing reshaped natural coastlines and converted wildlife habitats into luxury resorts. Pressure from the tourism industry greatly depleted the conch and lobster fisheries, while modern banana plantations pushed deforestation farther up mountain slopes.

Today, however, the local people are speaking out to halt the destruction of their fragile island ecosystems. One of the most successful mergers of environmental preservation and economic development has evolved on the islands of St. Kitts and Nevis, which were once world leaders in sugarcane cultivation.

Two-Island Federation

St. Kitts and Nevis, now a tiny two-island federation—an independent British Commonwealth country since 1983 and the smallest sovereign state in the Western Hemisphere—exists today much like the Caribbean of the 1950s: uncluttered, uncrowded, and virtually undiscovered. The nation's 48,000 inhabitants, who rank second in literacy in the Caribbean, enjoy a rural village lifestyle that has little poverty or unemployment.

Thanks to the rugged terrain of St. Kitts and Nevis that blocks access to miles of beaches, developers bypassed the country during the rush to construct tourist destinations for winter-weary travelers from the north. Recreational divers have also been slow to discover the country's rich network of reefs, walls, coral grottos, and old wrecks. Although archival records list more than 390 wrecks between 1492 and 1825 in coastal waters, divers have generally opted instead for the more heavily advertised underwater attractions of nearby St. Martin, Antigua, Barbuda, and Guadeloupe.

The two-island nation is shaped like an exclamation mark. Long, slender St. Kitts sits across a two-mile strait atop circular Nevis. The islands are closely bonded by the friendly competition of an annual sailing regatta, the country's largest sporting event. Among the divisions is one for fishing boats whose design dates back 500 years to the canoes of the Kalinago, the Indigenous people of the Lesser Antilles.

Both islands are dominated by their own extinct volcanic peaks, beacons for moisture-laden clouds that drench lush rainforests clinging to their upper slopes. Four life zones, each with its unique fauna and flora, are found within a quarter mile of the coast—attractions for the research-minded eco-tourist.

St. Kitts is home to a UNESCO-recognized stone fortress built by the British in 1690. Exhibits detail the harsh lives of slaves forced to construct the seven-foot-thick walls with black volcanic stone. Other exhibits at The National Museum of St. Kitts in its capital, Basseterre, trace the island's history from the Kalinago people through the enslavement and plantation era up to independence in 1983.

The other main attraction is the old eighteen-mile narrow-gauge train, billed as the "Last Railway in the West Indies," which offers scenic tours around a northern portion of St. Kitts. Established in 1926, the railway was used for sugarcane transport until the last crop in 2005.

Drawing the Line in the Sand

With fewer than twenty small country-style inns, St. Kitts and Nevis have lately been targeted as the newest destinations for large-scale tourist developments. A recently completed road on St. Kitts penetrates the natural blockade of steep hills, opening up one-third of the island's southeast coast, a region fringed with some of the finest beaches and most diverse underwater marine habitats in the world. Developers have gobbled up waterfront properties and are poised to begin construction.

But government authorities, armed with an Environmental Country Profile developed by the Caribbean Conservation Society and funded by the U.S. Agency for International Development, anticipated this move by several years and were waiting to regulate the developers before permitting bulldozers ashore. As a safeguard to ensure environmental law and order, the country has enacted some of the toughest environmental regulations in the Caribbean. Pesticide laws, endangered species acts, an anti-litter law, and fish-protection legislation are all on the books. Even more far-reaching, the National Conservation and Environmental Protection Act enables the National Conservation Commission to take whatever steps necessary to prevent damage to the nation's ecosystems.

Reefs, Seagrass, and Sea Turtles

Some observers contend that the environmental protection laws of St. Kitts and Nevis are too severe. However, a spokesperson for the Commission responds emphatically, "We live here and don't want our homes destroyed. We're preserving our island for ourselves and our children."

The St. Kitts and Nevis government is not alone in standing up to those who would harm the environment in the name of progress. Citizen activist groups are adamant about protecting their islands' fragile ecosystems. Both the Nevis Historical and Conservation Society and St. Christopher National Trust circulate periodic environmental newsletters to all schools and businesses. These publications discuss reef protection, solid waste disposal, water conservation practices, wetlands preservation, bird monitoring, and marine habitat protection, along with other ecological issues. Environmental awards are regularly bestowed upon individuals, businesses, and communities. There's even an Environmental Hall of Fame!

Nowhere have preservation efforts by the government and citizenry been more focused than along the coastline where the proposed hotels and resorts are to be built. A near-shore, intricate reef system offers some of the best scuba diving in the world. Artificial reefs have been created and regulations established to protect conch, juvenile lobsters, and turtles. Four species of sea turtles—all protected under the Protocol for Protection of the Wider Caribbean Region—are found in the waters of St. Kitts and Nevis. Beds of seagrass are closely monitored to ensure the large migratory turtle population continues to thrive in the islands' bays.

The country's three underwater dive operators begin each trip to the reefs with lectures warning divers not to touch the coral or disturb the marine life, and they all refuse to take anyone with a speargun. Kenneth Samuel, founder of Kenneth Dive Center on St. Kitts, has placed more than fifty mooring buoys over dive sites to protect them from anchor damage. When anchoring is necessary, he instructs his dive masters to descend with the anchors to position them away from the reefs.

Negotiating with Giants

Visiting cruise ships are restricted to areas where their anchors can do no harm, and mooring buoys have been proposed for anchorages near reefs. Years ago, operators of luxury liners threatened to bypass the islands unless a deep-water channel and an extended pier were installed, so passengers could disembark directly on land. Government authorities, having assessed the adverse impact this construction would have on the marine environment, initially opposed any such installation. After several years of negotiations, however, the government, recognizing the potential economic benefit, authorized dredging to allow large cruise ships shore access at a single area on each island.

One marina construction proposal was dismissed when the developer planned to dredge a red mangrove swamp. But marina construction remains a high government priority, and many smaller marinas have been built in recent years to accommodate the burgeoning traffic of cruising sailors aboard charter yachts from neighboring islands.

When four-mile-long Pinney's Beach on Nevis began to recede rapidly in the mid–1980s, the problem was traced to the new pier half a mile away in the Nevis capital of Charlestown. Studies showed that the rock-filled jetty deflected coastal currents, causing them to eat away at the popular beach, then considered the most eroded beach in the Caribbean. Learning from this experience, the government prohibited the Four Seasons Resort, one of the country's first luxury resorts, from adopting this berm-type construction method for its dock. The contractor was told to install pilings so as not to disturb the coastal currents. Negotiations on this and other points lasted almost three years before construction of the resort was allowed to begin, all to ensure minimal environmental impact.

When similar sand erosion problems occurred at the west end of the island, a noted coastal protection expert from the British Virgin Islands traced the problem to rock moles: solid stone jetties jutting perpendicular from the beach of the Nisbet Plantation Beach Club. The owners of the elegant Country House Inn immediately removed the problem-causing rock jetties and rebuilt two others angled slightly into the prevailing current.

David Has Stood Up to Invading Goliaths

Beach mining, though illegal, takes an even greater toll on the coastal sand than erosion does. Midnight backhoe raids frequently target beaches to mine this non-replenishable resource for cinder-block manufacture and concrete construction. To control this abuse, several environmental groups have developed alternative inland sand quarries to provide sand for construction.

Perhaps the world should pay more attention to this two-island sovereign federation. Government leaders of St. Kitts and Nevis have long recognized that their economy, previously dependent on the now-in-decline sugar industry, must refocus on tourism as its mainstay. Today their long-standing tough stance on environmental protection allows them to offer an attraction no other Caribbean island can claim—namely, a largely undisturbed tropical environment.

Over the decades, this diminutive David has stood up to invading Goliaths from the outside world—the would-be colonial rulers, giant cruise lines, and powerful resort developers. St. Kitts and Nevis have ultimately prevailed in protecting their natural environment for the benefit of its people, both present and future generations.

Miles of beaches fringe jungle lowlands

Typical plantation great house with wrap-around veranda

Chapter 29

SEA OF CORTEZ - SAILING IN STEINBECK'S WAKE

"Let us go into the Sea of Cortez, realizing that we become forever a part of it. This smooth blue water runs out of time very quickly, and a kind of dream sets in. The abundance of life here gives one an exuberance, a feeling of fullness and richness."
The Log from the Sea of Cortez, John Steinbeck

It may be blatant showmanship, but charter skippers in the Sea of Cortez can seldom resist the opportunity to show off to customers new to the area. The first night out to sea, a skipper will serve drinks, then wait until everyone settles back to watch the tequila skies of a Mexican sunset. Before long, someone asks if there are snacks. Grabbing a mask and snorkel, our performer flips overboard, returning minutes later to surprise the charterers with a selection of hatchet clams, scallops, and oysters. Such is the bounty of the Sea of Cortez!

The Peninsula of Paradoxes

Teeming with marine life, the Sea of Cortez, sometimes referred to as the Gulf of California, has changed little since John Steinbeck noted its abundance in his 1940 marine biology expedition travelogue. For decades a wealth of marlin, yellowtail, dorado, bonito, and shellfish have lured anglers and divers to the lower Sea of Cortez. But recently, word has spread about a different richness along the east coast of the Baja Peninsula—word of steady winds blowing through a 250-mile chain of plum-colored islands with anchorages rivaling the finest in the world.

Over the years, I have sailed in many of the world's prime cruising areas: the British Virgin Islands, Australia's Whitsunday archipelago, Chesapeake Bay, Denmark's North Sea islands, and the Pacific Northwest's San Juan and Gulf Islands. All these destinations offer marinas, restaurants, and marine services.

In contrast, I learn that Baja California offers hundreds of miles of isolation and dozens of uninhabited islands. For many cruising sailors, this would be a disadvantage, but for adventurers, this is an attraction—cruising grounds the way they were meant to be—a place where one can sail for days without seeing anyone except the occasional fisherman who will sell a few lobsters or fish for bargain prices.

Three friends from my hometown join me for a ten-day cruise starting in La Paz, the boating center for the region and capital of Baja California Sur. After a turbulent, not-so-peaceful past, La Paz—the name means "peace"—is now a laid-back city of 310,000. Paceños describe their city in Ps—a peaceful port city on a peninsula in the Pacific known for pirates, priests, privateers, prospectors, plagues, and pearls. (La Paz is the setting for Steinbeck's short story, "The Pearl.") By the end of our trip, my friends and I add another P—Paradise.

Cliffs, Cactus, and Quiet

After provisioning at the well-stocked CCC (Centro Comercial California) Food Emporium, we motor out of La Paz Harbor on an elegant, spacious Hylas 44 chartered from Palmira Marina's bareboat division. This center-cockpit offshore cruiser features graceful lines with a sleek, low profile and carries a mini-winged fin keel.

The five-mile channel, which hugs the city's attractive Malecón (boardwalk), has a bit of historical whimsy. In preparation for Queen Elizabeth's visit on the royal yacht *Britannia* some years ago, the twisting, narrow channel was straightened and upgraded with freshly painted red and green buoys. However, the upgrades extended only from the channel's mouth to the municipal marina in front of the Abaroa Boat Yard where the queen disembarked. Beyond this point, the winding channel, with its old, rusty buoys, remains unchanged, presumably not to be updated until some other dignitary travels its full length.

Once clear of the harbor, we hoist sail in a brisk northwesterly. Beaches and small fishing villages slip away behind us as we head into the open expanse of the sea. A twenty-mile sail brings us to the island of Espiritu Santo. As the island's hazy mountain contours sharpen, we discern burnt-orange slabs of rock jutting out of the sea. Along the island's shoreline, deep coves twist back to white beaches edging quiet, isolated bays. High above, giant cardon cacti, towering up to sixty feet, stand guard over parched desert hills dotted with patches of prickly scrub brush.

After passing Espiritu Santo, we hug the shoreline of neighboring Isla Partida all afternoon searching for the perfect anchorage for the night. Depth is not a problem except where the water color indicates the obvious. No need to consult charts to decide which cove is the best choice—they are all perfect. Steep cliffs offering protection from the prevailing winds surround small, golden-sand beaches all along Partida's coast. The beauty of each cove makes it difficult to decide. After making an arbitrary selection and dropping anchor, we swim, wiggle our toes in the sand, collect shells, and allow ourselves to be absorbed into the isolation and the quiet. This, after all, is the reason we are here.

San Francisquito—A Jumping Bean Anchorage

Leaving Isla Partida the next morning, we continue our upwind course, heading twenty miles north to the tiny island of San Francisquito. Predictable sunny skies and gentle 15-knot winds make us wonder why we had troubled to pack any clothes other than our bathing suits. Languid living quickly becomes routine.

With great expanses of open water between islands, we decide to get our money's worth from the fishing licenses Mexican law requires of all boaters. Within the hour we get a strike on our hand line, validating the guarantee given to us by our Palmira check-out agent. Reeling in a twenty-five-pound bullnose dolphin (which lives up to its Hawaiian name, mahi-mahi, meaning "strong-strong") is challenging and exciting. But to our surprise, when we pull it on board, the middle one-third of the fish's body is missing! Some enormous round jaw has made a clean chomp.

Then we remember the six-foot-long hammerhead sharks we saw hung up to dry on makeshift crucifixes at the villages we passed yesterday. No worries, however. Shark attacks on humans are unknown here where for decades skindivers have been diving without concern in these clear waters with 100 feet of visibility.

By afternoon, golden beaches begin to appear ahead on the horizon as we near our destination. In the evening, San Francisquito, a tiny jumping bean of an island, provides our most serene anchorage of the trip. To the southwest is a perfect crescent beach protected by the characteristic sheer cliffs where cormorants and brown pelicans swoop and glide in the updrafts. To the north, protection is provided by a mangrove peninsula. Apart from a flashing light on the southern cusp, no hint of human life is evident here or anywhere in the vicinity. By government decree, all the islands are uninhabited. One benefit: no evidence of plastic litter, garbage, or man-made debris. Only glistening shells jumbled among grains of sand litter these pristine shores.

Over the course of a few days, we crisscross between the mainland peninsula and the scattered islands lying off Baja's east coast. Dark ruffled waters contrasting with shimmering golden beaches form a perfect backdrop for sailing at its finest, and here and there along our way, we drop anchor to explore coves and bays.

One day we discover a mangrove swamp extending inland on Isla San José. Another day we explore old salt ponds carefully cut into the landscape. As we dinghy inland through the mangroves, we come upon Indian mounds and 800-year-old cave paintings. Along the mainland coast, we visit fishing villages where local inhabitants are happy to sell us fish caught earlier in the day. Although these villagers survive on centuries-old fishing methods, sixty-five-horsepower outboard engines mounted on the sterns of fiberglass 22-foot pangas hint at the encroachment of modern times.

Austere Land, Abundant Sea

The barren browns of rugged desert and jagged mountains provide a dramatic contrast with the bright blues of waters that harbor a great wealth of marine life. Although the islands themselves appear barren, we discover they are not entirely deserted. Hidden in shady cracks and under sunbaked rocks are scaly, menacing creatures that, as we chance upon them, slither into crevices. Scorpions, lizards, kangaroo rats, toads, and snakes—including the indigenous rattlesnake—convince us this land is not a friendly place.

While most cruising areas elsewhere are surrounded by lush, inviting landscapes, Baja is no garden spot. Only a few yards above the narrow beaches, one finds harsh, inhospitable desert where droughts can last for years. Such vegetation, as exists here—mostly cactus and chaparral, the heat-tortured plant life that has evolved to survive in Baja's tough environment of desert and mountain—is sparse. Though this parched, rugged landscape reaching almost down to the water's edge may be brown and barren, my friends and I nevertheless find it strangely, savagely beautiful.

In contrast to the barrenness of the land itself, the birds in the area are a delight. Brown pelicans—the clowns—transform at any moment from lazy gliders into screaming bombers, wings tucked tight as they zoom in upon a glint in the water. All the other birds—frigates, herons, storm petrels, terns, and brown boobies—are more subtle performers, soaring, gliding, and weaving in and out among the cliffs.

Locals claim the meagerness of the land and the richness of the water and air are simply Nature's way of maintaining a balance: on land, no excesses; in the sea, plenty.

With almost 600 species of fish, the variety and abundance of sea life are overwhelming. We soon lose our earlier excitement about fishing because we can haul in as much as we can eat without ever having to wait more than an hour to reel in a fresh catch.

Although we see no whales, which are said to be common in these waters, playful encounters with porpoises, mantas, turtles, and seals are daily delights. The highlight of our trip is snorkeling with sea lions at the rookery on Los Islotes. Hesitant at first, the curious creatures ultimately can't resist the fun of playing tag. As they become bolder, they swim straight toward us at full speed, only to blow bubbles in our masked faces before turning away at the last instant.

Where Geology Meets Weather

Geologists tell us the Sea of Cortez is one of the youngest seas on the planet. The 760-mile trench extends from the mouth of the Colorado River, fifty miles south of Arizona, down to the tip of Baja. Volcanic upheavals, geologic uplifts, and the ubiquitous southern extension of the San Andreas Fault worked together to split the Baja Peninsula from Mexico's mainland twenty million years ago, leaving behind debris of scattered islands in this northward-poking finger of the Pacific Ocean. The 3,000-foot peaks of the Sierra de la Giganta Range, a jumble of cliffs, volcanic peaks, and lava sheets strung along the coast of the peninsula, create an imposing rampart holding back the wild Pacific storms blowing in from the west.

The best sailing in the Sea of Cortez is in the southern third where meteorology and geology converge to create a near-perfect cruising area. Farther to the north, protected anchorages are few, and winds tend to be light and shifty. To the south of Baja's tip, the Mexican coast is again short on harbors, and, worse yet, the coast is exposed to the full fury of the Pacific. But the tranquil middle region where my companions and I sail is a sailor's dream come true: winter winds here are steady from the north at 10–20 knots; warm waters are protected; and secure anchorages beckon on all sides of the islands. Unlike the upper Sea of Cortez, tides and currents are negligible. A dozen major islands and more than 100 smaller islets invite exploration.

The only problem can be the Coromuel wind—a south to southwest wind with speeds up to 45 knots—that can blow throughout the night. However, the Coromuel occurs primarily in late spring and summer on the Bay of La Paz. Because we sail in the winter, the Coromuel is no issue for us.

When our cruise ends back at Palmira Marina, we find that readjusting to civilization and by-the-clock life is a bit of a challenge. We have sailed and explored a somewhat stark and compelling face of Nature in what, for us, is a timeless, isolated paradise. John Steinbeck was right. Here, indeed, is abundance—nothing is missing.

~

Approaching Espiritu Santo

Cardon cacti march from mountains to seashore

Hole-in-the-Rock, Partida Island

Mariachi band performs on jetty

Playing with sea lions, Los Islotes

Quiet anchorage, Partida Island

Chapter 30

EVEREST OF SAILING - BOC CHALLENGE

One day, while I'm reading a sailing magazine at home in Seattle, a short news article catches my eye. Little do I realize at the time how this notice will lead to one of the greatest travel adventures of my life! The article refers to a farmer from inland Washington State who plans to enter a single-handed sailing race around the world.

First, I can't imagine how a farmer, presumably with little sailing experience—let alone knowledge of ocean navigation—would dare take on a challenge like this. I, a lifelong sailor with many blue-water miles under my belt—and my sailing friends with similar experience—would never consider such a voyage.

Second, I don't understand why I haven't heard about this upcoming race, which bills itself as the "Everest of Sailing." I regularly read all the monthly boating magazines. Why have I never seen anything about this proposed around-the-world race before now?

The Race is On

In the days that follow, I dig a little deeper and discover that such a race is indeed being organized, but little promotion has gone out. The organizer of the event is Robin Knox-Johnston, a famous English sailor who was the first to complete a single-handed nonstop circumnavigation in 1969. Robin has lined up a sponsor for the race, British Oxygen Corporation (BOC), a U.K.-based industrial gases producer. The event is to be called the "BOC Challenge."

After further research, I learn that, despite the lack of publicity, this event has captured the imagination of sailors around the world. Entries have been received from France, Finland, Czechoslovakia (now Czech Republic and Slovakia), Australia, Japan, England, Canada, and the U.S. The competition will include two classes—50-footers and 60-footers—with only minimal restrictions on design. I suspect the entrants must be a special breed of men (all male), not typical recreational sailors. Rather, these will be sailors who have a daredevil thirst for a challenging adventure.

The event has also attracted the world's most prominent naval architects representing as many countries as the contestants themselves. The challenge for the yacht designers is to create a hull and rigging configuration that can stand up to the rigors of the oceans, particularly the Southern Ocean encircling Antarctica with its constantly swirling gale-force winds and turbulent waves that can exceed 100 feet.

Furthermore, the steering controls, navigation electronics, and operating systems must be designed for a single individual, securely ensconced in a protected cockpit. Because the skipper will be exposed to wild seas breaking across the deck while he is changing sails to adjust to varying sea and wind conditions, harnesses, lifelines, and tethers must be laid out to maximize safety without restricting his movements while he sorts through halyards, sheets, and sails.

The race is scheduled to start in August 1986 in Newport, Rhode Island, with three stopovers: Cape Town, South Africa; Sydney, Australia; and Rio de Janeiro, Brazil, before finishing back at Newport. Although the 27,000-mile event (including stopovers), expected to finish nine months later in May 1987, is billed as a "Race around the World," when I study the routing, I realize it will actually be a race around Antarctica.

The first leg will follow, as close as weather conditions allow, the great circle route from Newport to Cape Town. The strategy for the next leg: head south from the Cape of Good Hope and Cape Agulhas, at the southern tip of Africa toward Antarctica into the Southern Ocean as far as the skippers dare. Then they will head east as they dodge icebergs and contend with treacherous seas that constantly encircle the icy continent, where knockdowns are common and a collision with an iceberg can sink a boat in no time. Once through this turmoil, the skippers will turn north toward Sydney.

The challenge of the third leg is to round treacherous Cape Horn, where hundreds of ships have been lost over the ages. If sailors navigate too close to the Horn, they risk being swept by unpredictable, turbulent tidal currents into scattered rocks and shoals. If they stay safely off the coast, it will cost them several extra days to cover the additional distance.

The shortest distance to Rio de Janeiro would be hugging the east coast of South America, but this must be balanced with stronger winds and favorable currents farther offshore.

The final leg is the home run back to Newport, with the challenge of finding the optimum routing to cross the windless doldrums and enter the north-flowing Gulf Stream.

Planning My Strategy

I learn about this amazing single-handed sailing race around the world about a year before the event is scheduled to begin and expect to receive details in press releases over the following months. Surprisingly, the boating publications in the spring and summer leading up to the event all fail to even mention it. Either minimal interest—along with a lack of promotion—keeps this first-of-its-kind event out of the press, which is hard to believe. At this point, I contact the race organizers in England and am told, yes, the race is still on, and yes, BOC is the title sponsor.

Then my mental wheels start clicking. If this extraordinary event really does take place, and if the boating press either doesn't know about it or doesn't care, here is an outstanding opportunity for me as a relatively new boating writer and photographer. Once again, I contact the race sponsors in England—this time to request details on the timing of each leg and exact location of the stopovers. The starting gun is to be fired at 3:00 p.m. on August 30, 1986, and the first leg to Cape Town is expected to take six to seven weeks for the first boats to arrive.

Now it's just a matter of waiting to see if the race really will take place. Sure enough, I subsequently learn that on the scheduled date, twenty-four contenders sail out of Narragansett Bay from Newport Harbor. Destination: Cape Town. The major U.S. sailing magazines send reporters to cover the start, but considering that eight nations are represented, it's surprising that none of the foreign boating publications show up. During the months leading up to the start, I have become more and more excited about the possibility of reporting on the boats, not at the start or finish, but at the stopovers along the route. Time now to take action.

Securing Assignments and Flights

I quickly send a number of faxes (email is still in its infancy) to all the major sailing publications in the countries represented by the participants. I don't request financial support but instead ask if they would be interested in photos and articles about their skippers at each of the three race stopovers. I explain the offer depends upon my arranging flights to each location. Within two weeks, I receive affirmative responses from every magazine I contact.

Only two major airlines (both foreign carriers) offer convenient connections from the U.S. to Cape Town. Both depart from JFK Airport. South African Airways schedules nonstop flights and British Airways flies via London. Opting for the most direct route, I decide to contact the South African carrier. I figure I can afford to buy my own air ticket from Seattle to New York but can't begin to afford the cost of the intercontinental flight. So, I revert to my business-school days to make a plan outlining what I could offer in exchange for a free intercontinental flight.

After a lot of back-and-forth with the media relations supervisor, South African Airways offers a free ticket to fly from New York to Cape Town. Elated, I arrange for my flight from Seattle to New York.

Upon arriving at JFK, however, I am faced with a major setback. The very day I am scheduled to catch the Cape Town flight, President Reagan announces new sanctions against South Africa, and the national airline immediately loses its landing rights at JFK. The U.S. Comprehensive Anti-Apartheid Act of 1986 bans all flights by South African–owned carriers, including SAA. Quite apologetic, the airline spokesman says the best he can offer is a flight from London to Cape

Town, but I would have to make my own way to England to catch the flight.

Stranded, I call the JFK media relations manager at British Airways and, after explaining my predicament, ask for the cheapest ticket to London. I anticipate I will have to pay because there is no time to make a professional presentation of my credentials as a journalist. However, the BA agent makes an unexpected proposal. He offers me a free ticket to London. Then he insists I fly with BA from London all the way to South Africa, so he won't have to share credit with a rival carrier. He points out that this routing has the advantage that British Airways can fly south from London directly over the African continent, whereas South African Airways, because of overflight restrictions by many African countries, is required to fly around the continent over the ocean, making for a much longer flight. To make a good situation even better, the BA agent offers me a free ticket on my return to fly nonstop from London home to Seattle, bypassing New York entirely. Needless to say, I immediately accept this wonderful offer.

Cape Town

Cape Town has to be one of the world's most beautiful cities. As our flight approaches, I recognize Table Mountain, a prominent flat-topped landmark overlooking the city, and the Twelve Apostles range, a backdrop to the city nestled around Table Bay.

As I deplane, I look around for a clock to reset my watch from London time. I have a momentary lapse when I realize that both cities are on the exact same time—except six months apart! The only time difference is that I had left London in the autumn and arrive now at Cape Town in springtime.

A half-hour taxi ride deposits me at the Royal Cape Yacht Club, where the early race finishers are busy repairing their boats after the ocean's beatings. Crowds of spectators line the docks awaiting the next arrivals. The skippers, who have been at sea for more than forty days without talking to anyone on this 7,100-mile first leg, appear so hyped up that I decide to bide my time a few days before interviewing them.

Besides recounting their adventures to friends and families who have flown in to greet them, their immediate priority is to repair and replace broken equipment and reprovision for the next leg. The layover is scheduled for three weeks, so not until a week has passed and the frantic activity subsides do I begin to interview the eighteen skippers still in the race.

And indeed, they have many fascinating stories to tell. Two Class II boats from Finland are in a personal competition to determine who will be the first Finn to go down in the history books to complete a single-handed circumnavigation. The rivalry is particularly intense because one competitor is a so-called Swedish-Finn, whose ancestors once ruled Finland, and the other is of pure Finnish heritage. (The Swedish-Finn finishes overall in third place in 168 days, beating his compatriot by a mere seven days.)

Equally intense is the rivalry between the two South African entries in Class I 60-footers, pitting a young commander in the South African Navy against a more senior and well-seasoned sailor who has weathered tens of thousands of miles of ocean sailing. (The younger of the two South Africans finishes fifth in 147 days, beating his elder by 16 days.)

A major controversy arises when two skippers accuse the Czechoslovakian entrant of cheating by using his engine as propulsion. Before the start of the race, the organizers wrapped the propeller shafts of each boat with a seal that would be broken if the engine was used for any purpose except to charge the yacht's batteries.

Because each boat is required to call in its position daily during a mid-morning radio schedule, and because of the pattern of daily Argos satellite positions for all boats, contenders can monitor one another's locations. As three boats were semi-drifting through the doldrums, where light puffs of wind come and go, the Czech yacht sailing between the other two was making steady progress. The other boats' skippers speculate that the Czech skipper, an engineer, must have devised a way to bypass the seal. Although most feel sure he cheated, at the official hearing the jury dismisses the protest because of insufficient evidence.

Six of the twenty-four starters who departed Newport dropped out during the first leg. As repairs on the remaining contenders' yachts near completion, skippers help each other get ready for the next leg. But motives aren't entirely altruistic. They all know that if anyone has a major breakdown in the raging storms of the Roaring Forties, Furious Fifties, and perhaps farther south into the Screaming Sixties (as sailors commonly call them), only their fellow contenders could have a chance to rescue them.

Continuing my interviews with the solo sailors, I learn that the first leg had been near mayhem for the fleet. At the start on Narragansett Bay in Newport, collisions with spectator boats caused two competitors to delay their start for a day while making repairs. In the third week, Hurricane Earl wreaked havoc, causing several knockdowns (mast and sails dip into the water temporarily until the boat rights itself). When one of the 50-footers pitchpoled (end over end) in the South Atlantic, the mast bent into an "S." The skipper jury-rigged his spars and limped into Rio, where he notified race headquarters that he was withdrawing from the race. One of the 50-

footers hit a submerged object at night, believed to be a sleeping whale, and sank. The skipper was rescued by helicopter from his life raft.

One of the French competitors lost his autohelm and steered with the tiller day and night for seven days until he arrived bleary-eyed at Cape Town. Two other 50-footers withdrew due to rigging failure. When his satnav (satellite navigation unit) failed at the start, an American skipper had to navigate to Cape Town by sextant, relying on the sun and stars.

Another sailor lost his engine in an electrical fire, and his water-driven generator failed at the same time, leaving him without power. He managed to get the water generator working by employing a sardine can as a makeshift spare part. One contestant fell through a hatch and couldn't move for several hours. For the next three days, he could only crawl around his boat as he sailed toward Bermuda to receive medical attention.

Another skipper landed in Brazil to repair his rudder and, after continuing, stopped again when his keel was in danger of falling off. Another withdrawal. The Japanese entry encountered rigging and steering problems, and he too was forced to withdraw. The Australian skipper lost his mast near the equator and diverted to Recife, Brazil, to await arrival of a spar. However, the mainsail did not fit the new mast, so after further delays to make modifications, he raced down the South Atlantic and joined the fleet only a few days before the start of the next leg.

When asked why he entered this race, one of the American competitors said, "I am doing this for three reasons: I'm excited about adventure and competition; I love sailing; and given the choice, I prefer to be alone." After hearing these stories, I quickly repackage them into articles and send them along with photos from Cape Town to the sailors' home magazines and newspapers.

A Short Diversion

Deciding to take a break from my interviews, I contact Brian Steele, a South African classmate from Stanford Business School. At dinner he recounts an interesting story about his work as chief financial officer for a major South African conglomerate. With many U.S. companies in the process of divesting their South African holdings because of the apartheid boycott, Brian, with his knowledge of American business practices picked up during our business school days, negotiated the buyout for pennies on the dollar of major South African–based U.S. corporates like Merck and PepsiCo. The negotiations mainly took place in the U.S., and he said the Americans seemed comfortable dealing with a management team whose CFO was a Stanford MBA and whose core values relating to equality and non-discrimination were acceptable. Later, as the apartheid era was ending, Brian negotiated the sale, this time at full value, of the same divisions that he had earlier purchased, back to the U.S. parent companies.

Leg Two to Sydney

Six of the twenty-four starters are out of the race, which leaves nine entries in each of the two divisions. The first leg had essentially proved to be a qualifier for the rigors that lie ahead in this 27,000-nautical-mile race.

As the start of the second leg draws closer, contenders are constantly checking weather conditions in the Southern Ocean. How far to head south is the question on everyone's mind when they sail through the notorious forties toward the foreboding latitudes farther south. Some maintain that 42° is far enough. Others intend to push the limits of high 40°s and low 50°s.

How much fear and anxiety can these intrepid sailors endure?

With a farewell send-off by hundreds of spectator boats on November 15, the fleet gets underway to the south with the early arrivals expected in Sydney by mid-December. A day later, I'm on a British Airways aircraft flying home to Seattle, happy to enjoy my creature comforts, including the first-class seats they offered, as I think in horror of the rigors that lie ahead for the solo skippers.

The twenty-two-hour flight, which included a London stopover, is made especially comfortable with endless servings of tasty food and South African wines—wines no longer allowed to be imported to the States due to the embargo.

Once home, I need a week to recover from jet lag and readjust to being back in autumn again. After spending weeks sorting out my notes and photos, I send off another dozen feature articles to sailing magazines around the world profiling the incredible stories of the BOC Challenge's brazen sailors. Naturally, each article conveys due credit to British Airways for making these articles possible.

Shortly after the start of the second leg of the race, 50-knot storm winds sweep down off the Cape Peninsula, catching the skippers unprepared. Many boats are knocked down and damaged—autopilots are broken, rigging is weakened, equipment is lost—forcing several to return to port for repairs. Just past the halfway point when another storm bears down on the fleet, several boats are rolled 360 degrees, and two pitchpole and capsize but then right themselves. Nevertheless, all boats somehow survive the treacherous southern seas as they dodge icebergs along the way.

By now my credentials as a sailing journalist are so well established that Qantas Airways provides complimentary air tickets from Seattle to Sydney to meet the solo skippers upon their arrival. Whereas in Cape Town I had to fend for myself for accommodations, the Intercontinental Hotel at Circular Quay in Sydney is responsive to my request and hosts me for the duration of my stay with the tacit understanding that they will be acknowledged in my subsequent articles.

In a semi-crippled state, the fleet approaches the hazardous Bass Strait, 500 miles of steep, choppy waves between Tasmania and the Australian mainland. Funneling, constricted winds blast between the two land masses while savage rips and crosscurrents tear through the meeting zones between the Pacific and Southern Oceans.

The skippers, not daring to get more than one hour of sleep each night in this section of the journey, thread their way through heavy commercial traffic in crowded shipping lanes and among the numerous oil rigs and low-lying, fog-shrouded islands. An American competitor whose mast breaks just 100 miles short of Sydney expects to continue the race after making repairs. But when the repaired mast breaks yet again—his fifth setback since the beginning of the race—the devastated skipper chooses to withdraw and flies home.

Tragedy marks the finish of this leg when, only two days from Sydney, one of the French skippers, who was leading his class, either fell or was swept overboard and lost at sea. This was the first and only loss of life during this demanding event. All the skippers attend a memorial service for the lost sailor, held in a small Sydney chapel overlooking the sea. The sailor's body is never recovered.

With my interviews finished and nothing to do but sit around until the start of the next leg, I discover an opportunity for additional assignments. The stopover in Sydney coincides with the America's Cup Regatta on the other side of the country, at Fremantle, where Dennis Conner's *Stars & Stripes* and the Australian defender *Kookaburra* are sailing match races. Once again through Qantas Airways, I obtain a free flight across the country, where I plan to research an article covering the competition that I could sell to a U.S. sailing publication.

Imagine my surprise upon arriving in Fremantle to discover 2,500 journalists from around the world digging into every angle of the story imaginable. Not only are the world's major boating magazines represented, but their correspondents, all on expense accounts, are booked at the best accommodations, eat at the finest restaurants, rent private chase boats and helicopters to follow the racing, hire local staff to assist with research, and have priority in interviewing the skippers and crew. There was no place for a guy like me on a shoestring budget without an assignment. Goodbye, Fremantle.

On to Rio

On January 18, 1987, hundreds of recreational boaters jam Sydney Harbor to give the fleet a gala send-off as these global gladiators set out for Rio de Janeiro on the third leg of the race. This leg entails rounding Cape Horn, the world's southernmost cape, at the headland of the Tierra del Fuego archipelago of southern Chile, where the Atlantic and Pacific Oceans meet.

Although these waters are particularly hazardous owing to strong winds, large waves, strong currents, and icebergs, only one boat suffers a mishap. The lone Canadian entry, with the youngest skipper at age twenty-seven and the smallest boat at 41 feet, is dismasted. Mounting twin spinnaker poles to fly a small jib, the skipper rounds Cape Horn with this jury-rigged configuration and navigates to the Falkland Islands, where a new mast is waiting. Once underway, he continues on to Rio, but the delay puts him six weeks behind the previous finisher, and when he arrives the fleet has already departed on the final leg back to Newport.

Home to Newport

After the mandatory stopover in Rio to make repairs and re-provision their boats, the skippers set out on April 11 without the

Canadian entry, for the final journey to the finish at Newport. With relatively calm seas and favorable weather conditions, the boats suffer no mishaps along the way. The eight Class I boats all arrive within one day of each other, and the remaining seven Class II contenders arrive within a span of four days.

Determined to finish the race in time for the awards ceremony, the young Canadian skipper waives his right for a seven-day stopover in Rio and immediately takes to the sea again. He arrives at Newport elated to be part of the final celebrations where he is awarded the "Spirit of the BOC Challenge Award" and cited for his outstanding seamanship and spirit of determination.

Having no interest in meeting the fleet at the finish in Newport, I fly home from Rio to Seattle. But I do want to angle a way to attend the final BOC award ceremonies, and, thanks to a major international airline, it becomes possible. When the airline offers me an air ticket from Seattle to London to write an article about yacht cruising in the Baltic Sea, I jump at the opportunity to stopover on the East Coast to attend the BOC Challenge Awards Ceremony.

I have been following these skippers for the past nine months and, from the extensive interviews with each of them at the three stopovers, we've developed strong friendships. The skippers have all thanked me innumerable times for the many feature articles and news reports I submitted to their hometown newspapers and their national sailing magazines. Now I look forward to attending the final gala event as they receive the recognition they each deserve.

Award Ceremonies

Upon my arrival in Newport on May 30, I join 1,000 guests for the festivities in an enormous blue-and-white tent on Goat Island, where the race began last August 30 when twenty-four boats representing eight nations set out on this 27,000-mile Everest of Sailing. Only sixteen boats finished the marathon—six dropped out due to equipment and rigging failure, one sank after hitting an object, and one skipper was lost at sea.

As each skipper proceeds up to the podium to receive his trophy from race chairman Robin Knox-Johnston, he also receives the traditional gold loop earring signifying he has rounded Cape Horn. Tradition has it that it's worn in the ear that faced the Horn as it was rounded. For these sailors it would be the left ear. (If they were to round the Horn twice, once in each direction, they would be entitled to wear a gold loop in each ear.)

A couple of skippers, more interested in rounding the world's five southernmost capes than in winning the race, diverted south of Tasmania to round the South East Cape. (For the sake of completion, the other four capes, which every entry rounded, are Cape Agulhas, South Africa; Cape Horn, Chile; South Cape, New Zealand; and Cape Leeuwin, Australia.)

I had interviewed all the skippers at each stopover in the four-leg event—Cape Town, Sydney, Rio de Janeiro—and had reported their ordeals in the articles I wrote. Throughout the evenings, the skippers would talk readily and with precise detail about the technical aspects of their boats and the race.

Each racer sailed alone, tested to the limits of his skills, stamina, ingenuity, and courage as he faced severe winds, powerful waves, gear failures, injuries, and exhaustion, all while racing against unseen competitors. The race took these men to a region where Nature is without mercy—the Southern Ocean. Waves there tower to 100 feet, knockdowns are common, and drifting icebergs are silent threats. Some dropped out as their boats buckled under the punishment.

The sailors often point out that, although oceans are remote, they're not desolate—day and night they encountered whales, albatrosses, shearwaters, storm petrels, prions (whale birds), and a constant variety of fish and various forms of marine life.

Their biggest concern was pushing the boat hard, and to do so, they must stay physically and mentally fit. Backup equipment was key because everything breaks. With the tragic loss of one sailor, each must come to terms with the race's true challenge: survival.

One French skipper commented, "I feel lonely on land but peacefully alone at sea. I prefer being alone at sea rather than isolated in a city."

The race director, Robin Knox-Johnston, puts the event in stark terms: "We expect casualties; we hope there will be no fatalities. But there can be no chance of triumph without the possibility of tragedy, and no ultimate challenge without ultimate demands."

Once again, I reflect upon that persistent question: What was it that motivated these willing adventurers to risk their lives by participating in this event? When I ask the skippers why they decided to do this, they inevitably fall into a long pause. Fumbling for words, they haltingly mumble something about testing themselves, accepting an ultimate challenge, or living out a dream. But they aren't quite sure. Uncomfortable with this question, they always turn the conversation to a more tangible aspect of the race.

I never push this question because I realize I touch upon something deep within that these intrepid sailors would not—or could not—share, perhaps because they themselves don't fully understand the real reason they wanted to undertake this "Everest of Sailing."

Overall and each leg detailed results:

Class 1 yachts:

Place	Final	1st leg	2nd leg	3rd leg	4th leg
1	**Philippe Jeantot** 134d 05h 23m 56s	**John Martin** 42d 01h 10m 36s	**Tit. Lamazou** 28d 07h 13m 22s	**Phil. Jeantot** 36d 17h 46m 53s	**John Martin** 26d 00h 50m 20s
2	**Titouan Lamazou** 137d 17h 36m 06s	**Philippe Jeantot** 42d 16h 57m 35s	**Philippe Jeantot** 28d 12h 52m 43s	**Tit. Lamazou** 36d 21h 15m 45s	**Tit. Lamazou** 26d 05h 02m 37s
3	**Jean-Yves Terlain** 146d 10h 58m 10s	**Guy Bernardin** 43d 05h 58m 43s	**Jean-Y. Terlain** 31d 04h 55m 25s	**Jean-Y. Terlain** 40d 09h 54m 18s	**Philippe Jeantot** 26d 05h 46m 45s
4	**Guy Bernardin** 146d 12h 51m 34s	**Warren Luhrs** 44d 17h 41m 39s	**Ian Kiernan** 32d 11h 41m 54s	**Guy Bernardin** 43d 20h 52m 50s	**Guy Bernardin** 26d 05h 59m 37s
5	**John Martin** 147d 08h 14m 00s	**Tit. Lamazou** 46d 08h 04m 22s	**Guy Bernardin** 33d 01h 01m 14s	**John Martin** 43d 22h 56m 44s	**Ian Kiernan** 26d 06h 17m 51s
6	**Ian Kiernan** 156d 16h 03m 38s	**Jean-Y. Terlain** 47d 16h 44m 50s	**David White** 34d 14h 23m 25s	**Bertie Reed** 45d 23h 10m 31s	**Bertie Reed** 26d 10h 42m 54s
7	**Bertie Reed** 163d 21h 42m 56s	**Bertie Reed** 50d 17h 39m 48s	**John Martin** 35d 04h 16m 20s	**Ian Kiernan** 46d 18h 43m 23s	**Jean-Y. Terlain** 27d 03h 23m 37s
8	**David White** 164d 23h 05m 22s	**Ian Kiernan** 51d 03h 20m 30s	**Warren Luhrs** 37d 15h 00m 24s	**David White** 51d 08h 56m 20s	**David White** 27d 06h 25m 17s
9		**David White** 51d 17h 20m 20s	**Bertie Reed** 40d 18h 09m 43s		
10		**John Biddlecombe**			
11		**Rich. McBride**			

John Biddlecombe - after many problems withdrew at Cape Town
Richard McBride - broke his mast during the first leg and had to stop at Recife, Brazil for repair
Warren Luhrs - broke his mast few hundred miles before Sydney during second leg

BOC Class II Yachts

Class 2 yachts:

Place	Final	1st leg	2nd leg	3rd leg	4th leg
1	**Mike Plant 157d 11h 44m 44s**	**Jac. de Roux 45d 14h 47m 10s**	**Mike Plant 34d 16h 03m 52s**	**Jean Luc Van Den Heede 42d 21h 56m 09s**	**Jean Luc Van Den Heede 26d 21h 10m 20s**
2	**Jean Luc Van Den Heede 161d 07h 37m 16s**	**Mike Plant 47d 15h 30m 30s**	**Harry Harkimo 36d 09h 34m 11s**	**Mike Plant 47d 03h 00m 00s**	**Mike Plant 28d 01h 13m 22s**
3	**Harry Harkimo 168d 09h 21m 13s**	**Jean Luc Van Den Heede 51d 11h 16m 55s**	**Jean Luc Van Den Heede 36d 17h 43m 52s**	**Hal Roth 51d 08h 47m 17s**	**Harry Harkimo 28d 01h 28m 13s**
4	**Hal Roth 171d 20h 05m 38s**	**Rich. Konkolski 51d 11h 34m 15s**	**Mark Schrader 38d 09h 02m 20s**	**Harry Harkimo 51d 10h 42m 20s**	**Hal Roth 29d 13h 21m 39s**
5	**Rich. Konkolski 172d 06h 41m 03s**	**Harry Harkimo 52d 11h 36m 29s**	**Hal Roth 38d 09h 43m 25s**	**Rich. Konkolski 51d 11h 25m 58s**	**Pentti Salmi 29d 19h 10m 59s**
6	**Mark Schrader 175d 14h 23m 52s**	**Hal Roth 52d 12h 13m 17s**	**Rich. Konkolski 38d 18h 42m 00s**	**Mark Schrader 52d 08h 42m 24s**	**Mark Schrader 30d 09h 39m 38s**
7	**Pentti Salmi 175d 18h 02m 39s**	**Penti Salmi 53d 18h 55m 22s**	**Pentti Salmi 39d 18h 27m 32s**	**Pentti Salmi 52d 09h 28m 46s**	**Rich. Konkolski 30d 20h 58m 50s**
8	**John Hughes 224d 13h 55m 24s**	**Mark Schrader 54d 10h 59m 30s**	**John Hughes 39d 23h 49m 40s**	**John Hughes 92d 11h 27m 38s**	**John Hughes**
9		**John Hughes 55d 00h 23m 52s**	**Harry Mitchell 55d 03h 56m 21s**		
10		**Harry Mitchell 66d 07h 46m 31s**			

Dick Cross - his boat Air Force sunk during first leg
Eduardo Louro de Almeida - rudder breakage during first leg
Takao Shimada - rigging damage during first leg
Mac Smith - retired during first leg
Jacques de Roux - lost at sea during second leg
Harry Mitchell - run aground in New Zealand during third leg

BOC Challenge Race Results

Chapter 31

SIX METRE YACHTS - A LOOK AT YESTERYEAR

Co-written with Risa Wyatt

She sits on sawhorses, cocooned in Visqueen plastic wrap, as yet another coat of varnish sets. Replaced elm ribs strengthen her interior, and new mahogany gleams on her planked deck. Arguably the finest yacht ever designed by Olin Stephens, *Goose* is considered the most famous Six Metre racing yacht from the "Golden Age of the Sixes."

Built in 1938, she won nearly every major regatta from the late 1930s through the 1990s, including the British-American Team Race Challenge, the Scandinavian Gold Cup (four times), the Seawanhaka Cup, and the Australian-American Challenge Cup.

Some years back, *Goose* underwent reconstruction in owner Peter Hofmann's backyard shop on Bainbridge Island in Puget Sound, where she was prepped to reenter the international Six Metre racing circuit.

"My goal was to bring her back to her earlier condition and get her into racing form for the next century," says Hofmann. "It took about 2,000 hours of labor, and I've lost count of how many rolls of sandpaper and coats of paint we applied. We spent so much time on the boat that one of the guys who worked with me joked, 'This is getting way too personal—you're treating the boat like she's your daughter.' But that's how it is with the Sixes—they become members of your family."

The renaissance of *Goose* early last century marked a turning point in the resurgence of interest in the Six Metre Class in North America—and underscored the importance of these venerable yachts on the West Coast.

History

Often cited as the smallest of the "big boats," the Six Metres—like their Eight and Twelve Metre cousins—descend from the Metre Rule design, established in 1907. Like the larger Metre classes, the Sixes sail stiff and heavy. The first race under the Metre Rule was held in 1907 at Cercle de la Voile de Paris on the Seine.

Over the years, Six Metre owners have included royalty and magnates such as Norway's King Olav V, France's Baron Edmond de Rothschild, America's J.P. Morgan and his son Henry, and Sir Thomas Lipton. Although Lipton won many Six Metre campaigns, some for cups that still bear his name, he famously remarked that he had two regrets: Despite repeated attempts, he never won the America's Cup, and he never found a woman to share his life.

From the outset, the class was a gentleman-of-wealth pursuit steeped in the Corinthian spirit. Owners paid all the bills and skippered their own boats with amateur crews of family and friends. Although competitors took the racing rules seriously, they adhered even more strongly to the noblesse oblige of decorum and respect.

The appeal of the Sixes lies in the sheer beauty of the boats and the challenge of sailing them well. "Instead of sailing on your boat, we sail Sixes from inside the boat," observes Matt Cockburn, former head of the North American Six Metre Association, who races *Buzzy III*, a 1956 Sparkman & Stephens design. "The boat is basically sailed from below deck, and you seldom see the crew on the rail. When you stand up inside a Six, your knees are still below the waterline. It gives a unique feeling of power and connectedness. Each Six is unique. They're all one-offs, but they've all been built to the same Metre Rule since 1907."

During the early twentieth century, Sixes competed for such legendary trophies as the British-American Cup, Scandinavian Gold Cup, King Edward VII Gold Cup, Bermuda Gold Cup, One Ton Cup, Lipton Cup, and the Seawanhaka Cup, the oldest U.S. match-racing trophy. From 1908 through the Helsinki Games in 1952, Sixes vied for Olympic gold. They lost Olympic status because the boats had become too expensive to build and maintain, and their elitist image clashed with the egalitarian spirit of the Games. Consequently, the prestigious trophies were transferred to other classes. Although vibrant fleets existed on Lake Ontario in the 1950s and on Puget Sound in the 1960s, the Sixes almost vanished everywhere else.

However, the fortunes of the Sixes revived in 1958 when Twelve Metres were chosen as America's Cup racers. Since Sixes are basically scaled-down versions of the Twelves, the smaller sibling became the low-cost, beta test platform for improvements to the America's Cup contenders. And innovate they did. The Six Metre class introduced advances such as the genoa jib, parachute spinnaker, rod rigging, tank testing, and cold-molded construction. After Ben Lexcen's winged keel design, introduced in 1982 on Pacific Highway and revealed to the public on *Australia II* at the 1983 America's Cup, the Sixes were among the first to adopt the design as a class. Further refinements included winglets, flips, lips, razor-edges, and the upside-down. In addition, designers used the Sixes as trial horses for canards, trim tabs, bustles, and the infamous bow bulb.

After Twelve Metres ceased to be the America's Cup class in 1987, Sixes again fell into near oblivion. Not wanting to get stuck with nautical white elephants, owners around the world sold their boats as fast as possible, and owners on the West Coast bought them. It wasn't until the International Six Metre Association (ISMA) divided the Sixes into two classes—Classic (pre-1965) and Modern—in the early 2000s, that new life surged into the fleet as sailors became interested in restoring the classics.

Racer Retirement Home

The coastal waters of Puget Sound and lower British Columbia became a sanctuary for aging Six Metres. Rather than being scrapped, these boats found new life as many owners and boat builders restored the vintage racers.

Credit for establishing West Coast waters as a safe harbor for old Sixes goes to Peter Hofmann's late father, Harry Hofmann, who began buying the classics in the 1970s and 1980s. "Tracing the history of the boats around here that have survived is very simple," recalls Cockburn. "Whether the racer was successful or not, Harry Hofmann bought it."

Scouring the region, the senior Hofmann began a formidable collection that ultimately rescued ten yachts, including *Lulu* (1937, winner of the Scandinavian Gold Cup and King Edward VII Gold Cup), *Llanoria* (1948, two-time Olympic gold medal winner in 1948 and 1952), *Sockeye* (1978, multiple Lipton Cup 1997 winner and 2002 North American Championship), and, of course, *Goose.*

Classic Restorations

Only a handful of builders other than Peter Hofmann had the skills and boatyards to restore the classic wooden yachts built in the 1930s and 1940s. One of the longest-established companies is Jespersen's Boat Builders in Sidney on Vancouver Island, founded in 1973 by Bent Jespersen and later directed by Bent's son, Eric. One of Canada's most renowned sailors, Eric crewed on two America's Cup Canadian Challengers—*Canada I* in 1983 and *Canada II* in 1987—and competed in the World Championships for the Twelve, Eight, and Six Metres. In addition, he represented Canada in the Olympics in 1992 (winning the Bronze in the Star class) and in 1996, and he won the Star Worlds in San Diego in 1994.

"I'm quite passionate about these old boats, having raced, built, and restored Twelve, Eight, and Six Metres for many years," says Eric. "Modern boats being built today are future 'has-beens', nothing more than flashes in the pan. We don't need any more new boats. Saving an old boat is as much fun as building a new one, and you're keeping the old spirit alive."

In 1984, the Jespersen boatyard built its first Metre boat: the Bruce Kirby-designed Eight, *Octavia*, which won the Eight Metre World Cup in Toronto that same year. The following year the Jespersens constructed their first new Six Metre, *Capriccio*, while at the same time Martin Yachts in Vancouver built the Brian Wertheimer design, *Steverino*. These boats were two of the first winged-keel Sixes and two of the last in the class to be built in North America.

Jespersen has since resurrected several other Sixes, including Cockburn's *Buzzy III*, and *Saga*, a 1936 Bjarne Aas design owned by Seattle's Kimo Mackey. A winner of other regional trophies, Mackey represented the U.S. at the 2005 Six Metre World Cup in Sweden. In his own racer, *Frenzy* (1977, Britain Chance design), Jespersen and his crew dominated Six Metre racing in the Pacific Northwest for several years throughout the early 2000s.

Stradivarius of the Seas

High-gloss mahogany hulls that mirror sunshine and spray, the power of nearly five tons, and booms so low that you tack blind, ducking below deck for three seconds—sailors who race Six Metre yachts feel the magic even if they can't fully describe it. The appeal of the Sixes lies in the sheer beauty of the boat and the century-long tradition of campaigning the boats on both sides of the Atlantic.

"They don't bob or hobby-horse through the waves—it's an old-school aesthetic, like driving a vintage Ferrari," explains Mackey. "The Sixes are very challenging to sail, but when you find the groove, you get an incredible feeling. The boat is so powerful, and you're constantly on the edge," adds Bernard Haissly, former Swiss president of ISMA.

"My specialty is restoring classics of any type built from the 1930s to the 1960s," says Mark Wallace, a cabinetmaker turned boatbuilder based in Sidney on Vancouver Island. "They represent the craft at its pinnacle: beautiful boats with care and great engineering sophistication." Wallace particularly loves the Six Metre racer. "In their day, the Sixes were the Stradivarius of boats, meticulously constructed and varnished inside and out," he explains. "The trick to restoring them is to use old materials and good mahogany."

Wallace found *Saskia II*, a 1934 William Fife design on Lasqueti Island in Canada's Gulf Islands and restored it to its original design complete with wooden spars. Next, he undertook major repairs on *Ça Va*, a yacht built in Denmark in 1938 for the Royal Danish Yacht Club. It was plundered by the Germans when they invaded Denmark. After the lead keel was melted down to make bullets, the boat was abandoned until she was imported to Canada and eventually made her way to Vancouver Island. Wallace's restoration includes replacing the stem, stern post transom, ring frames, planking, wedges, seaming, and deck. The narrow-waisted racer is now at the Vancouver Maritime Museum.

Fintra II, another Six Metre Fife design (1933), sat for years under wraps at Wallace's boatyard waiting its turn to be restored. "Old boats don't just die," muses Wallace. "People become attached to them and want to see them preserved."

The Racing Scene

The Sixes have maintained a long racing tradition in the waters of the Pacific Northwest and Coastal British Columbia. In 1973, the Port of Seattle deeded the Six Metre World Cup. The inaugural event brought to Northwest waters the top skippers of the day, including Tom Blackaller, who won on *St. Francis V*. In 1979, Puget Sound again hosted the World Cup. Sixes continue to compete today in Northwest waters for the Lipton Cup, Boundary Cup, and North American Championship.

The creaky image of Six Metres as a private club for blue bloods and blue blazers was scuttled by the Queen Christina Nations Cup, deeded in 2003 and first raced at Port Madison on Puget Sound. Emphasizing maximum fun at minimal cost, establishment of the trophy was spearheaded by Seattle's Mackey. To compete in the QCNC, teams from visiting nations merely have to arrange their own transportation. Meanwhile, the host nation provides lodging, meals, racing yachts, and overall management of the event.

"The idea is to have fun—competitors just have to show up with their foulies," says Mackey. Indicating the easy-going attitude, the regatta is also known as the "Battle for the Aquavit." The winner receives a beautiful trophy holding a flask filled with Linie Aquavit, a preferred quaff for Six Metre crew members.

For two years following its initiation, the Nations Cup was hosted in Europe before returning to Canada in 2006, when the event was hosted by the Kitsilano Yacht Club in Vancouver. Three years later in 2009, the event was held in conjunction with the Six Metre World Cup in Newport, Rhode Island—the first time since 1987 that the World Championship took place in the U.S. The return of international competition to North America expanded interest in the Sixes across the continent.

The Third Way

In July 2005, in the largest-ever turnout, up to that time in the history of any Metre class, fifty-three contenders from eleven nations gathered at Sandhamn, Sweden, for the Six Metre World Cup. The classics, defined as racers built prior to 1965, outnumbered the moderns by twenty-nine to twenty-four, thanks to owners who took pride in restoring the vintage craft.

In addition to the resurgence of restored racers, the Sandhamn regatta heralded another trend in the class. Winning the division for the older boats was the Danish entry, *Sunray*, the fleet's first classic replica. Launched only two months prior to the event, the yacht dominated the field with four firsts in the eight-race series.

With the victory came controversy. In the bar of the Royal Swedish YC, crews of several classic competitors grumbled that a newly built boat—even if it follows original line drawings—is inherently stiffer and benefits from the use of modern materials. Many contended that restored classic racers are, for all practical purposes, new boats. But no one lodged a protest since *Sunray* had been approved by the class chief measurer as a means of keeping the fleet strong.

"A replica is neither a classic nor a modern," said Henrik Andersin of Finland, who recently restored the 1938 Sparkman & Stephens *Djinn* to its former glory. "It's a third category. It doesn't compete with either the moderns or the classics. These older boats were badly neglected over the years and had suffered broken frames, rotted floor timbers, and cracked planking. To get them back in racing condition, many were stripped down to the lead ballast keel and practically started from scratch using new materials and modern-age glues and fasteners—just like the new boats are built."

Two-Tiered Fleet

Prior to the creation of the two-tiered fleet, a few older boats showed up at regattas. Although they consistently finished at the bottom of the rankings, they attracted attention as they gracefully swathed through the waters, while the comparatively drab, tank-tested, fiberglass racers with winged keels turned in the winning points. There were a few notable exceptions such as *Scoundrel*, a beautifully crafted wooden modern that won the World Cup in 1987, 1997, and 2023.

"A modern design races about forty to sixty seconds faster per mile than a classic in light to moderate conditions," explains Hans Oen, Danish skipper of the 2005 World Cup winner, *Sunray*. "Margins loom larger in heavy conditions when foils and wings—found on most moderns but not allowed on classics—kick in."

"When they divided the fleet, it spelled the death of the modern Six Metre," said one owner. The moderns were costly to build, and naval architects couldn't do much more to improve the boat's sailing performance. Consequently, money and talent were redirected into the classics—most of the modern class at the 2005 World Championship dated to the mid-1980s and earlier.

However, the establishment of a separate class for classics meant that the venerable yachts could compete among themselves, reviving many rivalries dating back over half a century—*Bobcat VI* and *Melita* had vied for the 1934 British-American Cup at Oyster Bay, New York. A new generation of sailors could race in yachts that they had only read about in history books.

Finland's Hendrik Andersin is a Six Metre devotee who searches the globe to rescue forgotten hulls. *Djinn* had been built for Henry Morgan, son of financier J.P. Morgan, who later sold the vessel to the Argentinian Naval Academy. After racing in the 1948 and 1952 Olympics, it was sold again and subsequently left for decades in an open field. Andersin purchased the legendary racer in 2003 and faithfully restored it using vintage shipwrights' tools and parts. Above deck, *Djinn* was equipped with aluminum spars, modern sails, and rod rigging. After restoration was complete, *Djinn* made its racing comeback at the 2005 World Championship.

"If God had a boat, it would be a Six Metre," according to British financier David Roberts, explaining why he purchased *Melita*. "It's one of the most perfect elegant yachts to sail close to the wind." Built in 1934, the William Fife design was sold in the 1940s and again in the 1980s, first to Ireland and then to Sweden. When Roberts purchased the boat in 2003, it had been abandoned for many years. After undergoing two years of restoration, *Melita* competed as the only British classic at the 2005 World Championship.

As the 1990s progressed, with only a dwindling pool of pricey originals left to refurbish, attention turned to 'Ghosts'—classics that had been destroyed or were beyond repair. After extensive debate in 2000, the class membership voted to allow the building of replicas of vanished classics.

A new Six Metre era had begun.

New Ghosts

According to Six Metre class rules, a classic replica can be certified if the original boat is a "constructive or absolute total loss." Such was the case with *Sinkadus*, the yacht on whose design the 2005 World Cup-winning *Sunray* was based. The original was built in Sweden in 1939 and destroyed during a storm on Long Island Sound in the 1950s.

Sunray was constructed by the father-and-son Jensen boatbuilders in Copenhagen. After finding Arvid Laurin's original line drawings for *Sinkadus* in the Maritime Museum in Stockholm, they were able to obtain copies. The Jensens worked four years in their small workshop constructing the new classic piece-by-piece following the drawings in exact detail. They improved the boat by using modern materials, which were permitted, such as epoxy between the planks. Rather than the Oregon pine of the original, the deck is of plywood overlaid with teak, which makes the boat strong and stiff.

How do the Jensens and other builders of wooden boats explain their passion for bringing back these racing icons? William Jensen explains, "My family has been building boats for four generations. Why? It's because we can turn this," he says, pointing to a stack of rough mahogany planks, "into this," as he gestures to a lovingly handcrafted Three Metre dinghy gleaming with fresh varnish. (Danish Crown Prince Frederik commissioned a similar craft from the Jensens as a wedding gift to his wife, Mary.)

"Boats are our life," he adds simply. In return, the Jensens give new life to classic ghosts. Since then, other boatbuilders have geared up to craft classic replicas. The Jensens rebuilt *Nirvana*, a 1939 Olin Stephens design, and a Finnish boatyard resurrected the classic *Violet.* Other destroyed and missing Sixes include the 1936 gold medal–winning *Lalage*, burned by an angry spouse; the Seawanhaka Cup winner, *Circe*, destroyed in Soviet Russia; and *Inga Lill XXVI*, which also perished. In modern times, these ghost yachts have found new life and have been very much in evidence on the current Six Metre racing circuits.

Looking Back for their Future

In 2007, the Six Metre Class marked its 100th anniversary, although just over two decades previously it had seemed unlikely this venerable racer would survive the century mark. The once sleek Olympic class, which had been skippered by legends such as Magnus Konow, Sven Salen, and Herman Whiton, and later by Ted Turner, Pelle Petterson, and John Kostecki, was a fallen icon. Some suffered indignities, such as cabins tacked to their cockpits or engines, berths, cooking stoves, and heads installed. Others languished in the corners of farmers' barns, their ribs serving as roosts for chickens. Others that were neglected and decayed simply vanished.

But now, the Six Metres are back, arising from their apparent demise as they have so often done in their 120-year history. The 2005 Six Metre World Championship in Sandhamn, in addition to sanctioning the building of replicas, forecast other changes for the Sixes. Although double-breasted blazers abounded at Sandhamn, so did T-shirts, cargo shorts, and denim jeans. In the following years, instead of the owner-driver at the helm, many owners were sitting in the middle of the boat. *Courage IX*, the German entry that won the modern division in 2005, was crewed by a mix of international pros and Olympic contenders.

Syndicates, corporate ownerships, and sponsorships became common after 2005 because of the expense of campaigning a race. In turn, backers required recognition in the form of advertising. Under ISMA Class Rules, commercial messages are limited to spinnakers and transoms with lettering size kept relatively small.

The resilient survival of the Sixes that began in the Pacific Northwest has rippled out to the international racing scene. Most recently, the World Championship was held in 2023 at Sanxenxo, Spain, and in 2025 at Seawanhaka Corinthian Yacht Club (SCYC) in Oyster Bay, New York. Restored classics such as *Goose* and *Djinn*, sister yachts and rivals designed by Olin Stephens and launched in 1938, hadn't competed against each other for seventy years. Both are now active in the international racing scene, thrilling a generation of sailors who had only seen them in photos.

In recent years, the World Championships and other Six Metre regattas are raced in three divisions: Open Division, Classic Division, and Corinthian Division. The Open Division is the most competitive and modern of the three. Yachts in this division are allowed to be fitted with the latest materials, technologies, and designs. This means the boats are typically very high-performance and often feature advanced construction techniques, including lightweight composite materials like carbon fiber. Sailors in this division are typically professional or highly experienced, and the racing is intense.

The Classic Division is for yachts that have maintained their historical integrity and adhere to the design and construction guidelines set out in the earlier years of the Six Metre class. The yachts in this division are typically older boats, and there are strict rules around preserving their original design and materials. The goal is to maintain the vintage aesthetic and sailing characteristics, and to preserve the heritage of the class.

The Corinthian Division is for amateur sailors. The idea is to make the sport more accessible by encouraging participants who are not professional sailors. Yachts in this division are usually similar to those in the Open Division, but no professional sailors are allowed. This division promotes a fair and fun atmosphere, where the focus is more on the spirit of sport rather than pure competition.

Labors of Love

The Sixes were never intended to last. As a development class, they were the temporary templates of naval architects who thought the yachts had a competitive shelf life of three to five years. But they were wrong—precisely because they got the design so right. Beautiful, headstrong, and demanding, the Sixes live on. At a recent World Championship, the oldest entrant was Norway's *Mosquito* built in 1913.

"Why do we spend all this money on these boats—is it just for love?" ponders Robert Leigh-Wood, owner of Conch Fritters. He smiles, "Well, maybe it is. It's terrific fun racing Metre boats. It's a different kind of boat that involves all of the crew seventy-five percent of the time to sail it, not just the helmsman."

It is estimated that more than 2,000 Six Metre boats were built in total, of which some 150 are still in existence today, thanks to the ever-active, over-the-years skillful management of the International Six Metre Association, which combined the elegance of the Classic Division with the cutting-edge development of the modern boats in the Open Division and also included a Corinthian Division.

Today, Six Metre fleets flourish, and the class has returned as one of the most exciting and important racing circuits in the world that takes competitors to some of the most spectacular yachting venues around the globe.

Or, summing it up, take the perspective of the helmsman who came dead last at a Six Metre World Championship some years ago; crossing the finish line, he exclaimed, "We're the last of the angels, but we're still in heaven."

Downwind leg

Downwind run to leeward mark

Rounding windward mark

2005 World Cup winner – *Sunray*

Chapter 32

1988 WOMEN'S WORLD SAILING CHAMPIONSHIPS - A FIRST FOR WOMEN

Although today it is taken for granted that women enjoy increasing parity with men in sports, it wasn't always so. A case in point is competitive sailing. For many years, world and national championships, including Olympic competitions, offered few divisions for women.

But that began to change in 1988. A decisive turning point is often cited as the Women's World Sailing Championships, held that year at the Búzios Yacht Club in Brazil. The event was organized by World Sailing, the international sports governing body for sailing, then known as the International Yacht Racing Union (IYRU).

Notable because it was part of the International Women's Sailing Program, the competition gathered top female sailors representing seventeen countries. Rather than teams, the racing featured individual sailors, testing their skills in various wind conditions. This championship helped further the visibility of women in sailing, paving the way for more opportunities on the global stage. Many sailors from the 1988 World Championships competed in the Olympics and other world championships, continuing to push for greater inclusion and opportunity for women in competitive sailing.

For Búzios, this was its first international yachting event, and, judging from the near-perfect racing conditions, there will likely be many more. The small fishing village was "discovered" in the 1950s when Brigitte Bardot and her Brazilian husband came here to escape the press. But instead of hiding themselves, they revealed Búzios to the world.

In the 1960s, hippies arrived to camp out on the twenty-six fabled beaches of this jutting peninsula. They left in the 1970s when the wealthy of Rio, fleeing the deterioration of their city, bought up the land and built elegant villas. But in the country's economic turmoil of the 1980s, they too were blown away, making way for the next group—racing and cruising sailors—to move into the area.

Local Brazilian Indian fishermen say it's the winds that bring these changes. The name they give it is the Teral—the wind that never stops blowing. It sweeps the northeast coast for a thousand miles before veering inland at Búzios, where it cleanses the land, purifies the soul, and blows away dust in both the physical and metaphysical senses.

Today, Búzios is a mix of sophisticated boutiques from Rio and rustic Indian craft shops lining cobblestone roads that more or less follow the coastline. Everywhere, profusions of bougainvillea and tropical flowers mix with flame-tree reds and towering casuarina greens. The cool colors and welcome shade soften the heat of the blazing sun, creating a tropical charm. Búzios is the kind of place that, after you discover it, you hope no one else will, for fear that any further intrusion will shatter its delicate balance.

But for the world's top women sailors who gathered for this event, there was little time to take in the scenery. Their main priority was to become familiar with the unusual sailing conditions and figure out how to rig for the strong winds and large South Atlantic rollers that curve around Búzios' coast.

One of the classes in the 1988 Women's World Sailing Championships was the Mistral board, a one-design windsurfer. The standout windsurfer was Caroll-Ann Alie, a Canadian athlete who claimed gold in the women's Mistral division. Silver and bronze medals in the Mistral class were awarded to French athletes Valérie Capart and Anne François, respectively. Alie went on to appear in three Olympic Games (1992 Barcelona, 1996 Atlanta, 2000 Sydney) and secured multiple Pan American Games medals (gold in 1995, silver in 1987 and 1999).

Windsurfing has been one of the Summer Olympics sailing events since 1984 for men and 1992 for women. Since the Mistral era, several iterations of Olympic windsurfing equipment have come and gone. The latest generation of Olympic windsurfers is the iQFOiL, which uses foils that promise higher speeds and spectacular action. The Paris 2024 Olympic Sailing Competition included forty-eight windsurfers—twenty-four men and twenty-four women.

Also competing at Búzios was the Laser Radial class, a single-handed dinghy that was relatively new at the time. The championship saw great performances with sailors from various countries showcasing their sailing prowess. While the Laser Radial class, beginning in 1996, would eventually become a focal point for women's sailing in future Olympics, the 1988 event helped raise the international profile of women sailors in the class.

At Búzios, another competition was the women's 470 class, a two-person dinghy, marking the first official inclusion of a women's-only 470 event in major sailing. Later that year at the Seoul Olympics, the 470s marked the first Olympic-class appearance for women.

Most sailing competitions today are "open" events in which men and women compete together on equal terms, either as individuals or as part of a team. Sailing has had annual female-only world championships since Búzios, encouraging increased participation by women. The inclusion of more female sailors in the Olympics over the years has been a testament to the growth of the sport.

Below is a roster of female sailors from this era who were top-level competitors with world rankings at major international regattas. Some of these women competed at the 1988 Women's World Championships, and forty-two women from twenty-one nations competed in the two-person 470 dinghy class at the Seoul Olympics that same year:

- Allison Jolly & Lynne Jewell (USA) — First women's Olympic gold medal in sailing at the Seoul Olympics '88
- Marit Söderström & Birgitta Bengtsson (SWE) — Silver, Seoul Olympics '88
- Larisa Moskalenko & Iryna Chunykhovska (URS) — Bronze, Seoul Olympics '88
- Christina Bassadone & Saskia Clark (GBR) — Seoul Olympics '88
- Stefanie Rothweiler & Vivien Kussatz (GDR) — Seoul Olympics '88
- Lorna Pardy (AUS) — Seoul Olympics '88
- Patricia Langois (FRA) — Seoul Olympics '88
- Susanne Theel & Silke Preuss (DDR) — Seoul Olympics '88
- Courtney Becker (USA) — Bronze, Atlanta Olympics '96
- Fernanda Oliveira & Isabel Swan (BRA) — Bronze, Beijing Olympics '08
- J. J. Isler (USA) — Barcelona Olympics '92 and Sydney Olympics '00

- Christina Bassadone & Saskia Clark (GBR) — Strong contenders internationally '80s–'00s
- Ingrid Petitjean & Nadege Douroux (FRA) — Strong contenders internationally '88
- Giulia Conti & Giovanna Micol (ITA) — Strong contenders internationally '80s–'00s
- Silvia Vogl & Carolina Flatscher (AUT) — Strong contenders internationally '80s–'00s
- Nike Kornecki & Vered Bouskila (ISR) — Strong contenders internationally '80s–'00s
- Nicole Ambrasas & Karola Lehman (GDR) — Multiple 420 championships
- Francesca Pavesi (ITA) — Laser Radial multiple championships
- Margaret Hibbert (AUS) — Laser Radial multiple championships
- Kirsten Neuschäfer (RSA) — First woman to win an around-the-world sailing race

~

German team rigging their 470

Judges— hear no… see no… speak no…

Layover day aboard *Murilla*

Swedish competitor rigging her Mistral

Chapter 33

CRUISING TRENDS - CHARTING A NEW COURSE

Every charterer dreams of the perfect getaway. For some, it's white-sand beaches lined with swaying palms. Others imagine the scent of tall pines drifting across an anchorage while fog lifts. Many simply want to escape modern civilization while indulging their urge for independence.

Although making landfall in paradise has always been possible through chartering, the dream had, until recently, its limits. Logistics were complicated, charter companies were few, and boat selections were limited. Now, however, the industry is changing dramatically. One no longer needs to travel somewhere to board whatever boat happens to be available there. A lot more choices exist today. Consider these top trends in the charter cruising industry.

Ashore or Afloat

Cruising charter bases are often located far from good shoreside accommodations, so charterers must sometimes travel overnight in less-than-perfect conditions at the beginning and end of their cruises. Or, equally inconvenient, charterers arriving at the charter base immediately after a long flight might be whisked directly on board, with no shoreside transition to allow for adjustment to the new time zone, climate, or setting.

Sunsail Yacht Charters was among the first to offer transition options to arriving and departing clients. The company owns resorts at nine of its fourteen Mediterranean charter bases and arranges for guests to stay at Cay Club at Soper's Hole Wharf and Marina on Tortola, British Virgin Islands.

The Moorings, which has 750 boats at thirty-five locations around the world, operates Club Mariner resorts at three Caribbean charter bases: Tortola, St. Lucia, and Grenada. It also owns the Mariner Inn on Tortola.

Some resorts have taken the concept a step further. For one all-inclusive price, guests have the option of enjoying accommodations either ashore or on fully provisioned charter cruises aboard one of the resort's cruising yachts. The scheduling allows plenty of flexibility, so customers can decide from one day to the next if, where, and how long to cruise. Clients have the choice of one or more nights ashore near the charter base or a shore option if bad weather delays the start of their cruise. Alternatively, these facilities are vacation spots in themselves, with boats available for day use. For families whose members are not unanimously enthusiastic about chartering, these resorts offer split vacations, part ashore and part afloat.

Dream Yacht Charter, with a fleet of 800 monohulls and catamarans at thirty-five destinations in twenty-two countries, also offers accommodations at most of its charter bases.

Cushy Cruising

Charter companies, which purchase large numbers of yachts, have been a major force in pushing naval architects to increase performance and upgrade amenities. The Spartan center-cockpit charter boats of the past have given way to speedy aft-cockpit designs with careful use of space for maximum comfort. The emphasis today is on pleasure and fun. Newer boats have wide passageways and cockpits, spacious interiors, and extra headroom. Many conveniences such as microwaves, blenders, air conditioning, ice makers, hair dryers, quality sound systems, cellular phones, internet service, and extra water capacity for showers on the scoop-stern platforms have been added.

The study of ergonomics—fitting people into an environment—has not been limited to the office. Its application to the charter industry has produced a 50-foot sailing design with four private staterooms, each with its own shower and head, plus separate quarters for the crew.

Deck layout and rigging designs on today's sailing charter boats make handling easier than in the past. Roller furling, slab reefing, self-tailing winches, anchor windlasses, and lazy jacks are standard equipment on most boats.

Crewed Charter Elegance

On larger-crewed yachts—especially motor yachts and sailing multihulls—the cushy factor has pushed the limits with color televisions, fax machines, oversized refrigerators and freezers, trash compactors, and washer and dryers. Extra generators ensure enough electricity to feed power-hungry appliances and entertainment centers.

Plush carpets fit lavishly around molded interior shapes that have changed the sharp edges and right angles of the past into soft, rounded contours. Gourmet cooks serve haute cuisine three times a day with plenty of snacks and drinks in between. And deckhands are well-versed about the area's history, culture, and native lore.

One-Way Charters

This option has always been available but at a steep price: charter customers paid for the return delivery crew, and the rate reflected the extra time it took to get the boat back to its base, with or without the customer on board. That's changing. In the Caribbean, for example, The Moorings does not charge drop-off fees on crewed charters, and sometimes on bareboat charters as well, between its Grenada and St. Lucia bases. Florida Yacht Charters offers one-way charters without drop-off fees between its Miami and Key West bases. Sunsail has eliminated return delivery charges for drop-offs in its BVI bases.

Companies often waive drop-off charges if a return charterer can be found. Other companies have reduced rates, charging only actual return delivery costs without per diem rates for extra days.

Delivery Charter Cruises

Several charter companies offer berths on delivery cruises when bringing new boats from the manufacturer to the charter base, or when moving a fleet on ocean passages to give clients experience in navigation, weather forecasting, and blue-water seamanship. A New Zealand yacht charter company offers berths when relocating its fleet between Tonga and New Zealand. Members of The Moorings Sailing Club can participate in deliveries all over the world. Sunsail will accept charter guests on delivery cruises from its base in Annapolis to Florida and the Bahamas.

Multihulls

The crewed and bareboat multihull charter business has grown dramatically in recent years. The influx has come on two fronts: novice cruisers who want a stable sailing platform and experienced sailors who seek the thrill of higher speeds. For years, multihulls could not be brought into marine surveys because they were not self-righting when capsized. However, improved designs with shortened rigs and greater spans between the hulls led to charter approval by marine authorities.

Because multihulls go fast, do not tip, and are often double the space of the same size monohull, they appeal to families with children and grandparents. Stoves don't have to be gimbaled, and glassware doesn't get knocked over. Non-sailors don't worry about heeling. With no keels to scrape bottom, charters can go just about anywhere, often sailing directly up to sand beaches where kids can jump off into knee-deep water.

The Moorings, Sunsail, and Stardust Marine have added multihulls to their Tahiti, Mediterranean, and bareboat fleets, as has Florida Yacht Charters in the Keys and the Bahamas.

Crewed multihulls are making an even greater impact as they command the luxury end of the market. Staterooms are large, with enough space between them to provide everyone with privacy. Typical is the 25-meter French catamaran (more than 80 feet). Built as a floating palace, the yacht includes seven double staterooms (the largest with 130 square feet) flanking a spacious saloon and bar with varnished pearwood floor and Sycamore paneling.

Boat Standardization

Jeanneau and Beneteau dominate the sailing charter business throughout the Caribbean, South Pacific, and Mediterranean. The

Beneteau Oceanis 430, 390, and 350 yachts, which are now the backbone of the industry, were among the first to be ergonomically designed, providing optimum use of space and equipment.

Astute marketing by Jeanneau and Beneteau has allowed the two companies to dominate the charter market. By working with their dealers to respond to charter companies' requests for special designs, they have produced the boat of choice. So, whether in the Bahamas or Tahiti, you'll get the same boat.

Florida-based builder Hunter Marine, once a dominant factor in the charter business, has in recent years become a smaller player in the charter market. Hunter was acquired by Lauren Marine after 2008 and continues under the "British Hunter" brand. Florida Yacht Charters is the only major yacht charter company that maintains a few Hunters in its fleet in the Bahamas and Florida Keys.

Cruise Clubs

For those who wish to cruise but don't want the hassle of working out their own itinerary and charter logistics, there are cruise clubs—sometimes called affinity groups—which have the economic clout to command discounted airfares and charter rates. The Moorings has developed a similar concept with its Moorings Sailing Clubs, the first of which was established in Saint Petersburg, Florida. Particularly popular in California, such organizations as Newport Sailing Club of Newport Beach and Olympic Sailing Club in Berkeley, have the economic clout to command discounted airfares and charter rates.

Special Programs

Combining a charter cruise with a specific activity has opened extended cruising to a wider market. Cruising programs devoted to ecology, archeology, history, or scuba diving are becoming increasingly popular. Many of these programs include an expert guide or instructor.

The Moorings organizes regattas with its cruise fleets in the British Virgin Islands, authentic Native feasts in Tonga, and Odyssey flotillas focusing on island antiquity treasures in Greece.

Moorings-Rainbow Yacht Charters in New Zealand offers instruction in German, French, Spanish, and Japanese through its "Accelerated Languages Afloat" programs. Queensland Yacht Charters in the Whitsunday Islands offers floatplane pickups from any anchorage to fly to the Great Barrier Reef for scuba diving. Sale North, the world's northernmost power and sail charter operator, mobilizes its sailing fleet each year for the Commissioner's Cup Regatta in Canada.

San Juan Sailing supports "America's Adventure USA" to teach teens to sail and cruise. The Bitter End Yacht Club and Resort incorporates an invitational regatta into its "Fast Tack Vacation," which lets sailors of all levels crew for world-class skippers. Sunsail offers regatta charters for Antigua Race Week, the BVI Heineken Cup, and other racing events in the Caribbean.

Those who want to bareboat, but are somewhat hesitant, can find comfort by signing up for flotilla cruises, rendezvous charters, and cruising-in-company programs, which allow charter parties to follow a professional skipper in a lead boat through unfamiliar waters.

New Areas

Charter operations have been established by Sunsail at Thailand's Phuket Island and in the Seychelles Islands in the Indian Ocean, by Moorings-Rainbow in Tonga and Fiji, and by The Moorings in Australia's Whitsunday Islands. Charter companies, responding to the demand to open new cruising destinations in remote corners of the world, have been establishing new bases in Costa Rica, Venezuela, the South China Sea, Gulf of Thailand, Vanuatu, Japan's Inland Sea, Cook Islands, and Turkey. And more are on the way. Wherever cruising sailors dream of going, a charter company will someday set up a fleet to offer the perfect getaway.

~

Epilogue

WATERY BACKYARD

I have always loved being by the water, which is why, at the end of each trip experiencing wonderful sailing adventures around the world—after blue-water passages, wild anchorages, and the thrill of finding new sailing grounds—I look forward to coming back to my very special home.

Behind my home, there are no trees. There are no plants or flowers. In fact, there is no vegetation at all. There are no rocks, no stones, no insects, no pests; there is not even soil.

Yet the back of my "yard" holds its own beauty—ever changing, endlessly watchable. My backyard is the same as the front, and, for that matter, it wraps me on all sides.

I'm one of those Seattleites fortunate enough to live in a floating home. Please note: it's not "on," but "in." And it's not "houseboat," but "floating home." We who live this way tend to be a little fussy about terminology, distinguishing ourselves from itinerant boat people. They indeed live on boats, but we live in homes. We are not drifters; we are not passing through. This is home, with real kitchens and real bookshelves and real lives, gently rising and falling on the skin of Lake Union.

Scattered around Seattle's Lake Union and Portage Bay are, by the latest count, 510 of us with watery backyards. This overlooked bit of statistical trivia puts our city at number one, with the largest floating-home community in the country. But it still feels like a secret, a small world hidden in plain sight.

What drew me here—and keeps me here—is a complete reimagining of what a yard can be. The views out my windows are never still. They fill and change with an endless variety of nautical choreography. The boats that pass come in all sizes—silent silhouettes or bright ribbons of color ghosting by at any hour of the day or night. Windy days send a fleet of sails skimming by. Windless afternoons entice water skiers to carve bright white arcs across the blue. Sunny days draw out recreational powerboaters. Fishing boats come and go according to the lunar cycle. And the working vessels—the tugs, the barges, the small freighters—are always moving, reminding me that this is a living waterway.

In the early morning and at dusk, rowers and kayakers—otherwise known as the water joggers—skim by. Because they're in view for just a brief moment, the only way to tell them apart is to note whether they are facing backward or forward. They are the die-hards who appear in any weather. Their predictability makes them dependable alarm clocks in the morning and heralds of cocktail hour in the evening. Their regularity comforts me, like the rhythm of a tide. Finally, at almost any time, a rowboat, canoe, rubber inflatable, or windsurfer is sure to be out cutting a colorful trail across the vista.

During those rare moments when nothing human is afloat, birds flock into the backyard. My bird feeder, tethered to my deck, lures white swans, songbirds, Canada geese, mallards, and coots—the chorus of my waterborne theater.

Occasionally, there are periods of intermission when all is still, and the world seems to pause. These are the times when I watch the light dance and the sky turn the lake to silver, then gold, then ink. The crystal clarity of the air on a chilly morning or frigid evening brings out the "Seattle Sparkles" across the water. When fog rolls in, the light erases the edge of the world and embraces me deep within a cloud. Whether the sun is beaming or hiding, light is always playing on the water. Sometimes it winks; other times it frowns. Always, it changes, acting out its moods.

All this is not to say I am passive in my backyard. There are plenty of things to do. I swim in it. I fish in it. I can't play croquet or pitch horseshoes, but perhaps one winter day I'll be able to ice-skate on it.

Most people don't know what lies beneath the surface of their yards. I do. When the water's smooth and the sun is just right, I can make out the tiniest markings on the bass, salmon, perch, and sunfish darting below. I know which like to poke about the old sunken drainpipe and which prefer the cracked bathtub tilted on its side.

Every so often, underwater currents bring in an assortment of debris—and then some days later, carry it all away—rather like having a neighbor with an ongoing garage sale. Over the years, my long-handled boat hook has hauled in a bounty of home decorations, offbeat gifts for friends, and loads of semi-practical junk—flexible tubing, scrap metal, curtain rods, car antennas—things I find a use for once and then store for years, thinking—but not truly expecting—that I might use them again.

Best of all, my backyard asks nothing of me. I don't have to mow, rake, fertilize, water, or tend it at all. It takes care of itself, and I love it. All the activity outside my living room window creates a mosaic of light and movement—a sea symphony with never-ending music. It is mine to play in and mine to watch.

But I admit there are those odd moments when I grow weary of it. When that happens, I have my escape. I turn to my other diversion: Down in the basement I have this terrific aquarium…

THE END

ABOUT THE AUTHOR

Peter Schroeder grew up in Louisville, Kentucky, where he learned to sail his 12-foot Penguin dinghy on the most heavily trafficked river in the United States, the Ohio River, the main shipping waterway of America's inland fleet. In those days, every tug (correctly called push-boats) was a stern-wheeler, its great paddlewheel throwing up four-foot waves that rolled on for nearly a quarter-mile.

As a kid, Schroeder's favorite thrill was sailing his little boat alongside a moving barge, then the instant he was abreast the tug's stern, turning head-on into the churning wake for the ride of a lifetime—while the tugboat captain leaned from his wheelhouse shouting, "What a damn fool!" which, in itself, became part of the fun.

Those reckless afternoons sparked a lifelong love of sailing and adventure.

Since his youthful days on the muddy Ohio, Schroeder has skippered vessels of all sizes and shapes on lakes, waterways, and seas across the globe. He merged his two passions—sailing and writing—into a career as an adventure travel writer specializing in cruising under sail. Over the past three decades, he has published hundreds of articles in boating and sailing magazines and newspapers worldwide. *Tight on the Wind* gathers many of those experiences, creating an anthology of his charter cruising adventures.

When ashore, Schroeder and his wife, Risa Wyatt, divide time between homes in Seattle, Washington, where they spend summers cruising the San Juan and Canadian Gulf Islands, and Sonoma, California, where they tend their Syrah vineyard and boutique winery.

Schroeder holds degrees from Princeton University (BSE), the University of New Mexico (MSE), and Stanford University (MBA). His previous books include a memoir, *The Rock Shall Dance*; a writer's guide, *Freelance Writing: How to Make Money*, and a factual and gentle analysis of the inevitable outcome we all face, *The Octogenarian Handbook: Delaying the 5 Ways of Dying (and there are only 5 ways to die).*

RICHTER
PUBLISHING

www.ingramcontent.com/pod-product-compliance
Lightning Source LLC
LaVergne TN
LVHW020050110826
845155LV00021B/56

9781954094741